If Britain had Fallen

If Britain had Fallen

NORMAN LONGMATE

STEIN AND DAY/*Publishers*/New York

First published in the United States of America in 1974
Copyright © 1972 by Norman Longmate
Library of Congress Catalog Card No. 73-91846
All rights reserved
Printed in the United States of America
Stein and Day/*Publishers*/Scarborough House, Briarcliff Manor, N.Y. 10510
ISBN 0-8128-1669-2

If Britain had Fallen is based on the BBC1 television film of the same name, first shown on 12 September 1972. It was written by Lord Chalfont, Basil Collier and Richard Wade. The film included excerpts from *Hitler's Table Talk* specially edited by Rosemary Anne Sisson. Producers David C. Rea and Christopher La Fontaine. Executive Producer Michael Latham.

Contents

	Foreword	11
1	Plans	15
2	Preparations	26
3	Anticipation	34
4	Bombardment	48
5	Assault	63
6	Break-out	76
7	Defeat	93
8	Wanted: a Quisling	110
9	The Merseyside spies	124
10	Whatever happened to Nelson?	135
11	To laugh at the Führer is forbidden	146
12	How long is a Crayfish?	162
13	Requisitioned	175
14	Deported	186
15	See Germany and die	196
16	Resistance	207
17	Collaboration	223
18	Which way to the Black Market?	231
19	The New Order	243
20	The end of the nightmare	258
	A note on sources	263
	Index	267

Illustrations

Between pages 64 and 65

1 Building a strongpoint, Trafalgar Square, May 1940
2 Weapon training for Members of Parliament, July 1940
3 Assault training for Southern Railwaymen, June 1940
4 Central London street scene, May 1940
5 Enemy aliens en route to internment, May 1940
6 A roadblock in Southern England
7 Home Guards erecting a wire trap across a road
8 and 9 Anti-air-landing obstructions, July 1940
10 A roadblock near the coast
11 The removal of place-names. A notice in the Bristol area, June 1940
12 A church notice board, Summer 1940
13 Anti-tank roadblock, July 1940
14 An anti-aircraft gun's crew taking post, 1940
15 Sea-bathing on the south coast, 1940 style

Between pages 144 and 145

16 Invasion barges, as seen by the RAF
17 Oil defences being tried out on the south coast
18 German storm troops under training
19 The defenders. Winston Churchill and General Sir Alan Brooke on the south coast
20 The attackers. Hitler with General von Brauchitsch and Admiral Raeder, on their way to an invasion conference, June 1940
21 An invasion barge, during an exercise at Calais
22 Embarkation exercise at Dieppe, September 1940
23 A cliff-scaling exercise on the French coast
24 and 25 A German parachutist and a Panzer break-through (a British artist's impression)
26 and 27 German motorised troops on manœuvres and a river-crossing exercise, with rubber boats

28 A pontoon bridge in use in Luxemburg, May 1940

29 German troops occupying Luxemburg

Between pages 192 and 193

30 German troops on Guernsey

31 Guernsey Occupation Orders, July 1940

32 German troops in St Peter Port, Guernsey

33 German tanks on occupied Guernsey

34 A German military band in the Royal Parade, St Helier

35 Guernsey cinema taken over by the Germans

36 Anti-invasion defences under construction at Anne Port, Jersey

37 A captured French gun being towed into position on Guernsey

38 and 39 A gas-driven van and a horse-drawn van on Jersey

40 Residents of Jersey collecting Red Cross food parcels

41 The Germans burying British servicemen with full military honours

42 The New Jetty, Guernsey, awaiting possible demolition

43 Parliament Square, July 1940

Maps

British Isles, showing possible German invasion routes *page* 10

The south-east in 1940 *page* 14

Acknowledgement is due for permission to reproduce the following plates:

Associated Press 26, 28; Central Press 3, 13, 43; Frank Falla 30, 31, 32, 33, 37, 42; Fox photos 15; Imperial War Museum 16; *Jersey Evening Post* 34, 36, 38, 39, 40, 41; Keystone 4, 23, 24; Radio Times Hulton Picture Library 1, 8, 9, 10, 14, 17, 18, 19, 25, 27; Wide World 2; Reece Winstone 11.

The maps were drawn by Nigel Holmes. The illustration on page 123 is reproduced by courtesy of Rupert Hart Davis Ltd.

To

J.C.L.

Growing up in freedom—because we won

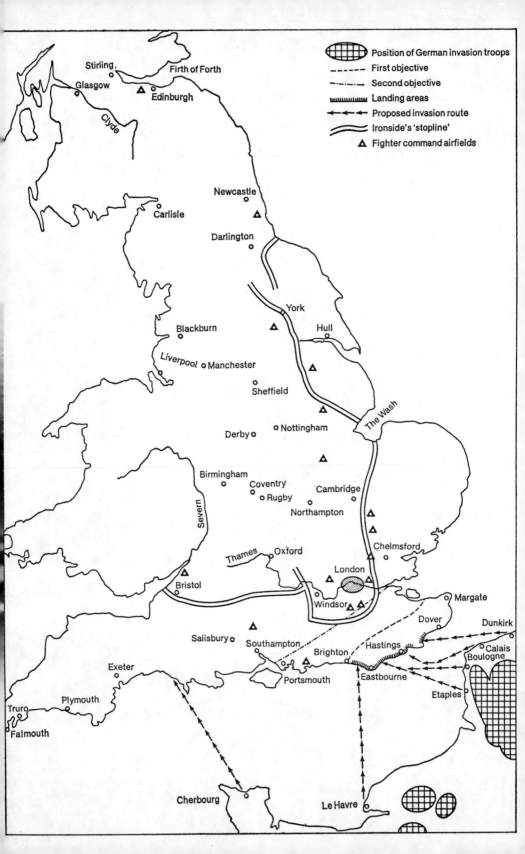

Foreword

A possible German invasion and occupation of the British Isles is a subject that has attracted many previous writers. Some, like Erskine Childers in *The Riddle of the Sands*, first published in 1903, have been concerned solely with the preparations for an attack; some, like 'Saki' (H. H. Munro) in *When William Came* (1913), have dealt solely with life under German rule; some, like C. S. Forester in *If Hitler had invaded England* (published posthumously in 1971), have concentrated on the actual landing and the subsequent military campaign. This book is different from these distinguished predecessors, and from various others less distinguished, in that it covers the whole subject, from the initial planning, through the assault and later operations, up to the German seizure of power and daily life under enemy occupation. It is, I believe, the first book to do so, and it also differs from earlier works, which have included at least one play and two films, in that it is based on fact. The first four chapters, describing German preparations and the British reaction to them, are wholly factual, while the last thirteen describe, in an entirely non-fictional way, what German occupation would have been like, by reference to captured documents and by the record of how the Germans actually behaved in other countries, especially the one small corner of Britain they did occupy, the Channel Islands.

Thus of twenty chapters only three deal with imaginary events, and even these are very far from being mere fiction. The military formations taking part on both sides are those which actually existed at the time, and the places where the invaders landed are those they selected for the purpose. The course of the battles which would have followed is inevitably a matter of speculation, but I have been guided by the conclusions reached by a panel of high-ranking military advisers to the associated television programme, who studied the problem at length, and by the narrative of the likely course of events prepared by the military historian, Mr Basil Collier, who is the author of the relevant volume of the official government *History of the Second World War* and an acknowledged authority on the subject. I have added a good deal of description and a few incidents to the factual skeleton, but have included nothing that could not have happened. The massacre of civilians by German troops, for example, did actually occur, though in 1944 in France and not in 1940 in the Sussex village where I have set it, and to which I have given the only imaginary place-name in the book.

Any historian must feel some diffidence about mixing fact and fiction, but I finally decided that, provided the three fictional chapters were clearly signposted as such, the technique was in this case legitimate, partly because, as mentioned earlier, such accounts have a long and respectable ancestry, but, more important, because the preceding events would directly have affected the nature of the occupation following them. Denmark, which capitulated without a struggle, had a far easier time than Norway, which put up a gallant fight, and life in occupied Britain, after weeks of bloodshed and with no government in being, would clearly have begun in a very different atmosphere from that of the Channel Islands where not a shot was fired and the civil authority was still in being.

The book has its origin in the television programme of the same name, but it is something more than the 'book of the programme', not least because a volume of this size can include more material than even a three-hour television programme. Although I have had the benefit of discussions with the producer about his intentions, and have had access to the documents assembled for the production and the transcripts of the interviews recorded for it, I had when I wrote the book seen neither a complete script nor any part of the final programme, which was then still being edited. Much of the material I have used is based on my own research and does not appear in the programme. Although on the military side I have closely followed the conclusions of the experts, my own military service, as a private in the Home Guard and an NCO in the Army, having been at less elevated levels, I have felt free to dissent in minor matters, and the account of the form occupation would have taken is wholly my own.

While writing the book I have constantly had cause to feel grateful that the whole of my military service, after preliminary training, was spent in studying, though in a very junior capacity, the problems of an occupied country, first from outside and then on the spot. From August 1944 to May 1945 I worked in London in the Supreme Headquarters Mission to Denmark, moving with the Mission to Copenhagen at the end of the war, and remaining there until I was demobilised in September 1947. It was, I now appreciate, a valuable experience to see the intelligence reports coming out of one occupied country during the final months of the war just as it was an exhilarating one to be among those cheered in the streets as liberators (not very deservedly, since we had taken no part in the fighting) in May 1945. Later, working as I did in an office formerly used by the Germans, and meeting every day people who had taken part in—or been sceptical about—the Resistance, I gained, I believe, some understanding of the meaning of Occupation, both to the occupiers and the occupied. I have allowed myself the small indulgence of including the training battalion in which I served among those which play some part in the fictional section of this book, although I suspect that it did not in fact exist in 1940.

When the BBC's plans to produce the programme of *If Britain had Fallen* were first disclosed a number of people expressed misgivings, apparently considering that even to acknowledge that this country could have been defeated in 1940 was unpatriotic. This reaction, even when not based on a complete misunderstanding of the programme's intentions, was, in my view, wholly misplaced, revealing in those who displayed it a surprising ignorance of recent British history. Almost every leading statesman in 1940, not excluding Winston Churchill himself, at least admitted the possibility that Germany might successfully invade Britain, and many eminent figures, such as President Roosevelt, actually expected this to happen. Nor were the generals then in command optimistic, at least in private, about a British victory; indeed, considering what had recently happened in Norway and France, and was soon to happen in Malaya, they had little reason to be. The authorities on both sides agreed that the success or failure of an invasion depended upon command of the air, and the desperately narrow margin by which this was retained, and the Battle of Britain won, has often been described and never disputed. In other words, we could well have lost the war in 1940, and most ordinary people who lived through that time will probably admit that, at least in their innermost hearts, they harboured such fears at the time, while some people at least openly voiced them.

I must record my thanks to Mr Michael Latham, the producer of the television programme *If Britain had Fallen*; to the staff of the BBC Reference Library, who dealt with many queries on minor points with their customary efficiency; to Mrs Sheila Bailey, who typed the manuscript at record speed; and to my secretary, Miss Judith Went, who was consistently helpful in my research into events that occurred long before she was born. The responsibility for what appears in the text remains entirely my own.

N.R.L.

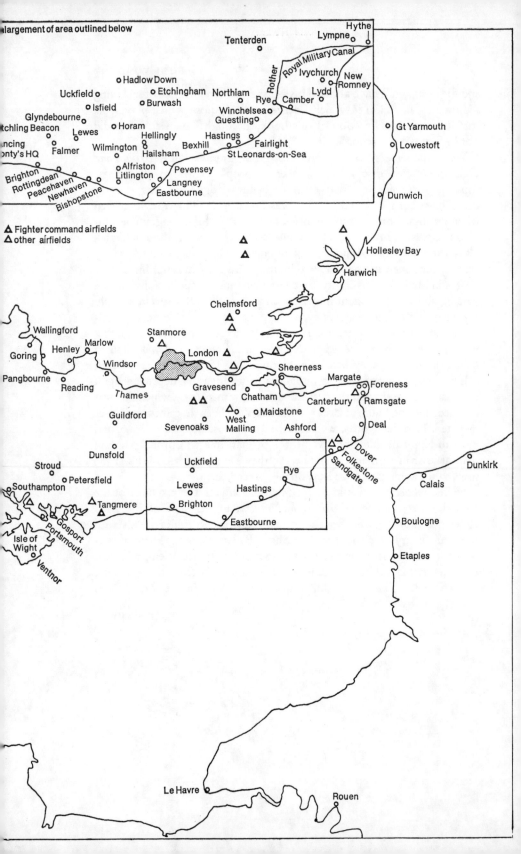

Chapter 1: Plans

Since England, despite its hopeless military situation, still gives no sign of any readiness to come to terms, I have decided to prepare for invasion of that country.

Adolf Hitler, Directive No. 16, 16 July 1940

In the Summer of 1940 it was a fine thing to be a German soldier. Even the most pacifically-minded ex-civilian, reluctantly called up a year before, could hardly fail to feel proud of his uniform as he looked back on the long, unbroken series of victories achieved by the Army in the past few months. It was an even finer thing to be a member of the German High Command, and thus one of the architects of these triumphs, but, curiously enough, the officers concerned felt less confidence in their abilities than the men they led. The British expected Hitler's generals at least to attempt an invasion; the German soldiers and regimental officers expected it to succeed. But those on whom the actual responsibility rested were by no means so optimistic, largely because this was one contingency for which they had never been asked to plan. Hitler had always maintained that he had no real quarrel with England. What possible concern was it of the British what happened to German-speaking Austria, or Germany's artificially created neighbour, Czechoslovakia, or her historic enemy, Poland? None of these states were within five hundred miles of Great Britain, but all lay on Germany's borders.

Hitler waited patiently, by his own standards, for the first peace overtures to come from Great Britain and finally, a month after the armistice with France, with no word from England except of defiance, himself extended the olive branch. It almost caused him pain, he told the Reichstag on Friday 19 July, the anniversary, had he known it, of the defeat of the Spanish Armada, to be responsible for bringing down a great Empire 'which it was never my intention to destroy or even to harm. . . . I can see no reason why this war must go on . . . I . . . appeal once more to reason and commonsense in Great Britain as much as elsewhere. I consider myself in a position to make this appeal since I am not the vanquished begging favours, but the victor speaking in the name of reason.'

For Hitler this was indeed unusually mild and the reception of his 'peace offer' in England confirmed his worst misgivings about the unreasonableness of the British. The government largely ignored it, and when, in August, copies of the speech under the title *A Last Appeal to Reason* were dropped from German aircraft they were auctioned for war charities and torn up for toilet paper in front of the newsreel cameras. In private Hitler did not conceal his disappointment at the rebuff. He was, he insisted, sincere in wanting to avoid a battle which he believed would be 'hard and bloody', but the British left him no alternative, and planning, which had only begun in earnest two days before his Reichstag speech, was now pressed ahead.

Although the German command system placed final power in Hitler's hands as Führer, the Chief of the High Command of the Armed Forces (OKW) was Field-Marshal Keitel, whose immediate subordinate was General Jodl, Chief of the Wehrmacht Operations Staff. They, or Hitler direct, issued orders to the Army High Command (OKH) under Field-Marshal von Brauchitsch, the Naval High Command (OKM) under Grand Admiral Raeder, and the Luftwaffe High Command, headed by Reich Marshal Göring, who was also Minister for Air. Hitler himself, and the staff of OKW, at first doubtful whether an invasion was necessary, eventually became convinced that it could be successfully achieved—given adequate naval and air support. The German Navy was always far more pessimistic and acknowledged frankly that it could not unaided achieve the necessary command of the sea; the Luftwaffe, under Göring, was more hopeful but during the following weeks their continuing failure decisively to defeat the RAF made the value of his opinions suspect. No one in fact was really enthusiastic about the invasion, and even as the preparatory work for it began the men at the top still hoped that Great Britain might be driven to seek peace by an air and sea blockade alone.

In prewar staff studies this had always been the textbook answer to this particular problem and when, on 23 May 1939, Hitler had informed his generals of his decision to attack Poland, he had predicted that, once Holland, Belgium and France had been occupied, Britain could be blockaded at close range by aircraft flying from bases in those countries and at longer range by U Boats operating from French ports. On 9 October, a month after the war had begun, another top-level directive confirmed that to secure bases for this purpose was one of the aims of 'Operation Yellow', the attack on France, and the policy of defeating Britain by destroying her trade and starving her into surrender, which had come close to success in 1917, was reaffirmed in another order, signed personally by Hitler on 29 November.

The first actual examination of the strategy needed to invade Britain was made by the Naval Staff Operations Division, whom Admiral Raeder ordered to look into the subject on 15 November 1939. Its report, submitted to him two weeks later, very understandably stressed the difficulties of the operation. The geography of the British Isles, they pointed out, favoured the defence, and excellent internal communications would make it easy to concentrate reinforcements against any German forces which did secure a foothold. It would undoubtedly be essential, before any landing of troops was attempted, to destroy the British Air Force and the Navy would still need to protect the invasion fleet by deploying a strong force of escort vessels on either flank and by laying extensive minefields.

The Navy's proposals raised for the first time one problem to which much thought was to be devoted in the next few months: should the attack be mounted from German bases on the North Sea, or even in the Baltic via the Kiel Canal, which would make embarkation much easier and reduce the chance of the British discovering, and interfering with, the vast preparations needed, but would mean a long sea crossing, increasing the risk of interception at sea and forfeiting the advantage of surprise? Or should the fleet sail from French and Dutch ports, more vulnerable to reconnaissance and aerial and naval attack, but offering a short sea crossing and making it easier for the Luftwaffe to provide air cover? The answer to this question largely dictated the answer to the second basic decision: where should the attack be directed? The short sea route meant the troops disembarking in Kent and Sussex, convenient for a thrust towards London but likely to be heavily defended and with relatively few ports and beaches suitable for landing, due to the area being commanded by cliffs with high ground, favouring the defenders, a little way inland. The long sea route would point to disembarking along the East Coast, with, between the Tyne and the Thames, at least thirteen excellent harbours, such as Blyth and Harwich, and a wide variety of suitable beaches all the way from Filey and Bridlington to Cromer and Clacton. The flat countryside here would make securing a bridgehead, and the subsequent break-out, easier though it was further to the enemy capital. Due to the gently sloping coastline along the East coast, however, the water tended to be shallow close in, with few sheltered bays, so the larger transports would have to lie off shore, exposed to the risk of attack, while discharging their cargoes into smaller lighters and barges, a slow and hazardous business even if the weather were favourable. The Navy nevertheless favoured the North Sea/East coast route, while clearly hoping the operation would never be necessary at all. The High Command, they urged, should not 'neglect, for the distant object of a possible landing, opportunities which are readily available for damaging the enemy', and the planners laid down one essential precondition for success: 'It seems to be indispensable that airborne troops should establish a bridgehead for landing.' But, if this and other requirements were fulfilled, they were cautiously optimistic, conceding that 'when forces are released from the Western Front . . . a landing in the British Isles, undertaken across the North Sea on a grand scale, . . . appears to be a possible expedient for forcing the enemy to sue for peace'.

Not long afterwards it was the German Army's turn and on 13 December, while the civilians in Great Britain and the British Expeditionary Force in France were settling down to that first, cold, dark, miserable winter of the war, the Army Commander-in-Chief, General von Brauchitsch, 'ordered an examination of the possibility of a landing in England . . . in a study to be called "North-West" ', the code-name which continued to be used for the invasion plans until July 1940. By now the German commanders knew that Holland, as well as Belgium and France, was to be attacked in the Spring Offensive, an important addition, for the Dutch ports and estuaries offered far better facilities for assembling barges and embarking troops and supplies than those so far available. The use of Holland as a base also made more attractive the idea of a 'middle route' aimed solely at East Anglia, and the Army favoured a landing on the East coast between the Wash and the Thames, involving some sixteen divisions. The plan was to capture Yarmouth and Lowestoft in a sudden combined sea and air assault, with further landings at Dunwich and Hollesley Bay. Two infantry divisions would land north of the Humber and advance towards the industrial area around Leeds, but this would be essentially a diversion, for the real thrust would come further south, where some four infantry divisions, with airborne support, would clear the way for two panzer divisions and a motorised division. These, it was hoped, would break through the British defences and sever London's communications with the North, the force's flank being protected by airborne troops landed on a captured airfield near Cambridge. Other forces would follow in later waves and, once the Germans had built up an overwhelming force, it would move on London, the capture of which would lead, they believed, to the collapse of the whole defence system.

Although the reputation of the Army General Staff stood high, the Army's confidence in its plan was not wholly shared by the other two services. The Naval Staff, perhaps recalling the defeat of the *Graf Spee* off Montevideo, displayed in its comments a healthy respect for the Royal Navy. 'The British Home Fleet will always be able to appear in greater strength than our own fleet, if the will is there', it advised despondently. Whatever support the German Navy received from the Luftwaffe it could not guarantee 'continuous control of the supply lines', and, it pointed out in a masterly understatement, it could not 'be assumed . . . that the major part of the enemy forces will be incapable of action' while the landing was in progress. Finally, the Naval Staff recalled what the soldiers seemed largely to have overlooked, that the ships needed to carry this force of men and vehicles across the North Sea did not exist. 'The transport required for the forces specified by the General Staff amounts to about 400 medium-sized steamers, with in addition a large collection of auxiliary vessels of the most varied nature, some of which must first be constructed.' And this was only to carry the first wave of seven divisions. In fact, concluded the sailors gloomily, to mobilise such a force would mean that 'during the period concerned all other shipping activity is virtually suspended', while to assemble ships needed in the number, and with the equipment required, 'presupposes that at least one year previously certain measures have been taken in the dockyards'. It was the classic reply of the Irishman asked the way: 'If I wanted to go there I wouldn't have started from here.'

The Luftwaffe, too, perhaps also fearful of being made the scapegoat for failure by the Army, threw cold water on the 'North-West' proposals, and the two other services abandoned their own rivalry to combine against the common enemy. 'The Airborne landing planned', warned the Air Staff in a note sent to the Army on 30 December 1939 and previously seen by the Naval Staff Operations Division, 'will run into the strongest point of the enemy air defence, which it will not be possible to eliminate. . . . The planned operation can only be considered . . . under conditions of absolute air superiority, and even then only if surprise is ensured. . . . Even weak enemy forces would suffice to make transport almost impossible. . . . A combined operation with a landing in England as its object must be rejected. . . . It could only be the last act of a war against England which had already taken a victorious course, as otherwise the conditions required for the success of a combined operation do not exist.' Here again was that circular argument to which so many discussions had already returned: an invasion could only take place successfully when it was no longer necessary.

And then, far sooner than the German generals had themselves expected, the situation changed dramatically. In April 1940 Denmark and Norway, in May Belgium and Holland, were overrun. On 4 June the last British soldier was lifted from the beaches of Dunkirk and two weeks later, on Monday, 17 June, France asked for an Armistice. The whole of the coastline of north-west Europe, from the north of Norway to the Spanish frontier, now lay in German hands, and the booty which had fallen to the victors was enormous. Though much had been rendered temporarily unusable, the British Expeditionary Force had inevitably abandoned enormous numbers of guns and vehicles and vast mounds of supplies of all kinds, while the French had not even attempted to prevent their huge accumulation of stores and weapons falling into German hands, or to send their fleet away to carry on the fight, though its most powerful warships were to be crippled by the Royal Navy in July on Churchill's orders. By many Germans the Führer, the real architect of all these triumphs, was now elevated to a status little below that of a god, and if the German General Staff did not share this view they certainly felt a new respect for Hitler's abilities as a strategist. It was not only in England, where emphasis tended, however, to be placed on the failure of his predecessor's invasion plans in 1804 and his final defeat, that Hitler was compared to Napoleon. So far the German Army had not been eager for an invasion, and the German Navy and Air Force had come close to predicting that it would fail. But now, if Hitler said it was possible, then, however much military habits of thought and training counselled caution, it could almost certainly be done.

In July 1940 planning for the invasion of the British Isles, which had hitherto been left to the initiative of the three services, became the concern of the High Command of the Armed Forces (Oberkommando der Wehrmacht, or OKW), to which all three service chiefs were responsible, and on 2 July Hitler issued a formal directive that staff planning was now to begin. This preliminary warning was followed on 16 July 1940 by the famous *Directive No. 16, Preparations for the Invasion of England*, which became the basic blue-print for the whole operation, now given the name *Sea Lion*. Even in the preamble, however, there was a hint of Hitler's continuing reluctance for a confrontation with Great Britain on her own soil:

Since England, despite its hopeless military situation, still gives no sign of any readiness to come to terms, I have decided to prepare for invasion of that country and, if necessary, to carry it through. . . . The aim of this operation will be to eliminate England as a base for carrying on the war against Germany and, should it be required, completely to occupy it.

Hitler's plan, presumably drafted for him by the OKW staff, accepted the previous findings of the Navy on the need for air supremacy and for protection of the flanks of the invasion corridor against naval attack.

The English air force must be beaten physically and morally to a point that they cannot put up any show of attacking force worth mentioning. . . . The Straits of Dover must be cut off on both flanks by thickly laid minefields and the Western entrance of the Channel in a line from Alderney to Portland will be blocked as well. . . . The coastal area on the immediate front will be held under fire by strong coastal artillery to form an artillery screen. . . . It will be an advantage to pin down English

Naval forces, shortly before the operation, in the North Sea, and in the Mediterranean (by the Italians) and an attempt will now be made to cripple naval forces based in England by air and torpedo attacks.

Hitler also came down firmly in favour of the Navy's final preference for the 'short sea crossing' against the Army's old 'North-West' scheme for landing in East Anglia:

The landing will be carried out as a surprise crossing on a broad front from the neighbourhood of Ramsgate to the area of the west of the Isle of Wight; some air force units will play the role of artillery and some naval units will act as engineers. . . . Preparations for the entire operation must be completed by the middle of August.

With only a month to go, and the invasion clearly 'on', the service commanders had more than enough to occupy them, but Hitler kept up the pressure from above with *Directive No. 17*, on 1 August, in which, in his lordly way, he declared:

I have decided to carry on and intensify air and naval warfare against England in order to bring about her final defeat.

For this purpose I am issuing the following orders:

1. The German air force with all available forces will destroy the English Air Force as soon as possible.
   The attacks will be directed first against airborne aircraft, their ground and supply organisation, and then against the aircraft industry, including the manufacture of Anti-Aircraft equipment. . . .
2. In view of our own intended operations, attacks on harbours on the South coast will be kept to a minimum.

The Directive also declared that 'I am reserving terror attacks', i.e. the bombing of cities, 'as reprisals' and ordered that 'intensification of the air war can begin on 5 August 1940', though the actual date was to be fixed by the air staff according to weather and other conditions.

During the next few weeks Hitler's Commander-in-Chief, Field Marshal Keitel, and Keitel's subordinates, General Jodl and Major-General Warlimont, Chief of the Operations Branch, issued a steady stream of orders which can have left the three service commanders in no doubt that the Führer was in earnest. On 5 August Keitel himself signed a somewhat grandiose signal declaring 'The Great Air Offensive against England will begin within a few days', and two days later he issued further orders 'On deceptive measures to maintain the appearance of constant threat of invasion of the United Kingdom'. It was not only in the title of this document that a note of hesitation crept in:

Regardless of whether or when we invade England, the constant menace of invasion must be maintained against the English people and armed forces. . . . The main German operation shall appear to be preparing for landing on the English East coast as well as invading Ireland. . . . The various services must extend their preparations . . . to cover the actual intentions by deploying considerable forces in Norway and Denmark (landing on English East coast), Netherlands (landing North of the mouth of the Thames), Brest and area Biscay (landing in Ireland). . . . After the completion of preparations the denying of certain areas to civilian traffic may be considered in order to increase the verisimilitude of the preparations. . . . Those individuals below a specified grade of the High Command who are concerned with the preparations are not to be informed that their tasks are aimed at deception.

One of the problems confronting the German General Staff which had not yet troubled their British opposite numbers was that of maintaining a reputation for infallibility, and the *Summary of the Situation referring to Invasion of the United Kingdom* which General Jodl circulated on 13 August reflected this unwillingness to be associated with failure. 'The landing operation', wrote Jodl, 'must not founder in any circumstances. Failure can have political repercussions far outweighing the military set-back'—among them, perhaps, that the Führer might have sought a new Chief of the Wehrmacht Operations Staff. Jodl went on:

As far as it is humanly possible to eliminate failure, I am in agreement with the Army that it is essential that:
(a) landing must be simultaneous from Folkestone to Brighton Bay.
(b) within four days ten divisions should be landed in this sector.
(c) within the succeeding four days at least three divisions with complete equipment should follow across the Straits even if sea conditions do not permit the use of flat-bottomed craft (barges), while the troops landed further to the West will be reinforced by airborne troops. . . .
Should the Navy, however . . . not be in a position to fulfil conditions (a), (b) and (c) then I consider the landing to be an act of desperation which . . . we have at this stage no reason whatever to contemplate. . . . England can be brought to her knees in other ways.

The 'other ways' Jodl contemplated were, it seemed, intensifying the U Boat offensive and air war, with the help of the Italians, 'taking Egypt, if necessary with Italian help, and taking Gibraltar in agreement with the Spanish and Italians', suggestions made, perhaps, rather on diplomatic grounds than as serious military proposals.

Meanwhile, at lower levels, work on *Operation Sea Lion* was pressed ahead. On the day after Hitler's *Directive No. 16* the Army General Staff had already begun to earmark troops for the operation and to move these favoured, or unfortunate, formations to the coast. Six divisions, it was proposed, should cross from the Pas de Calais and land between Ramsgate

and Bexhill, four more would embark near Le Havre, destined for the
Sussex and Hampshire coast between Brighton and the Isle of Wight,
and three more from Cherbourg, to make passage for Lyme Bay, where
they were to come ashore between Weymouth and Lyme Regis, the
beautiful stretch of coastline, though the Germans did not mention this,
hitherto famous chiefly for the unique pebble ridge known as Chesil
Beach and the ancient swannery of Abbotsbury. Altogether the Army
planned to put ashore 90,000 in the first wave, building up to 260,000
men by the third day, a force roughly equal to the British Expeditionary
Force rescued from Dunkirk. The Army Commander-in-Chief, von
Brauchitsch, had now become highly enthusiastic about the whole
operation. Bridgeheads, he believed, could be secured without difficulty,
a total of forty-one divisions could be poured into England as smoothly
as they had recently spread out into France, and within a month the
British government would, he prophesied, have capitulated.

The Naval Commander-in-Chief, Admiral Raeder, failed totally to
share this optimism. On 17 July he warned von Brauchitsch that the risks
were so appalling that the whole invading force might be lost, and two
days later his staff produced for his use a list of difficulties enough to daunt
the stoutest heart. Carrying the numbers proposed the required distance,
they insisted, was a task beyond the Navy's strength, the ships would be
threatened by mines, there would not be sufficient landing-craft available,
the harbours and canals needed for their assembly had been damaged and
could not handle the numbers needed and—a factor that mere landsmen
were always liable to overlook—the tides, current and weather might all
conspire to upset the plans prepared ashore. Worst of all, it was only too
likely, after the first wave had successfully got ashore, that the Royal Navy
would prevent reinforcements arriving, leaving the troops in the beach-
head, cut off from their base, to be picked off by the enemy at leisure.

Hitler's confidence in his own powers had never extended to the sea,
which he personally disliked, his favourite retreat being deep in the
mountains. He had never crossed the Channel, even as a day-tripper, much
less made an ocean voyage, and he was, he said in private, prepared to
leave England her traditional command of the sea provided she would
recognise Germany's supremacy on land. The Navy's anxieties about *Sea
Lion* made a deep impression on him and, wiser than his generals, he did
not accept their description of the operation as merely an opposed river-
crossing on a large scale, at which they were past-masters. 'This is not
just a river crossing, but the crossing of a sea which is dominated by the
enemy,' he reminded von Brauchitsch and General Jeschonnek, Chief of
the Luftwaffe General Staff, on 21 July. *Sea Lion* was an 'exceptionally

daring undertaking' and 'the most difficult part will be the continued reinforcement of equipment and stores'.

Ten days later, on 31 July, a long procession of powerful staff cars carried Field Marshal von Brauchitsch, Admiral Raeder and other senior officers through the ugly little town of Berchtesgaden and up the steep and winding road leading to Hitler's magnificently sited mountain retreat, the Berghof, for a major conference on the coming invasion. Britain, Hitler told his commanders, seemed determined to fight on and bombing and U Boat operations might take as long as two years to win the war unaided, so that a 'positively decisive result can only be achieved by an attack on England'. The first step was the air offensive, which should begin at once, and if this failed preparations for the invasion would have to be abandoned. 'But if we gain the impression that the English are being crushed . . . then we shall attack.'

Soldiers and sailors now confronted each other, under the Führer's chairmanship, and Raeder made the most of his opportunity. The Navy was, he reported, pressing on energetically with preparations for *Sea Lion* and assembling shipping and converting landing-craft, but even granted favourable weather and air superiority the Navy could not hope to be ready before 15 September, and the earliest period when all the requirements for the landing would be met would be between 19 and 26 September. Raeder pleaded, too, for the invasion area to be narrowed still further, and for landings to be confined to the Straits of Dover.

Although Hitler replied that 15 September should remain the target date, subsequent events showed that Raeder's arguments had, as in the past, made a deep impression and on 7 August Raeder's Chief of Staff, Admiral Schniewind, and his opposite number, Colonel-General Halder, Chief of Staff to von Brauchitsch, continued the argument without the Führer. Halder indignantly rejected the Navy's demand for the landing to be on a narrow front, declaring that 'I might just as well put the troops through a sausage machine', and a week later Schniewind riposted with a written reminder that the airborne landings behind the beaches, in which the Army placed such faith, could not assist the Navy. 'The airborne troops', he pointed out, 'can influence neither the weather nor the sea; they cannot prevent the destruction . . . of the few harbours, nor hold off the enemy fleet.'

The Navy won its argument. On 16 August Field Marshal Keitel signalled to the three services that Hitler had decided that 'preparations for a landing in Lyme Bay will be suspended', and on 27 August the planners were informed that the assault to be mounted from Le Havre, aimed at the coast between Brighton and Portsmouth, would also be scaled down. Hitler had decided, reported Keitel, a little superfluously it may be felt, that 'Army operations will be adapted to fit in with the given facts in relation to the available tonnage and cover for embarkation and crossing'.

On 3 September, one year to the day after the outbreak of war, Keitel issued the timetable for the campaign designed to force Great Britain to surrender. It read:

1. The earliest date for
   (a) The departure of the transport fleets will be 20 September 1940.
   (b) S day (Invasion day) will be 21 September 1940.
2. The order for the start of the operation will be given on S—10 days, probably on 11 September 1940.
3. The final decision on S day and S time (beginning of the first landing) will follow at the latest on S—3 days at noon.
4. All measures will be taken so that the operation can still be held in suspense 24 hours before S time.

So *Operation Sea Lion* was definitely on. The commanders had taken their decisions, the planners had done their work. Now all rested upon 'the field-greys', the ordinary German soldiers, who, with their superbly trained, battle-hardened officers and NCOs, made up the most formidable army in the world.

Chapter 2: Preparations

'How much do you charge for swimming lessons?'—*British propaganda leaflet dropped on German invasion troops, August 1940*

To land upon a hostile shore is one of the most difficult operations known to military science, and the greater one's knowledge of the sea the more respect one has for it. When, in July, the Army which had conquered France got down in earnest to training for the coming attack on England, it was the recruits from inland provinces like Bavaria and the Tyrol, many of whom had never before seen the sea, who were most light-hearted about their approaching ordeal. Even they learned fast; a single panic-stricken moment floundering out of their depth when bathing, a single bout of sea-sickness during a disembarkation exercise, was enough. To many orderly-minded Germans the apparently capricious behaviour of the tides also came as a disagreeable surprise. General von Manstein himself, commanding 38 Corps, was disconcerted, after leaving his Mercedes high up the beach to go swimming with his ADC, to find the waves lapping round it on his return, and the commanding officer of a Mountain Division in the same Army Group, whose role on S day would be to scale the Kentish cliffs, suffered an equal shock when he ordered a daily parade on the beach at 0900 hours for a swimming lesson. On the first morning the sea was in the expected place, but on the second it had unaccountably moved much further out. A Naval liaison officer helpfully explained that tides did vary from day to day but the commander firmly refused to revise the divisional training schedule, so that each morning the men faced a longer and longer march across the foreshore before bathing could begin.

There was prestige, as well as pleasure, to be gained that summer from being stationed on the coast, as it meant one's unit was likely to be among the first to land. Training was hard. The troops practised musketry and drill, unarmed combat and patrolling, digging trenches and standing guard, like all soldiers in every army. Time after time they packed their belongings into knapsacks and haversacks, loaded their packs with cartridges and, in progressively more orderly and rapid-moving files, climbed on board barges or steamers and then, the loading exercise completed, climbed back on the jetty again. Sometimes, after a short and often all too rough voyage, the landing-craft were run aground, and the men dashed down the ramps and charged up the beach led by their officers, pistol in hand. It made an impressive sight, but more than one old soldier, recalling tales of Gallipoli, must have wondered whether it would all go quite as smoothly on the day.

But there was not much training afloat, for there were few vessels to spare. The 8th Division, preparing to cross to Newhaven, complained as late as 23 August that its men had so far been assigned only one steamer for practice purposes, and this had now been sunk. Other troops, scheduled to make the crossing by barge, were not reassured by the sight of the broken-down and battered old river-craft scraped up from somewhere to carry them. The soldiers grumbled, too, about the horses which cluttered up the roads and embarkation areas, for 4000 were due to go in with the first assault and 7000 in the second, to drag guns and supply wagons across the soft sand and loose pebbles of the landing beaches, and then up the steep and narrow roads leading inland. But the horses, too, had little opportunity to become accustomed to life afloat, for as soon as vessels were collected they were hurried into boatyards, to be given concrete floors to carry tanks and guns, and collapsible ramps down which men and vehicles would (in theory at least) charge eagerly to confront the enemy.

Shipping, it was soon clear, was going to be a major problem. Admiral Raeder estimated that even for the much smaller first-wave and follow-up landings which the Army had now accepted more than 1700 barges were required, with nearly 500 tugs, 1200 motor-boats and 155 larger transports. Although, with typical German speed and thoroughness, most of the barges needed were rapidly assembled, mainly from the canals and rivers of Western Europe, a few were self-propelled. The rest would have to be towed, a difficult operation for shallow-draught craft built for use on inland waterways, and some of the largest, with a capacity of 1300 tons—the average was only 500 to 800—would only move when fully loaded if wedged between two minesweepers to half-pull, half-push them across the Channel. The watermen who had operated these craft under sheltered conditions on the Rhine or the Scheldt showed little desire to man them on their cross-Channel journey, and their owners were content for the invasion to be put off indefinitely, due to the unexpectedly generous rate of compensation for each day their vessels were retained.

As the troops lounged in the sunshine on the beach that August, or paraded by the estuaries and harbours of France and Holland, there was plenty for them to watch as the barges were manœuvred into place by the ubiquitous tugs, and the motor-boats which were to ferry troops ashore from the larger ships steamed urgently about on exercises. The finest spectacle was provided, if one were fortunate enough to see it, by the high-speed landing-craft, driven by an aircraft-engine, which it was hoped would roar across the Channel and charge up the enemy beach like racing-boats. Unhappily, however, the *Truppentransporttragflachen- schnellboote* proved to have a more impressive title than performance and very few sailed except on the air-waves of the 'black' German radio, which darkly referred to them on 10 September as one of the reasons why England should make peace.

The approaching invasion was already providing inventors on both sides of the Channel with a field day, and with the need to obtain tactical surprise in mind the German authorities were unusually receptive to new ideas. As early as April Professor Gottfried Feder, no mere crank but a senior official in the Ministry of Economics, had prepared plans for *his* contribution to what he called 'the great war aim', the destruction of England, the 'war tortoise' or 'war crocodile'. This consisted of a large hollow slab made of reinforced concrete, ninety feet long, twenty feet wide and twelve feet high, powered by an engine which would either drive it through the water, just below the surface, or, as it touched bottom, operate caterpillar tracks. The sight of these monsters, nearly the size of four buses placed end to end, crawling up the beach of Folkestone or Bexhill, might well have caused surprise among the defenders, and the 200 armed men, or detachment of guns and tanks, which each would disgorge would, Feder hoped, strike terror in their hearts. Like most inventors he had an answer to every objection; the craft's bulk, he believed, would guarantee its seaworthiness, while production presented no problem since the German concrete industry had easily coped with the demand for blockhouses for the Siegfried line. Rather surprisingly, discussions were held between the Army and the Navy (which was sceptical about it) on the feasibility of the new weapon, but no 'crocodiles' were ready by September.

Designed to serve much the same purpose, but far more practical, were the amphibian and submersible tanks on which the Germans were already working. Both types consisted basically of ordinary armoured vehicles which had been waterproofed, but the former were designed to float in the sea while the latter were virtually small submarines, which crawled along the sea-bed, steered by periscope and obtaining their air through a tube fixed to a floating buoy, not unlike the 'Schnorchel' device later fitted to U Boats. A successful demonstration in front of the German Armaments Minister was held on 25 June, and the conversion of existing tanks was pressed ahead so rapidly that by late August 262, sufficient for a whole armoured division of four tank battalions, were ready for use, 210 of them being medium tanks of a submersible kind, and the remainder light amphibians designed to float. By late September even larger numbers would be available, though already Field Marshal von Brauchitsch had

been supplied with more adapted tanks than he had asked for. The only
delay came from instructions, issued in mid-July, to keep in France a number of Mark III and Mark IV Panzers, earmarked for return to Germany
to be modified, so that they could lead the planned Victory Parade
through Paris. But they went after all, for plans for the big parade were
abandoned after someone had courageously reminded the Führer that the
RAF might turn up as an uninvited guest.

Such anxieties were the officers' concern. For the ordinary soldier
life was agreeable enough in between training sessions, as he lay on his
back in the sunshine and watched the Junkers 88s and Heinkel 111s
streaming over the Channel with their protective swarms of Messer-
schmidt fighters buzzing about them, and every night the radio boasted of
the great victories won that day in the skies over England. On the camp
notice boards were appeals for volunteers with experience of handling
boats and a few men who had boasted of sailing a small boat in peacetime, or of canoeing holidays with the Hitler Youth, proudly gave their
names in, and departed to a new unit, with many a joke from their comrades about hoping one would not be sent to face the Tommies in a boat
they were manning.

Although they had not yet been generally distributed, the enterprising
individual could also obtain without too much difficulty, from the heaps
stacked in the camp office, a *Bildheft*, or picture book, prepared for issue
to the invading forces to explain what sort of country they were about to
occupy. From the pictures it seemed that England was a country of
picturesque little harbours (like Mousehole, pronounced Maushohl, in
Cornwall), romantic ruins, like Tintern Abbey, and spacious country
houses. There seemed to be little industry and nothing like the German
Autobahnen, unless one counted the Mersey Tunnel (of which the official
opening in 1934 was shown), though the pictures of Blackpool Tower
and beach proved that the English did sometimes enjoy themselves.

For officers a good deal more information was available. The really
enthusiastic had already pored over the set of seven maps of the British
Isles, showing its population, transport and other features, prepared by
the German Intelligence Branch, and some had looked curiously at the
street-plans (based, had they known it, on those prepared by the Automobile Association) of towns like Dover and Hastings. At divisional
headquarters the staff might be seen earnestly studying a solid handbook,
Military-Geographical Data about England, which made it clear that East
Anglia and Salisbury Plain were the areas to which the keen tank-man
must hope fortune took him, while the narrow lanes of Devon were to
be avoided. The more pessimistic meanwhile studied the helpful lists of

the number of beds in the main hospitals of Southern England. Attempts at speaking the English sentences contained in the glossary were always good for a laugh in the mess at night, like 'Where is the next tank?'—not 'Vere', the booklet stressed—and there were such helpful phrases as 'War Office' (not 'Vor Ofiz'), 'sewage works', 'lunatic asylum', and, a little ominously, 'the bottom of the sea', or 'bot'tim ov dhe sie'.

Off duty, for all ranks, there was no lack of entertainment. French wines, brandy and champagne were cheap and plentiful and the initial surliness of many Frenchmen was beginning to wear off, as it became clear that the invaders would pay for what they wanted. The French girls, disdainful at first, were proving, at least in private, to be all that soldier's legend had claimed for them; there were, it was clear, advantages in occupying what Dr Goebbels had so often described as a degenerate country. Victory had brought, too, some unexpected spoils. The English had left behind, among their medical stores, box upon box labelled 'Sheaths, protective, 1 gross', each containing, for some curious English reason, not a sensible Germanic round number but the odd figure 144. Already everyone who had taken advantage of this unexpected gift reported that this was one British product vastly superior to the standard Wehrmacht issue.

The resulting pleasantries at the expense of the absent English were especially welcome when, as so often happened, one was turned out of bed in the small hours by an air raid alarm, while the Wellingtons and Blenheims bombed the barges and harbours on the coast, and occasionally the planes dropped leaflets, though there were orders that these must be handed in if found. They seemed at first, under the familiar heading *Wir Fahren Gegen Engelland*, to offer a number of helpful phrases in German, French and Dutch, but all proved on closer inspection to have a distinctly pessimistic ring: 'Was that a bomb—a torpedo—a shell—a mine?'; 'We are seasick. Where is the basin?'; 'How much do you charge for swimming lessons?'; and, most upsetting of all, in view of the rumours about British plans to set the sea on fire, 'See how briskly our captain burns!'

But the waiting Armies were reassured by the programmes which they, and the listeners at home, heard over the national radio network, now retransmitted in France. The Germans were a highly wireless-minded people; a higher proportion of people owned sets, and more people listened to each set, than in almost any other country in the world, and from their first seizure of power the Nazis had exploited the propaganda possibilities of radio to the full. Little outright propaganda was needed that summer for Germany's victories spoke for themselves, and German radio relied largely on quotations from the world's press to drive home the message of Britain's impending downfall. When foreign newspapers failed to come up to expectation German radio commentators filled the gap, especially the Propaganda Ministry's star performer, Hans Fritzsche, later head of its Radio Division. In thirteen talks between the beginning of August and the original target date for *Sea Lion*, mid-September, he assured his hearers that the British were doomed to defeat, either—the commonest reason quoted—because they were inefficient and unsoldierly, a greater crime perhaps in German than in British eyes, or because they were immoral and 'overage', meaning apparently that the British Empire had been there a long time.

The Propaganda Ministry was sensitive to the suggestion that perhaps the Germans were not going to invade England at all. The British, suggested German radio on 13 August, had invented the story that Hitler had boasted that he would be dining in Buckingham Palace by the 15th, this being their 'old trick' of announcing the date on which Hitler proposed to celebrate victory so that they could say 'The Germans have again missed the bus'. It was, announced the same broadcaster on 3 September, briefly elevating his own boss to a position he had never claimed, 'Dr Goebbels and the Führer', not the British, 'who would decide the decisive hour'.

Most of the bulletins which the soldiers heard that summer, however, were concerned with the air war, and every day yielded some new superlative: the recent attacks were 'the worst', 'the longest', 'the heaviest' that any country had ever undergone. 'While German bombers stream uninterruptedly towards England, our motor torpedo boats assure a sea rescue service in the Channel', boasted a reporter, allegedly posted on the French coast on 27 August, a little tactlessly. Another favourite theme throughout the summer was the supposed demoralisation of the British people. The 'most fashionable sickness' in England, the radio commentator assured the Fatherland, 'was parachutist fever', while English plutocrats, a favourite if vaguely identified group in German propaganda, 'soothe their feverish nerves by indulging in wild orgies'. On the same day, 27 July, it was claimed that 'a lady coming from one of the very best families told a reporter that it was easier to die when drunk than sober'. The radio speakers mocked any suggestion that the British might give as good as they got. 'The conception of the Fortress of England was invented by Churchill personally', Radio Berlin assured its audience. When a public appeal was made for arms for the LDV the Germans were delighted, drawing the all too accurate deduction that Britain must be desperately short of weapons, and the gift of several shotguns from the King's gunroom at Sandringham caused their commentator particular glee.

Obviously, he suggested, King George would not be needing them since he and his government were now packing their bags to leave for Canada.

Music of every type had always made a strong appeal to the Germans and all over conquered Europe *Deutschland über Alles* and the Nazi Party anthem, the *Horst Wessel Song*, were heard constantly that summer, alternating with other songs of lesser musical merit. Loyal Dutchmen or Danes might hurry away when a German band, playing in the park or a public square, struck up *Wir Fahren gegen England*, the best and oldest of these works of musical propaganda, but to anyone within earshot of a radio it was difficult to get away from it, although like most soldiers' songs it was more popular with the civilians at home than with the men in the field. Significantly, German radio played it on 21 June, at the end of its report on the French armistice negotiations, and it was heard again on 6 July after a description of the Führer's return through the flower-strewn streets of his capital to the Chancellery – Berlin's Buckingham Palace – where he appeared on the balcony to greet the hysterically applauding crowds. As he strode forward to acknowledge their ovation, the girlish voices of a choir of the Bund Deutscher Mädchen, the female equivalent of the Hitler Youth, sang out (although they were far too young to fight anyone, and also the wrong sex):

> Our flag waves as we march along.
> It is an emblem of the power of our Reich.
> And we can no longer endure
> That the Englishman should laugh at it.
> So give me thy hand, thy fair white hand,
> Ere we sail away to conquer Eng-el-land.

Soon afterwards it was the turn of Field Marshal Göring, never one to be left out of the act. The Luftwaffe's first entry into the popular music field was not perhaps a very happy one:

> We fly against England
> How red the roses bloom.
> We fly against England
> And with us flyeth doom.

But the Reich Marshal's song-writers made amends with the far more successful *Bombs on England*, played for the first time at the end of the edition of the regular programme *Front Reports* on 7 September, in which it was announced that the Air Minister and Luftwaffe Commander-in-Chief had arrived on the French coast to direct operations personally. Thereafter it became the programme's closing signature tune and was heard daily:

We challenge the lion of England
For the last and decisive struggle
We sit in judgment and we say,
An Empire breaks up.
Listen to the engine singing, Get on to the foe!
Listen, in your ears it's ringing, Get on to the foe!
Bombs, oh bombs, on England!

The song-writing division was not the only part of the Propaganda Ministry busy during those weeks. Recognising that 'on the day' everyone would be too busy to pose for the cameras, and that poor light and enemy fire might lead to inferior pictures, Goebbels's men filmed in advance a full-scale invasion exercise on the French coast, which they proposed to pass off, on cinema audiences in Germany and throughout the world, as the real thing, once *Sea Lion* had been launched. In this pre-scripted version of events, German soldiers were seen cheerfully embarking on their assault craft and leaping bravely into the surf off the 'enemy' shore, German casualties, wounded in photogenic places, were shown lying, uncomplaining, on stretchers, and British prisoners were filmed surrendering in droves and being marched off to captivity. It all looked remarkably convincing, but was a total fake. Only the shots of the prisoners were real, and they had been taken during the retreat to Dunkirk.[1]

By now summer was giving way to autumn. The leaves on the trees in the Bois de Boulogne and in the fields of the Pas de Calais would soon be turning brown. Already the golden days of May and June during which the Army had 'swanned' through the Low Countries and France seemed only a memory. The weather was still mainly fine and warm, but there were occasional showers and in the evenings it was chilly, as a reminder that winter was not so far away. The troops marched and trained and embarked and disembarked. But still they didn't set sail.

[1] This memorable production was never shown to its intended audience and vanished, not even catalogued, into the vaults of the German film archives, where, thirty years later, it was unearthed by researchers for BBC Television. Ironically, therefore, its first-ever showing was to a British audience.

Chapter 3: Anticipation

The English fear of an impending German military invasion is weighing like a huge nightmare on the inhabitants of the British Isles.

German radio commentator, 18 July 1940

Great Britain really began to prepare to resist an invasion on 10 May 1940. At dawn that morning Germany began her great offensive in the West – but early that evening, on the far side of the Channel, Winston Churchill became Prime Minister. Henceforward, even if the means to fight were still lacking, the spirit was not. When, at the end of May and during the first days of June, the British Expeditionary Force, driven back from the Belgian frontier to the sea, had to abandon all its equipment and take to the boats to escape capture, it seemed to the German generals and the German people a great victory. To the British the sight of their retreating soldiers, lacking weapons, uniforms awry, weary, travel-stained and apparently decisively beaten, far from spreading gloom merely seemed to generate resolution. The reaction observed by one woman in Kent was typical:

We lived near the railway line from Dover to London. One day we noticed, from our field, a trainload of very tired, dishevelled-looking soldiers. Then another and another, day after day, night after night. Lots of people came from the village to stare. It was very hot, and we took out bottles of water and handed them up. . . . They wanted to know whether we had been bombed. 'Not yet.' At the next station, Headcorn, three miles away, arrangements had been made for feeding them. Local residents worked day and night, cutting sandwiches in an old barn, strings of sausages, hundreds of cans of tea. We did two or three nights and still the trains piled up along the line. The station was littered with tins and paper. It was intensely dramatic—the eager work in the dim lantern light in the old barn, us with our backs to the wall, and the fleeing army crowding back. . . .

More alarming as a reminder of what might be in store for the country, for the British troops were now at least back in their own country and no longer reliant on untrustworthy allies, was the arrival of boatload after boatload of civilian refugees, driven from their homes, and finally from their country, by the irresistibly advancing Germans. One thirteen-year-old Dorset schoolgirl now saw for herself what invasion could mean:

Weymouth was one of the main ports for the refugees and my mother was in charge of cooking for them, in a park called the Alexandra Gardens. She had six wash boilers for coffee, six for tomato soup, and a working party of about a dozen matelots to help her. They stirred the soup with cricket bats and were tireless and gentle with the babies. . . . My job was to wander around finding anyone who needed clothes for themselves or their babies, and taking them backstage in the theatre to fit them out. . . . One lady held a tiny baby, and the severed hand of a toddler. She had bent over the baby when the bombs fell, and the blast had killed and taken away the toddler. We could not take that gruesome hand away from her and she had to be sedated and taken to hospital. . . . The refugees were all trying to dry their photos from home, and one little Parisian was trying to sort out his photos near the heat of one of the boilers. He was an incredibly handsome man and looked so funny in his bloomers, but he wouldn't let go of one of these photos, it was all he had left of Paris.

In London, too, the arrival of the refugees made a deep impression. One woman, working all day at Victoria on 27 May as an interpreter for the Belgians flooding in from the Continent, found the policeman beside her growing more and more silent. At last he voiced what was in his mind, a fear almost unthinkable to someone living in a country not invaded for nearly a thousand years: 'Why, Miss, this is really serious. . . . This may happen to us.'

Already, too, some residents of Great Britain were being uprooted from their homes, as the government reluctantly bowed to public pressure and began to round up male Italian citizens, to join in captivity the Germans detained since the start of the war. To at least one family, living in Londonderry in Northern Ireland, the realisation that they were now technically 'enemy aliens' came as an appalling shock.

When Italy entered the war on 10 June 1940, my parents were already in this country for thirty years. We, the family, were all born here. . . . It was a shock to us, to be declared enemy aliens, to be awakened at 6 am on the morning of 11 June, by a dozen or more policemen, who told my father, regretfully, that they had come to detain him, my brother and a young relative who lived with us. We were called from our beds and came down to find the place surrounded by policemen. We were in the catering business, cafés, ice cream and fish and chip saloons. Each door was guarded by a policeman, the back gates were similarly guarded, while others swarmed over the house and cafés, searching for 'enemy' signs. You can imagine our bewilderment, my mother's distress, our tears as we watched my father, brother and cousin being led away by police escort to the barracks. Shortly afterwards the phone started ringing, my sisters in other towns told us of our uncles and various friends who had also been detained. By this time, the news had spread all over the city. 'The Italians have been arrested', and as we opened our shops that morning we did not know what to expect. But we were soon to find out. People who walked past stared in, some even stood and jeered, and I saw several who spat in our doorway. Our hearts were heavy as we noticed that none of our usual customers came in. One young office junior, who came every morning for milk and biscuits for the office across the way, and paid at the end of each week, told us sheepishly that they would not want anything else after this weekend. . . . I answered him sharply that he need not wait until the end of the week to finish with us, he could finish right now. . . . It was painful indeed to stand in our empty cafés, to watch our one-time customers outside, warning others not to go into 'enemy' shops. For some weeks this upheaval in our lives continued, our houses were searched, our car and radio confiscated; we were suspect. . . . Customers of years' standing, whom my parents had seen growing from childhood to manhood, ignored us and forbade others to come into our cafés. . . . And we were lucky that we did not get our windows smashed, as happened in many other places.[1]

Since no one liked to admit that they had been beaten by orthodox means, the myth that the defeat of Belgium, Holland and France had been due to mysterious and underhand tactics was readily accepted, and between May and September 1940 tales of the achievements of the dreaded 'fifth column' of traitors, lurking undetected within the garrison like wolves in sheep's clothing, or soon to be dropped by parachute in a variety of cunning disguises, spread from mouth to mouth The vice-admiral in command of Dover warned the Admiralty on 31 May that there were 'indications of numerous acts of sabotage and fifth-column activity', though the only overt sign was 'second-hand cars purchased at fantastic prices and left at various parking places', the supposed spies apparently being too honest simply to steal a car if they needed one. Five days later the Commander-in-Chief, Home Forces, soon to be replaced, warned a conference of LDV commanders: 'We have got examples of where there have been people quite definitely preparing aerodromes in this country. . . . We want to know from you what is going on. Is there anything peculiar happening? Are there any peculiar people?' Apart from a few harmless bird-watchers, holiday-makers sketching beauty-spots, and over-eager aircraft-spotters, lurking near aerodromes, all of whom were detained at various times, no 'peculiar people' were forthcoming, but the hunt for them continued. One schoolmistress, on holiday in a Dorset village, assisted the local mounted Home Guard unit, which patrolled the area on horseback, to search for 'arrows supposedly acting as pointers for incoming German bombers . . . cut in the middle of areas of standing corn', which, it was believed, an observer on horseback could detect more easily than anyone at ground level. She made no more exciting discovery, however, than a courting couple, meeting secretly because of parental disapproval.[2]

The really suspicious figures at this time, however, were nuns, it being

---

[1] In fact, both this woman's father and brother, after being well treated, were released the same day and with the arrival of troops in the area the business was soon booming again.

[2] A similar fear of secret signals to aircraft infected the Germans on Guernsey, who suspected that tomatoes had been planted in some fields to point towards hidden gun batteries.

widely believed that Holland had been captured by battalions of tough storm-troopers descending from the skies dressed as members of religious orders. The Dutch foreign minister, who started the story, also told a press conference in London in May of invaders arriving disguised as nurses, monks and tramcar conductors, but these categories never enjoyed the same popularity as fifth-columnists. Before long everyone knew someone who had encountered a nun in a train who had worn heavy jackboots beneath her skirt, or when trodden upon had uttered a manly oath, though why the Germans, with so many alternatives to choose from, should have selected a form of fancy dress that was both conspicuous and impractical was never explained. As one woman, involved in anti-invasion preparations in a remote village in Essex, remarked, any nun arriving there even in peacetime and by bus, let alone parachute, would have set the villagers speculating for days.

Among the measures taken to frustrate the knavish tricks of fifth columnists was the taking down of all the signposts in the country, ordered on 31 May, and the removal of milestones, station nameboards, place names on war memorials, and any other sign that could enable a town or village to be identified, a measure that could not have caused more trouble to the defenders, and less to the potential invaders, if it had been the inspiration of Hitler himself. *Punch* reflected the traveller's problems when it published in late July a cartoon showing a small boy telling a group of obviously lost staff officers, clutching maps, 'I'll tell nobody where anywhere is'.

Other restrictions, like the ban on carrying a car radio, caused less concern and one change introduced in May 1940 was positively popular, the identification by name of announcers reading the news, prompting many ponderous imitations by humorists declaring with an exaggerated, supposedly German accent: 'Hier ist ze news and hier ist Alvar Lidell reading it.' The possibility was, however, less fanciful than it seemed to the general public for (although the British government did not wish to advertise the fact) already four 'black', i.e. unacknowledged, German radio stations were bombarding the British Isles with misleading information, each claiming to be operating 'underground' as part of a secret resistance movement against the British government. The New British Broadcasting Station, which used as its signature tune 'The Bonnie, Bonnie Banks of Loch Lomond', had been broadcasting since February, and it was followed in July by Workers' Challenge, which depicted the war as a capitalist ramp, Caledonia, appealing to nationalist sentiment with a Scottish accent and 'Auld Lang Syne', and the Christian Peace Movement, pleading for an armistice on pacifist grounds. The stations also did their best to spread

fear by describing air-raid injuries in horrifying detail, and by prophesy-
ing the use of such secret weapons as a death ray and artificial fog, under
which airborne troops could drop unseen. As the appointed date for the
invasion drew nearer the stations grew more frenzied, urging their supposed fellow-countrymen to hiss Churchill when he appeared on the
newsreels and break the 'warmongers'' windows. The broadcasters also
did their best to confuse the British commanders by mentioning a whole
range of possible targets for an attack, Glasgow, the Black Country, South
Wales and Ireland all being suggested, and, since its omission would have
been suspicious in itself, South-East England. By early September the
stations' warnings were becoming increasingly strident: 'Invasion', listeners were told, 'may come any day. The time is fast approaching.' And
this at least was true.

More open attempts to undermine British morale were made by the
chief broadcaster of the German service in English, William Joyce, universally known as 'Lord Haw Haw', who openly broadcast as a spokesman for the enemy, but his efforts were far less successful than during the
winter of the 'phoney war'. The government paid Haw Haw the compliment of an advertising campaign urging people not to listen to him and
even created an imaginary 'Silent Column' of citizens pledged not to pass
on the rumours he tried to launch, a short-lived body which soon collapsed, being aimed at a danger which did not exist. Apart from an in-
significant minority of Fascists, pacifists and other traitors preaching
defeatism or non-resistance, no one in Great Britain even contemplated
surrender.

Spirits almost everywhere were high that summer. The reports which
reached the Germans telling them, as one did, 'Workers fed up . . .
Troops not keen . . . Churchill not popular', could not have been wider of
the mark. Morale, already solid in May, was sky-high by September, sus-
tained by the sense of purpose with which the new government had in-
fused the country, by the rescue of the Army by the 'little boats' at
Dunkirk, by the losses being suffered by the Luftwaffe, and by the visible
signs of preparation to meet an invasion. Most important of all were the
speeches of Winston Churchill. When on 4 June, the day the last troops
left Dunkirk, he made the famous declaration in the House of Commons:
'We shall defend our island, whatever the cost may be. We shall fight on
the beaches, we shall fight on the landing grounds; we shall fight in the
fields and in the streets; we shall fight in the hills; we shall never surrender',
it seemed to the Germans mere empty oratory; by the British it was taken
as a plan of action and a pledge.

The French decision to ask for an armistice, reported to the nation in the one o'clock news on Monday 17 June, produced not the desire to stop fighting the Germans had expected, but the universal resolve, voiced in a famous cartoon of the time, 'Very well then, alone'. Some people hoped for divine intervention. 'That week people were praying everywhere,' one Welsh miner noticed, 'on the pit top, underground, in factories, as well as in places of worship.' With its conquest an imminent possibility, people everywhere that beautiful summer began to look at their familiar landscape with newly-opened eyes as one Scotswoman remembers:

Nobody who lived through it can forget the effect of the news of the fall of France. I remember going immediately after having heard it to change my library books. It was a slack time for traffic, and it seemed as if a hush had descended on the whole world, and that I was walking in a vacuum, the last person left alive. . . . Later in that week of wonderful weather, my brother, who was recovering from an illness, took his first outing to call on my mother and me, and we sat for a time on the terrace behind the house. Across the valley, the road northwards to Edinburgh wound round the hill, and over it came a convoy of army vehicles. I at once thought with a pang, 'What would it be like if ever a stream of German armour appeared in that loop of road?' Apparently the same thought had occurred to my brother for he said, out of nowhere: 'If I had a machine gun I could enfilade that road awful nicely.' (He was a gunner in the first war.)

The ease with which small forces of Germans had roamed about France and the Low Countries, often behind the front line, causing chaos and demoralisation out of all proportion to their numbers, had deeply impressed the opposing generals and to prevent this happening in the British Isles an elaborate system of roadblocks was set up to slow down and contain any German advance. As the summer wore on the first impromptu obstacles of farm-carts, old cars, empty tar-barrels filled with earth, builders' rubble, broken bedsteads and discarded mattresses, were largely replaced by properly built, if not always well sited, barriers of 'concertina' wire, massive concrete blocks and, sufficient to delay a motor cyclist or a single lorry, tree trunks mounted on a pivot which could be wheeled into position at strategic points. The first ingenious expedients, like the plan at Margate to seal off the beaches with ancient bathing machines filled with sand, were now supplemented by the biggest programme of fixed military defence works since the Roman legions had built Hadrian's Wall. Soon every river or crossroad of any size in the South of England and East Anglia had its tank trap, consisting of concrete blocks or cylinders the size of a large barrel, and during July and August an army of 150,000 labourers toiled in the sunshine, stripped to the waist, to build the blockhouses and pillboxes which, it was hoped, would enable even lightly armed units to give a good account of themselves.

The British government's main anxiety was about the threat from the air, for, misreading what had happened on the Continent, where airborne forces had played only a minor role, they had a disturbing vision of parachutists being scattered about the countryside, capturing strongpoints and generally wreaking havoc, and of whole planeloads of tough German infantry descending upon unprotected fields far behind the front line. To cope with these dangers, between late May and early September every open space on which an aircraft might land was covered with obstacles – sections of sewer pipe, farm machinery, wigwam-like tripods of posts. (In one place 'fire ships' of old cars loaded with explosives were contemplated but they proved impractical.) To stop gliders swooping down on wide roads, vast hoops of metal were erected over them like those which in happier times formed processional arches. The commonest type of obstacle was a simple wooden post, well planted in the soil, and one volunteer left behind him a detailed account of the effort involved in making this vital, if unspectacular, contribution to the nation's security:

Having helped a number of local men to obstruct one meadow I came to the conclusion at the end of one day's work that even a butterfly would crash if it attempted to land on that field. . . . The work was extremely hard. . . . You could not let up . . . because that gave the man digging the next hole a chance to get ahead and triumphantly to thrust his old railway sleeper, or young pine log, into the earth and begin on another. . . . This business of digging a hole four feet six in depth, and not much more than eighteen inches in diameter, may sound simple enough until it is tried. The first two spits may be dug out without complication; but after that, difficulty increases unless you have made a narrow trench for your feet. . . . A dry summer had made the earth cement-like . . . but, apart from this, a flinty stratum immediately under the tough matted turf made plain digging impossible and called for a pick and shovel. After eighteen inches of this a semi-rock layer had to be delved through, a slow and strenuous process owing to lack of space in the deepening hole. . . . At four-thirty . . . we dropped our tools and enjoyed excellent cups of tea and neat little buns . . . [brought by two local women]. The work was hard, but it exerted a powerful fascination. At last we were permitted to do something for the country.

The Germans did their best to encourage the preoccupation with parachutists by dropping on the night of 13 August instructions on their conduct in the forthcoming invasion to imaginary agents in the Midlands and Scotland, confirmatory evidence being provided by haversacks containing maps, wireless transmitters and high explosive, though many of the parachutes landed in standing corn, which had clearly not been disturbed by the foot of any spy. The government had, however, already taken active steps to combat the threat from the skies with the formation on Tuesday 14 May 1940, following a broadcast appeal for recruits by the Secretary of State for War, of the Local Defence Volunteers. The LDV, which two months later was renamed the Home Guard, consisted of volunteers aged, officially at least, from seventeen to sixty-five, who had offered to serve as unpaid, spare-time soldiers, becoming full-time when enemy troops actually landed. Their purpose, stressed Mr Eden, was to cope with parachutists; a seaborne invasion was not mentioned. But, however the enemy came, the readiness to challenge him was unmistakable. By the end of the month 300,000 men had enrolled and by the beginning of September a million and a half, if not under arms for arms were still scarce, were at least on the units' nominal rolls.

Many of the earliest recruits, as the government had hoped, were ex-servicemen, like one who was now a Whitehall Civil Servant living in Berkshire:

I think that none of us will forget our first LDV route march. On it a quarter of a century slipped away in a flash. There came memories of the Menin Road, of loose, shifting, exasperating cobbles, of the smell of cordite and the scream of shrapnel, of the mud and stench and misery of Flanders. . . . Our first route march was a silent one, with each of us busy with those thoughts of the past, trudging a Berkshire road with that almost automatic one-ness of movement which the old soldier can never lose. . . . I remember too, that none of us fell out, although more than one of us badly wanted to.

Here was a spirit that Hitler, himself a veteran of the first world war, might have envied, but his spokesman on German radio preferred instead to abuse the new 'murder bands', which, he threatened, would be treated as civilian partisans and shot out of hand when captured. Sometimes these tirades were replaced by mockery of the new force and this, had the Germans realised it, was a far more effective tactic. More than one recruit, disillusioned by being put to guard a roadblock equipped only with an armlet and a home-made club, resigned in disgust, and others' visions of martial glory faded fast when set to doing arms-drill with a broom-handle. It was also deflating to patriotic spirits to be chased off the municipal lawns by a park-keeper when training, or when practising grenade-throwing with a brick on a patch of wasteland, to be urged by the small boys playing cricket there to 'Go away and play somewhere else, mister, 'cos we was 'ere first'.

Yet the Germans made a mistake in simply ignoring the Home Guard. In May and early June it had been, perhaps, a militarily negligible force, though already doing useful work in scanning the skies for parachutists and guarding bridges and power stations, but by September, although many units were still virtually unarmed, the situation over the country as a whole had been transformed. The newly-formed battalions of 'Sunday soldiers', as their critics disparagingly called them, were now integrated into the defence plans for every locality. Most men now had a uniform of some kind, even though it was usually only ill-fitting denims topped, if at all, by a steel helmet that was too small, and rounded off with boots far too large; the Army, ordered to hand over its surplus stores, had, naturally enough, disposed of the sizes of which it had no need. The key factor, however, both in morale – the will to fight – and in fire-power – the ability to fight – was a unit's weapons and here the months of waiting had been well used. Even in May most of those who had gone on the first patrols in the coastal areas of Kent and Sussex had been armed, though very little ammunition was available, but the arrival of half a million old American rifles in mid-July, though at first with only ten rounds of ammunition apiece, made an enormous difference, and 20,000 more revolvers and shotguns trickled in as a result of the appeal which had already attracted Dr Goebbels's amused attention. If, as the British feared, the Germans planned to drop marauding parties of parachutists far inland it might go badly with the Home Guard for weapons. Away from the coast not merely in the Home Guard but in the Army weapons were still desperately few. In the South-Eastern counties, however, few men, whether regular soldiers or Home Guards, whatever their other deficiencies of training and equipment, would have had to confront their country's enemies totally unarmed.

Already by September the original conception of the Home Guard as a small force of part-timers, concentrated in rural areas and designed only to deal with lightly armed airborne troops, had been forgotten. It was now far larger than the government had at first intended, much of its strength lay in built-up areas, and it might well have had to cope not merely with motor-cyclists and parachutists but with enemy tanks. Since there were far too few anti-tank weapons to equip even regular units with them, the Home Guards had to do the best they could from their own resources, and many entered eagerly into the manufacture of Molotov cocktails, which consisted of bottles filled with petrol, with a wick through the cork, lighted just before the bottle was thrown. The value of this dangerous device was highly questionable and one veteran of the Spanish Civil War considered that 'if lobbed on the top of a tank . . . they merely warm it slightly', but any weapon to halt the Panzers seemed better than none. A captain in one Kent company toured his village one Sunday morning with a farm cart collecting several hundred whisky and soft-drink bottles – beer bottles were considered too hard to break easily – and then set up his own private filling plant in a wood, where a mixture of warm tar and petrol was poured lovingly into each container, the wives of his men obligingly making canvas carriers for the bottles from old mattress covers and sackcloth. Other devices had an even more desperate air. The news that one inventor had converted an ARP stirrup pump into a flame-thrower, discharging inflammable dry-cleaning fluid, and that a Hampshire unit was equipped with its own cannon, consisting of a metal tube filled with gunpowder, fired by hitting it with a hammer, was more likely to have struck joy into Doctor Goebbels's heart than terror in Field Marshal Keitel's.

The loyal Englishman could buy at the station bookstall on his way home that summer a variety of books on irregular warfare, written by experts who had already fought the Germans in Spain, and much of the advice given was sound and easily followed. One author recommended that men manning roadblocks should be posted 'all on one side of the road, in case they fire on each other at moments of excitement', and there was a simple way of dealing with a dive-bomber: 'It is said to be a good idea to swear at it; even if you cannot hear what you say, you know the meaning of the words and thus get psychological relief.' Although still warning against clergy and – inevitably – nuns who were parachutists in disguise and even, a new tenor, 'adolescent enemy agents . . . dropped in the uniforms of Boy Scouts or Sea Scouts', the writer urged a reasonable measure of caution, which had rarely been mentioned in the first hectic days back in May: 'The business of the Home Guard is to be soldiers first and heroes afterwards and . . . live heroes are usually better than dead ones.'

Another booklet published that summer admitted that the keen Home Guard was also up against a difficulty not encountered in less peaceful lands: 'Unfortunately our history, having been very different from that of the Spanish, gives us very little information on the tactics of street fighting. In Spain almost any villager can tell you the exact street corner where barricades have always been raised in the past.' However, there was sometimes an unexpected repository of knowledge in the district, as a third paperback book suggested: to obtain information on the use of cover, 'ask your local scouts', having first, presumably, ascertained that they were not Germans in disguise. 'Don't be ashamed to learn from some cocky kid! This is not your personal life only; it is everyone else's.' The same author offered instructions on how to make an anti-tank grenade as casually as if advising his readers how to prune their roses: 'Take an eight-ounce stick of ordinary commercial blasting glycerine . . .' it began. To hold up enemy vehicles he recommended broken glass, boards studded with nails, and a blanket slung from a rope across a narrow street, to blind an enemy tank or force a patrol to slow up and become a more vulnerable target. The writer summed up: 'Your weapon may be a tin can of explosive or a shotgun that will only hit at fifty yards. Treasure it until you have a good chance to kill a German. Even if you only get one, you have helped to beat Hitler.'

Such publications were private ventures and the government was not enthusiastic about private armies outside the regular forces or the Home Guard, conducting campaigns of their own with weapons more likely to harm their users than the Germans. The most useful contribution the ordinary civilian could make to victory in an invasion, the authorities urged, was more passive, to stay where he was, to leave the roads clear for military traffic and to avoid becoming a refugee, spreading panic and hindering the defending forces. As a first step, all those living in coastal areas of Kent and Sussex were advised to move inland, being given practical help and a warning that, if they stayed, they might later have to go compulsorily at a few hours' notice. Many schools and businesses evacuated to the South-East had already moved, now that so much of Southern England was within easy reach of German bombers, and in June every household in the country received a leaflet, *If the Invader Comes*, which, besides some barely needed patriotic exhortation—'Think always of your country before you think of yourself'—insisted that 'Your first rule . . . is IF THE GERMANS COME, BY PARACHUTE, AEROPLANE, OR SHIP, YOU MUST REMAIN WHERE YOU ARE. THE ORDER IS "STAY PUT".'

To stay put, with roads blocked and supplies cut off, every community would need to be fed, and arrangements were hastily made to establish dumps of food in every village, the rectory, which usually had ample space and a trustworthy occupant, being a favoured spot. While the boxes of biscuits, corned beef, tinned soup, sugar, condensed milk, margarine and tea, were being stacked in attics or outhouses, the invaluable women who were the backbone of every local fête or flower show were called in to plan emergency feeding arrangements. A woman who attended one such meeting, in Smarden in Kent, recalled later how 'Mrs R, a famous voluntary local caterer, was asked if she would undertake the organisation of public meals. She looked seriously at the chairman and said, "Well, everyone must wash up their own knife and fork." Good old Mrs R. Germans or no Germans, down to the practical details in a moment!' Mrs R's morale was also unshaken as the same witness discovered. 'I asked her later: "What would you do if a German soldier appeared at your back door?" ' Her answer: 'I should say to 'im, I should say, "What are you a-doin' of 'ere?".' At Cranbrook, in the Weald of Kent, the older children were pressed into service. 'When the Germans came everyone was to stay in their houses as much as possible,' one schoolgirl later remembered, 'and each side of the village street had an emergency food dump. Our job was to go round the backs of the houses, over walls and through hedges and make sure all was well with the inmates and take food and medical supplies to any in need.' Their prize item of equipment was an enormous tin opener labelled, a little ironically, 'Made in Germany'.

Despite all its requests to 'stay put', the government realised that there would still be an exodus from some of the invaded districts, by people whose homes had been destroyed, by those in whom the instinct to flight was irresistible, and, most commonly of all, by residents ordered by the British military authorities to leave an area about to become a battle-ground. The then Chief Constable of Essex remembers that, to prevent these retreating evacuees becoming entangled with the (one hoped) advancing British forces, a map was drawn up for 'yellow roads' to be used by refugees, and 'red roads' to be used by the Army. It became some-thing of a joke within the police force, who had to see that the two streams of traffic were kept apart, that the authorities' preparations had not extended to ordering sufficient coloured ink. A note on the map they received explained that 'yellow roads' were in fact shown in purple, as no yellow had been available.

Another experienced police officer, then serving in Kent, in the very front line of the expected invasion, was personally involved in drawing up plans to deal with the expected flood of refugees. Some places were in fact to be evacuated, such as 'nodal points, which were going to be subjected to all-round defence and in those cases all "useless mouths"—women and children and the aged—would be compulsorily removed. The 'Stay Put' order applied everywhere else. 'The idea was, of course, that they should remain where they were, but,' he admits, 'I don't think we were so naive as to expect that they would. Certainly some of them would have bolted and the whole idea was that they should be kept away from main routes which the defence forces might be expected to use and they should be headed off into woods and more remote villages, and there looked after as best we could by putting them in village halls, churches and that sort of thing. It was our purpose to turn them away from those areas where they could do any harm until the battle had rolled over them and then to try to get them back whence they came.'

It would, he believes, have been a difficult and, of course, unfamiliar job for the police, but not impossible. 'Crowd control', he points out, 'is usually a question of having enough policemen. . . . It would have been a question of having officers at suitable strategic road junctions and ensur-ing that they followed the routes that we wanted them to.' Occasionally, he admits, peaceful persuasion might not have been sufficient. 'If you get a difficult person who simply won't go the way you want him to well then you have to shove him the way you want him to go. And I suppose if the worst comes to the worst, you have to knock him down and hand him over to someone else to cart off.'

Prewar governments had sometimes dreamed, in the days when the reality of air attack and the capacity of the ordinary citizen to resist it were both unknown, of bombed cities having to be ringed by an armed cordon to stop the inhabitants fleeing in terror. By September 1940 such fears had subsided, although a good deal of thought had been given to arming the police, not to keep order among the civilian population (though conceivably in an emergency it could have come to that) but, since they were already well organised, uniformed and disciplined, to serve as a kind of second-line Home Guard. Churchill was an enthusiastic advocate of this policy, which he proposed at his first Cabinet meeting on 11 May, and ten days later the Cabinet agreed to it 'as far as the arms available permitted' – an important qualification, since at that time the Army and LDV had first claim on any firearms that could be found.

During the next few weeks ministers returned to the question on several occasions, and it was even suggested at one meeting that the 'police should become part of the Armed Forces' in the event of invasion, though it was then pointed out that some were over military age and that this essentially civilian body could not be transformed 'as a whole and automatically into a combat force'. A good deal of anxiety existed within the Cabinet about the role of the police during an invasion if they were not to be combatants, and the Home Secretary tried to reassure his colleagues on 10 July by explaining that the police had been instructed that '*until* the enemy had obtained effective control of an area it was their duty to fight and to treat the enemy as miscreants', a phrase which conjures up a suggestion of some stalwart village bobby rounding up a German soldier who had strayed on to his 'patch' as though he were a Saturday-night drunk. But, Herbert Morrison added, 'should the police . . . find themselves behind enemy lines, they had orders to give up their arms and to look after the interests of the civil population'.

The thought of British policemen carrying out the orders of Nazi officers in some conquered corner of the country still troubled the government, and on 26 July the Cabinet was told that news of it had leaked out and 'become known in very misleading forms. It was suggested that it would be preferable if the police were instructed in this contingency to act at their own discretion and not, in any event, to afford assistance to the invader.' Some ministers felt that 'in no circumstances should the police be responsible for keeping order in an area which had been overrun by the enemy; such a task should be performed by the enemy'. Finally, on 5 August, the existing instructions were confirmed, to the effect that 'if any elements of the civil population remained in an enemy-occupied area, the rearguard of the police should also remain behind, and the Senior Officer of the police should offer the assistance of the police in maintaining order, any arms not previously handed over to the military authorities being surrendered'. Once again 'objection was raised to the idea that the police should put themselves under the enemy and give them any help whatsoever', but by now these fine professions of principle were being tempered with realism.•These rules, it was explained, 'applied only to the rearguard, and . . . if steps were to be taken to ensure that civilians stayed put, and did not obstruct the roads, some police must stay behind until the enemy occupation became effective'.

The original decision to arm the police was never formally rescinded, but the first weapons ordered for the purpose did not arrive from the United States until 1941. A scattering of weapons still remained in police stations for use against criminals, but the overwhelming majority of policemen in 1940 were, and remained, unarmed. If any refugees had poured out of the coastal towns of Kent and Sussex that autumn, they would not have found their way barred by some grim-faced gendarme flourishing a gun, but by a familiar, blue-helmeted figure armed with nothing more lethal than persuasion, cajolery and, as a last resort, a truncheon, reciting that often heard litany, 'This way please.'

The police, then, had their orders: To get out if they could, to keep order for the Germans if necessary, but not to collaborate. What of the ordinary civilian? Some people admitted, even at the time, that once the Germans had arrived they would do what they were told without question. A few talked of killing themselves and their children rather than allow them to grow up in a Nazi country, though the temptation to postpone such an irrevocable act would probably have proved almost irresistible. A number did, however, plan to make the Germans' arrival as disagreeable as possible. One wealthy woman in Buckinghamshire proposed to invite the officers in for champagne, privily dosed with weedkiller, and thus 'poison the lot', while even the normally kind-hearted ladies of the Women's Institutes, which officially took no direct part in the war effort, pondered how the home-made jam, for whose manufacture they were famous, should be denied to the enemy. At Langton Matravers in Dorset the best method of jam-interdiction was seriously debated: 'Was it', the women wondered, 'wise to hide one's store of jam under the floor . . . or imitate a Jael-like housewife who kept a hammer ready for a last-minute smashing, in hopes of the dire effect of powdered glass on jam-starved Germans?'

Chapter 4: Bombardment

The air war over England increases day by day and hour by hour. It is like a howling crescendo.

German radio commentator, 7 September 1940

The policy of 'No surrender', announced in the House of Commons, was, hard though the Germans found it to believe, no mere public gesture. In private, too, the government had determined to sell their lives dearly, as one minister learned when, on the afternoon of 28 May, the senior members of the new coalition government were summoned to meet the Prime Minister.

He said, 'I have thought carefully in these last days whether it was part of my duty to consider entering into negotiations with That Man'. But it was idle to think that, if we tried to make peace now, we should get better terms than if we fought it out. . . . 'And I am convinced,' he concluded, 'that every man of you would rise up and tear me down from my place if I were for one moment to contemplate parley or surrender. If this long island story of ours is to end at last, let it end only when each one of us lies choking in his own blood upon the floor.' There were loud cries of approval all round the table.

The defence of the United Kingdom against invasion first came before the Cabinet on 30 April, when the Secretary of State for War reported that the Chiefs of Staff were considering the subject, and the last meeting of the Chamberlain Cabinet on 9 May had before it a warning from the Chiefs of Staff that a landing might come anywhere between the Wash and Newhaven, though the Secretary of State for War, enjoying, though he did not know it, his last day in office, observed reassuringly that an attack on the South Coast was unlikely. When, twelve days later, the Cabinet returned to the subject, it was in an atmosphere far removed from the earlier complacency, the Home Secretary being instructed to consider collecting firearms in private ownership. There was, too, that day a quaint echo of an earlier war. The Cabinet discussed whether the Kaiser, who had fled to Holland in 1918 to escape the vengeance of the allies and the wrath of his fellow-countrymen, should be given asylum in Britain if he asked for it. It was decided that he should, but the request was never made.

Throughout the next few weeks the tempo of preparation mounted and the civil population were soon feeling the effects of many of the measures agreed, from the obstruction of football grounds where aircraft might land to the rounding-up of enemy aliens. Of other subjects discussed the public had no inkling, such as the Prime Minister's plea on 22 May that 'We should not hesitate to contaminate our beaches with gas if this . . . would be to our advantage. We had the right to do what we liked with our own territory.' In fact, though the Cabinet was not told this, one bomber squadron was soon busily practising 'crop spraying', dropping a pink powder, representing mustard gas, from tanks slung beneath the wings.

Recognising the eagerness of many citizens to teach a lesson to any German impertinent enough to land on British soil, the Cabinet was worried as to how far they could go without being shot as *franc-tireurs*, or partisans. The Minister of Home Security, Herbert Morrison, a former pacifist, comfortingly informed his colleagues that 'there could be nothing wrong in civilians helping to block roads under the orders of the military', but 'there was a clear distinction between defence measures taken in advance of invasion, which were perfectly legitimate, and action taken by civilians after the enemy were in effective control of an area, which were not legitimate. He was also advised that action by civilians against individual parachutists and Fifth Columnists was legitimate.' They could, it seemed, shoot first and ask questions afterwards.

On 21 May, General 'Pug' Ismay, Military Head of the War Cabinet Secretariat, submitted to Winston Churchill a formal warning that 'the grave emergency is already upon us', and that it must be assumed that the Germans had planned the invasion of the United Kingdom 'to the last detail. We can be sure that Hitler would be prepared to sacrifice ninety per cent of the whole expedition if he could gain a firm bridgehead on British soil with the remaining ten per cent.' Even the accepted doctrine that Hitler would need to capture a port was now questionable, for German air superiority might enable the enemy to land tanks and artillery across open beaches. Hence 'not a moment should be lost' in preparing demolitions to block the way inland.

During the next few hectic weeks, the Cabinet devoted much time to the problem of Ireland which, it was feared, might be seized by the Germans as a base for an assault on the British Isles from the rear. Eamon de Valera, the Prime Minister of Eire, insisted that the Irish would defend their independence, but the Chiefs of Staff believed that his country might easily fall to an airborne assault, perhaps by no more than 2000 determined men, or to a seaborne attack from men concealed in merchant ships, as had happened in Norway. The British government offered to help defend Eire if asked but the Irish, like other small countries before them, insisted that they could remain neutral or, if necessary, defeat a German attack. De Valera refused to come to London to discuss the danger in which his country and his own person stood (for the British government believed the Germans might shoot him to facilitate the take-over of Eire) and when a British emissary went to see him he refused out-right all British help. Some ministers, with the whole future of the British Isles in jeopardy, favoured Britain seizing the Irish ports needed to pro-tect her western approaches, to forestall a German landing, but wiser, or at least milder, counsels prevailed, for this, it was felt, would convert Eire from an uneasy neutral to an active ally of Germany. Plans for an All-Ireland Council came to nothing and a British division, badly needed in England, remained tied up in Northern Ireland, but it was estimated that no fewer than ten would be needed to garrison the whole of Ireland with a hostile population south of the border.

If Eire was a disappointment to the British government, so, too, was the United States, the Americans being clearly more concerned about the long-term threat to themselves than the immediate threat to Great Britain. Half a million old rifles, 2000 sub-machine guns, even some ancient artillery, they were willing and able to provide, but Winston Churchill's request for the loan of fifty old destroyers, first made in May, met with no success until August, when Britain offered in exchange a lease of various bases in the West Indies and Newfoundland, and was not finally settled until 5 September, far too late for them to arrive in time to affect the out-come of the daily-expected invasion. The American attitude was under-standable. Their ambassador in London, Joseph Kennedy, was pouring across the Atlantic a stream of pessimistic predictions and, as will be dis-cussed in more detail in a later chapter, the United States contained many people opposed to involvement in Europe. The most that President Roosevelt could promise was 'all aid short of war', and this seemed un-likely to be enough. Essentially, the United States faced the same dilemma as had confronted Great Britain when asked to send fighters to shore up the crumbling front in France: she might be throwing good money after bad and good money, furthermore, which would soon be desperately needed at home.

The American government's real anxiety all along was about the future command of the Atlantic, a fear shared with their Canadian neighbour, and on 24 May the American Secretary of State asked the Canadian government to send some reliable representative to Washington to meet the President privately, to discuss 'certain possible eventualities which could not possibly be mentioned aloud'. This meeting duly took place and others followed in an equal atmosphere of mystery, the Canadian Prime Minister, Mackenzie King, being thinly disguised in telephone conversation as 'Mr Kirk' and President Roosevelt as 'Mr Roberts'. Mr Roberts, it soon appeared, despite his cordial response to Winston Churchill's overtures, believed that France would collapse and that it would then not be long before the United Kingdom would be 'forced to sue for peace', and presented with the choice of total destruction or the 'surrender of the Empire and handing over of the British fleet'. Roosevelt believed that 'the temptation to buy a reasonably "soft" peace will prove irresistible' and the American government was desperately anxious that, once the battle was lost, 'the remnants of the British fleet should be sent out to South Africa, Singapore, Australasia . . . the Caribbean and Canada'. The Americans, the Canadian emissary reported, were comfortably philosophic about the consequences of this unselfish act. 'The people and government of the United Kingdom', they recognised, 'will probably be terribly punished for taking these steps but they will be no worse off than previous victims of German aggression and their suffering will have a real objective in that it will make possible the ultimate triumph of civilisation.'

Kinship now proved a more powerful force than mere neighbourliness and a common language. To King it seemed, at least 'for a moment . . . that the United States was seeking to save itself at the expense of Britain', and Roosevelt was told, politely but firmly, that if he wanted Britain to sacrifice herself for the benefit of the United States he must make the request direct. But the Canadians, being of British stock themselves, knew Winston Churchill and his countrymen better than the Americans. If Britain had to choose between a 'hard' peace if she sent the Fleet to safety to fight another day, and a 'soft' one if she surrendered her warships, Roosevelt was told on 29 May, she would opt for suffering – and honour. Ten weeks later the British Cabinet formally resolved to tell the Americans that, Ambassador Kennedy's doleful predictions and President Roosevelt's forebodings notwithstanding, they had no intention of surrendering. It was, the Cabinet agreed, 'of the utmost importance to make it absolutely clear to the United States that it was our firm resolve to fight it out here, and that even if, contrary to our belief, we should find ourselves being overwhelmed, we should retain entirely unfettered the right to decide when (if ever) we should send the Fleet away from these waters to defend our kith and kin overseas'.

While the Americans were already concerned about their own defence, to some British people the United States seemed a haven of refuge. A few inglorious poets and actors had already, as the current joke had it, 'gone with the wind up' across the Atlantic, and now many well-meaning and well-off people began to send their children to friends and sympathisers there. The government was reluctant to ban such evacuation altogether but the Prime Minister had little time for it. The flight from the British Isles, he told the Cabinet, 'encouraged a defeatist spirit, which was entirely contrary to the true facts of the position and should be sternly discouraged'. It was, too, unpatriotic, tying up shipping needed for more useful purposes, and, even more serious, had given rise to the ridiculous rumour that the two Princesses had been sent to Canada and that the King and Queen, escorted by the government, were even now preparing to follow. 'These rumours', the Cabinet agreed, 'must be scotched', and in the event only 2000 children went to the United States and 3000 more to the dominions.

But if people could not decently leave the threatened island, it made sense to deny to the Germans the funds that would enable Britain to carry on the fight overseas and on Sunday 23 June two special trains, planned in deep secrecy and heavily guarded – the origin perhaps of the rumours about the Princesses' departure – left London for Greenock with an undisclosed cargo. The next day the cruiser *Emerald* set sail for Canada, laden with 9000 gold bars and 500 boxes stuffed with documents – negotiable securities which could readily be sold on the world's markets. She was followed on 8 July by a task force which could ill be spared from the defence of the homeland, the battleship *Revenge*, the cruiser *Bonaventure* and three requisitioned liners, escorted by four destroyers, and other smaller convoys followed later in the summer. By late August £637 million-worth of gold, including some historic and valuable eighteenth-century currency, and £1250 million-worth of securities which had required seventy miles of tape to tie into bundles, had crossed the Atlantic and arrived in Canada without a coin or a share certificate being lost. The securities ended their journey in the vaults of the Sun Life Insurance Company in Montreal, and the gold was sent to Ottawa after being unloaded at the port of Halifax, as some Royal Canadian Navy recruits stationed there for basic training had cause to remember:

Very early one morning we were told to get out of our hammocks, put on our coveralls and report outside the barracks. There we were loaded into trucks, taken down through the city of Halifax to the dock area. We arrived to find one of the docks very well guarded by Royal Canadian Mounted Police carrying sub-machine guns. There were Canadian National Express cars inside the shed. We were taken to the dockside and detailed off, some of us on the ship, some of us on the dockside, to carry heavy wooden boxes from the ship to the railway cars. Naturally somebody got very curious, and accidentally or otherwise let one of the boxes drop back into the magazine where it broke open. And he leaned over and said 'Just as I thought, it's gold!' Down in the hold a voice replied, 'B . . . the gold, watch my head!' . . . We finished unloading the ship, after several hours' work, and we were warned in no uncertain terms that we were to say nothing to anyone about what we'd been doing the night before. Next morning we were back on the parade ground as if nothing had happened.

While the later consignments of Britain's gold reserves were still being ferried to Canada, the attack on the homeland had begun in earnest. Both sides knew that mastery of the air was the key to victory and the Luftwaffe general given the preliminary task of clearing the Channel of British ships and aircraft set up his forward command post in an old bus on the cliffs of Cap Gris-Nez, close to a statue of Blériot whose achievement in 1909 in flying the Channel had led to the premature observation that Britain was no longer an island. The opening shots in the Battle were fired on 3 July, when a Dornier dived suddenly out of a cloud, killing one man on a training airfield at Maidenhead, and on the following day twenty Junkers bombed Portland. From 10 July to 7 August it was the convoys in the Straits of Dover and the Channel ports which were the main target, supported with scattered sorties over many parts of England after dark, but Göring's men had been eagerly waiting for fine weather for *Eagle Day*, when the all-out offensive against the British mainland was to begin, and, after several postponements, it finally came on 13 August, when the Germans flew nearly 1500 sorties. This time the target was the RAF: aircraft factories, the Royal Aircraft Research Establishment at Farnborough and, above all, Fighter Command's airfields. Forty-five German aircraft were destroyed, largely the 'Stuka' dive-bombers which had done so much execution in fact, and even more by repute, in Holland and France, but which were appallingly vulnerable unless the skies were clear of enemy fighters.

Two days later the Battle reached is first climax and on a day of bright sunshine every available German aircraft rose into the air to press home the attacks on airfields all over the British Isles. From Norway and Denmark in the north to the Pas de Calais in the south the Junkers and Heinkels, Dorniers and Messerschmitts mounted a seemingly endless stream, and almost continuously from dawn until darkness some part of the British Isles was under attack. Several aircraft factories were badly hit, but far more serious was the damage done at one airfield after another. Vital bases like Manston, where Fighter Command squadrons were permanently stationed, forward landing grounds like Hawkinge and Lympne, whose role during an invasion would be vital, were badly damaged and some were put out of action, but even more serious to the defenders was the knocking out of several of the radar stations on which early warning, and hence interception, depended. Ventnor on the Isle of Wight, had already been silenced, leaving a gap in the centre of the protective chain covering the South-East, now others at such key spots as Rye, Dover and Foreness were temporarily 'blinded' as their electric power was cut off by broken cables. All over Fighter Command aerodromes resembled a battle-field, as indeed they were, with hangars destroyed, wrecked and smoulder-ing aircraft littering the dispersal areas, workshops and barrack buildings damaged and, worst of all, runways pitted with craters and control rooms knocked out. The British public, hearing that 182 German aircraft had been shot down for the loss of thirty-four British, were jubilant, and news-vendors' posters proclaimed the casualty figures as though they had been scores in a cricket match. The Luftwaffe High Command, knowing that in fact they had lost only seventy-five bombers and fighters – serious enough but not crippling – assumed that the figures for RAF losses were also inaccurate. The RAF, they believed, though not yet beaten, was now fighting desperately for survival. At Fighter Command headquarters, and in the Cabinet room, there was less rejoicing than in the press. The Air Marshal and ministers knew how badly the RAF had been hit and that the German tactics of concentrating on airfields and radar stations were potentially fatal to the very survival of the RAF, and hence of the country.

Throughout the last two weeks of August, while civilians in Southern England became accustomed to seeing the white vapour trails waving in the sky above them and to hearing the distant clatter of machine-gun fire or the sudden rattle of spent bullets falling to earth, the sinister pattern of the attack continued. Croydon, Kenley, Redhill, West Malling, Biggin Hill – the list of airfields knocked out or heavily damaged mounted. The supply of spare fighters from the factories and repair plants was still flowing well, but many arrived to be destroyed on the ground, and not enough experienced pilots were coming forward to replace those killed or wounded in action, for novices from the training units often rapidly be-came casualties. The shrinking band of veterans who taxied and took off along the crater-pitted runways were desperately tired. The spontaneous gaiety of June and July, the ready chivalry of early August had long since vanished. Fighter Command was fighting for its life; if its members had known that one Luftwaffe pilot, shot down near Canterbury, had arro-gantly sent a Home Guard to the nearest shop to buy him some 'State Express 555' cigarettes – no other brand would do – they would not have been very amused; if they had known that one German airman, clambering unharmed from the wreckage of his bomber on the beach at West Wittering, had instantly been shot they would not have been shocked. And, despite the fervent patriotism of BBC news bulletins and the press headlines, not everyone in England was dedicated to winning the war. Two WAAF officers who toured the village of Biggin Hill in search of billets for bombed-out airmen had more than one door slammed in their faces. It was, they were told, all the RAF's fault that the area was constantly being attacked.

By 4 September a thousand German aircraft had already been shot down, although the British believed the total to be far higher, which made it all the more ominous that the attack did not seem to be declining in strength. That day another 300 fighters and bombers crossed the Channel to attack the airfields and aircraft factories on which the defence depended, and Hitler addressed a mass rally of Nazi supporters in Berlin. For the first time since his 'peace offer' back in July the Führer referred in public to the failure of his last surviving enemy to come to terms. 'When people are very curious in Great Britain and ask, "Yes, why don't you come?",' he told his wildly cheering audience, 'We reply: "Calm yourselves. We shall come!" The hour will strike when one of us will break and it will not be National Socialist Germany. Our remaining opponent, Great Britain, the last island in Europe, will be broken!'

Hitler's speech, the undiminished fury of the air war, the unmistakable build-up of troops and barges across the Channel and the approach of winter all pointed to an early invasion and on the evening of Saturday 7 September the growing tension erupted into a false alarm. The event had its origins back in the hectic days of early June when the Commander-in-Chief Home Forces, General Ironside, had prepared plans to bring his troops to a state of readiness to repel invasion by issuing a single code-word, 'Cromwell'. Ironside himself may have chosen this highly appropriate word, making an oblique reference to his own name, for an admiring enemy commander in the English Civil War 300 years before had nicknamed Oliver Cromwell's troops 'Ironsides'. Or it may have been the choice of the Prime Minister, recalling Andrew Marvell's poem on the Protector's death:

> Thee, many ages hence, in martial verse
> Shall th' English soldier, 'ere he charge, rehearse,
> Singing of thee inflame himself to fight
> And with the name of 'Cromwell' armies fright.

Whoever was responsible, 'Cromwell' was certainly a more inspiring battle-cry than its predecessor, 'Caesar', for Julius Caesar had led the first *successful* invasion of the British Isles, but its meaning was by September largely forgotten. Its purpose was to warn the units who received it, but no others, that conditions were right for invasion and that they should move to their battle stations. It did not affect other units, or the Home Guard, and it did not mean that an invasion was actually in progress.

Since June, however, a great deal had happened. Units had moved, commanders had changed, and, on this Saturday evening, many senior officers were taking a well-earned night off after the frenzied activity of the past few weeks, leaving on duty junior officers who had only a hazy idea of the meaning of 'Cromwell', if they had ever heard the word before. Thus, when at 2007 hours (just after 8 pm to the civilian) the brigadier left in charge in London, while his two superiors were respectively touring the defences and attending a meeting, decided, very sensibly, to send out this preliminary warning, it caused consternation which in some places approached chaos. The vital signal took hours to reach some of the troops on the coast, who should have received it immediately, and many units which should not have been notified of it at all also received it and, though in the dark as to what they were supposed to do, resolutely decided to do *something*. Many rang the church bells, which had been silent since 13 June, being now reserved for use as a warning of invasion; some generously called out the Home Guard who, eager not to be left out and hearing the peals from distant churches, decided that it was their duty, too, to rouse the sleeping countryside and call their fellow-citizens to arms.

What happened in the Dorset village of Stoke Abbott, as recalled by the rector's sister, was not untypical:

It was 11.45 pm when I was woken by the telephone in the room below mine. I dashed downstairs and had just lifted the receiver and heard Admiral F's voice saying 'Tell the rector to ring the church bell', when my brother joined me. 'That means invasion,' he said, and hurried off to the church. My sister-in-law came downstairs and asked me to go and help him as she was afraid the effort might bring on his asthma. I still have a picture in my mind of our two pairs of hands pulling the great rope in the faint yellow light of a storm lantern set out our feet in the darkness of the church. . . . Then we heard other bells in the neighbourhood and . . . my brother went off in his car to fetch Home Guards from outlying farms and cottages. He told me afterwards that as he drove along the narrow lanes winding between steep banks and overhanging hedges, he kept wondering whether, round the next bend, he would run into a pack of grey-green uniforms. Meanwhile I returned to the house where my son, half awake, was stumbling downstairs fastening up his Home Guard uniform. He disappeared down the dark drive. My sister-in-law switched on the wireless, hoping to hear the midnight news, but it was over. Then she turned to me and asked, 'What do I do? I'm supposed to have a First Aid Post.' Hastily thinking, 'First Aid—treat for shock,' I said, 'Put on a kettle for hot drinks,' to which she retorted, 'Who for, the Germans?'

About 5.30 am my son returned saying Admiral F had decided to send half the Home Guard company home to get some sleep, while the others remained standing-to. He was evidently beginning to think it was a false alarm.

To the Home Guard the sudden turn-out came as the climax to the hurried weeks of training and brought home to them, if nothing else had done, the reality confronting them. One man farming on the Sussex coast near Lewes found himself manning a pillbox commanding the road from Newhaven. He knew the occasion must be serious for he had been issued with sixty rounds of ammunition instead of the usual five, and the post had been reinforced by two soldiers armed with a Browning machine gun, whose commander later arrived to announce, solemnly, 'There is to be no retirement.' Inland the Home Guard were not always so well organised – or so well armed. One Gallipoli veteran was warned, by a policeman at the door just as he was going to bed, that German parachutists were expected in the Midlands that night, and was soon manning his observation post near Northampton with only ten rounds of ammunition and the cheering admonition in his ears, 'This is it.'

The Army, despite the tremendous progress made since Dunkirk, was sometimes even worse equipped. A young Territorial officer in charge of an Army workshop near Stockton-on-Tees had had to hand in his revolver for use elsewhere, along with his men's rifles. On the arrival of a despatch rider with the dreaded code-word he armed them instead with the most formidable weapon his stores afforded, heavy spanners. Another wartime officer, defending the Ferrybridge power station on the Great North Road, was enjoying his first weekend for weeks with his wife, who had made a long cross-country journey to join him. 'I had got a room', he later recalled, 'in a little cottage in the village and . . . at four o'clock the next morning . . . there was a hammering on the door. I went down in my dressing gown and there was one of my soldiers, facing me with his tin hat on, with his rifle. I looked at him, he looked at me, and he said, "Sir, it's Cromwell!" I . . . went back to our mess and . . . we spent the whole of the rest of that day sitting in the mess waiting for the invasion which never happened.'

Even the newest, most junior recruits were affected by the crisis. At an RAF maintenance unit near Radlett on the outskirts of London, newly-joined airmen found themselves turned out of bed to load machine-gun belts, while at Cromer, on the east coast, a young sailor training to be a signalman found his class transformed into Britain's front-line defenders, unenthusiastically manning a trench and pillbox behind the beach, clutching Army rifles which most of them had barely seen before, and staring anxiously into the darkness of a cold but fine September night, waiting to hear the crunch of enemy barges on the beach. They heard instead an even more alarming noise, the faint thump of distant explosions, probably due to some over-eager sappers who were blowing up already-mined bridges, or perhaps to the explosions of mines laid prematurely on one East coast road, which killed some Guards officers, the only casualties of that night. In Lincolnshire some minor road bridges were blown up, while in Lincoln itself an Army despatch rider set the bells of five churches pealing and two engineer officers informed the District Superintendent of the London and North Eastern Railway that they proposed to destroy the main railway yard, to prevent the Germans, when, in the near future, they arrived, using it to load troops and supplies. Fortunately he insisted on checking with his Control Centre before the explosives were actually detonated and Lincoln station was saved.

When daylight came and, rather sheepishly, troops and Home Guards retired to bed, while their commanders held an inquest on the whole affair, rumours abounded. The Germans, it was whispered, had attempted landing and been repulsed by blazing petrol which had set the sea on fire. In fact not a German had sailed and not a beach had burned, although experiments with oil defences had been in progress for some time. The Petroleum Warfare Department, since its formation in July, had indeed been trying to set the ocean ablaze, but with little success. It had, it was true, managed on 24 August, by pumping twelve tons of oil an hour into the sea through ten pipes and igniting it with flares, to create 'a wall of flame of such intensity . . . that it was impossible to remain on the edge of the cliff and the sea itself began to boil', but this happy result, it soon transpired, could only be achieved under ideal sea and weather conditions and at prodigious cost in labour and equipment, and by September not a yard of coastline was yet protected in this way.

The British Isles did, however, have some flame defences in the shape of 'Flame Fougasses', forty-gallon barrels of petrol and tar, intended to stick to a tank, which were mounted in batteries of four at the bends of roads and in the banks of sunken lanes over much of Kent and Sussex. A few places also possessed Static Flame Traps, consisting of concealed pipes down which petrol could flow to flood a low-lying stretch of road and be set ablaze by a Molotov cocktail, crates of which were now stacked near every Home Guard roadblock.

Hitler had not come on 7 September. When would he at last arrive? Many people believed the invasion would begin on the 15th, a date invested with the same mystic significance as in August, and in fact the original target date chosen by the Führer himself, though S Day had since then been pushed back. But even more important to the British commanders than *when* the Germans would arrive was *where*. The British were no longer short of men: with nearly one and a half million men under arms in the Forces (or at least in uniform) and as many again in the Home Guard, although this played little part in the generals' calculations on either side, the British fighting units should comfortably outnumber the largest task force, estimated by the Admiralty at no more than 100,000, which the Germans could get across the Channel before the Navy intervened. If, however, the Germans had a chance to build up their forces beyond this point, and especially to land several divisions equipped with armour and artillery, in which the British Army was sadly deficient, the outcome of the battle would be in doubt. General Ironside's strategy had been designed, therefore, not to prevent a landing, since with 2000 miles of coastline in England alone to watch this was impossible, but to prevent any single assault building up to a major threat. He planned to achieve this by distributing his forward troops in a thin 'crust' covering all the threatened beaches, their job being to blunt and delay the first enemy onslaught and to give time for local reinforcements to arrive. If none the less the enemy succeeded in breaking out, he would, it was hoped, be further delayed by a series of 'stop lines' consisting mainly of anti-tank ditches and 'dragons' teeth' obstacles, covered by blockhouses and pillboxes designed to make up in defensive strength what the Army lacked in fire-power, and to give time for the strategic reserve to be hurried to the danger point. The main stop-line ran from Yorkshire to the Wash, then westwards to the outskirts of London, and from Maidstone in Kent to the Bristol Channel, with in front of and behind it small divisional stop-lines, all designed to slow up the enemy attack and prevent enemy forces, as had happened in France, roaming the countryside almost at will.

Ironside's plans made good sense at the time of appalling weakness when it was drawn up, for then sandbags and concrete were plentiful but weapons and trained troops were scarce. By late July, with arms, though still short, less desperately scarce than in June and the scattered units recovered from Dunkirk rested and regrouped, the first emphasis on thinly spread forces manning fixed defences was replaced by a demand for mobility, to enable a strong enough force to be assembled to crush any serious attack that developed. Churchill was haunted by the fear of large numbers of men tied up in sandbag emplacements and slit trenches, rather as the French had been in the Maginot Line, while the real battle was being decided elsewhere. He was shocked on visiting a young up-and-coming general, Bernard Montgomery, who had done well in France and now, from headquarters at Lancing College, commanded the 3rd Division, entrusted with the defence of the Brighton area, to find that his men were dispersed along thirty miles of coastline instead of being held back for use in force once landing had occurred. 'The battle will be won or lost,' wrote Churchill to the Chiefs of Staff, 'not on the beaches, but by the mobile brigades and the main reserve.'

This belief in 'mobile offensive action' was shared by General Sir Alan

Brooke, who had also distinguished himself during the great retreat in France, remaining calm when confusion reigned and all had seemed lost, and whom Churchill appointed to succeed Ironside at the end of July.[1] Brooke had at his command far greater resources than his predecessor – nearly 500 anti-tank guns by September in place of 170, 350 medium tanks insteady of eighty, 500 light tanks instead of 170, and nearly fifty per cent more artillery – and on his orders many men were withdrawn from the beach defences, but the main reserves were moved forward and the 'stop-lines' were stripped of troops, leaving them to be manned by whatever troops were available when the need arose. It was still essential to concentrate rapidly to throw back any serious challenge, for in a battle on anything like equal numerical terms the Germans were likely to win. Of Brooke's twenty-seven infantry divisions only four were fully equipped and fewer than half even had sufficient transport, while assembling forces for the counter-attack and transporting them across the Thames estuary or through the vast labyrinth of London, would be extraordinarily diffi-cult especially if, as in France, they were under constant attack from the skies.

It was therefore vital to decide – 'appreciate' in military jargon – where the main German attack would fall, and the British realised early on that the real choice lay between East Anglia and the south-eastern corner of England. Like the Germans, they at first favoured East Anglia, the large, flat area of England between the Wash and the Thames. Throughout June, July and much of August, Prime Minister, Commander-in-Chief, the Admiralty, and the special Combined Intelligence Committee set up by all three services to weigh the evidence, all believed that it was the East Coast which was threatened, probably by a force crossing from Holland and Germany itself. The concentrations of barges at Dunkirk, Ostend and further south, collected in full view of British aerial reconnaissance, were, they believed, meant to deceive the defenders into planning for a direct cross-Channel assault which, if it ever came at all, would be a mere diversion. The planners, if they reflected that both major successful in-vasions of England, by the Romans and the Normans, had come via the south-east, dismissed the thought, being more influenced by the fictional accounts of an imaginary German invasion with which authors of an earlier generation had made their contemporaries' flesh creep. From the classic *Riddle of the Sands* by Erskine Childers, first published in 1903, to Saki's *When William Came*, in 1913, a depressing tale which ended with Britain still in German occupation, every author had described a sudden

[1] General Brooke received his knighthood on 11 June, shortly after his return from France.

swoop across the North Sea on to the flat beaches and fields of Norfolk, Suffolk and Essex, none of them having foreseen a situation in which Germany would control the whole Continental coastline and thus be able to attack where she wished. The British experts recognised that the enemy would probably need to capture a port to mount a major invasion – the Germans in fact had their eyes on the nearest of all, Dover – but even this was uncertain. It seemed possible that 'the Germans with their renowned thoroughness and foresight' had 'secretly prepared a vast armada of special landing-craft, which needed no harbours or quays, but could land tanks, cannon and motor vehicles anywhere on the beaches'.

At last, however, the British High Command began to realise where the real danger lay. By early August General Brooke was warning of the danger to Kent and Sussex, and although on the 13th the Chiefs of Staff decided that they were 'slightly over-insured along the south coast', by early September the meaning of the build-up of forces and shipping across the Channel was unmistakable. While the Germans made the final preparations to pour not 100,000 men, as the British anticipated, but half a million into Britain, the defences along the south coast dramatically increased. Instead of eight divisions there were now, including reserves, sixteen, three of them armoured, a total of some 300,000 men, while the forces posted north of the Thames were cut from seven divisions to four, plus an armoured brigade, or about 90,000 men altogether, but with many more men still under training or in supporting units, a reserve denied to the Germans until they had gained control of the Channel. So long as the RAF controlled the skies above the British Isles, the British commanders could, Churchill believed, 'move with certainty another four or five divisions to reinforce the southern defence if it were necessary on the fourth, fifth and sixth days after the enemy's full effort had been exposed'.

And so as day after day the Luftwaffe and RAF met in bitter combat in the skies above Britain, the fate of the invasion was already being settled. Without mastery of the air, Hitler had said, there could be no invasion; without mastery of the air, Churchill had agreed, the invasion could not succeed. At his headquarters in the pleasant French town of Fontainebleau, General von Braüchitsch completed his plans, studied the signals from his subordinate commanders as they reported that one formation after another was fit for action, heard from the naval liaison officers that the growing fleet of barges was ready to put to sea and awaited from the Luftwaffe the news of victory in the air which would mean that his waiting armada could be launched across the Channel.

The events described up to this point all actually happened. The story recounted in the next three chapters is wholly fictional although the places, military units and some of the people mentioned are real.

Chapter 5: Assault

The Army Group will force a landing on the English coast between Folkestone and Worthing and ... take possession of a beachhead where the landing of further forces ... can be ensured.

Instructions of the Commander-in-Chief, Army, to Army Group A, 30 August 1940

When, at 9 am on the morning of Thursday 5 September 1940 the three German Commanders-in-Chief assembled under Hitler's chairmanship, as they had done seven weeks before, they found Air Marshal Göring in an unusually restrained mood. The attack on Fighter Command airfields had not, he admitted, proved decisive, although enormous numbers of British aircraft had been shot down or destroyed on the ground. Had the time not come to switch the attack to the cities, thus throwing the defences off balance, weakening the enemy's will to fight, and exacting revenge for recent British air raids on Berlin?

The Navy and Army representatives must have found it hard not to smile at Göring's confession of failure but they had no chance to speak, for Hitler was already launched on one of his tirades. He did not believe in the 'invincible' English Air Force, he shouted, any more than he had believed in the unconquerable French Army or the impregnable Maginot Line. The British *could* be beaten; they were isolated, outnumbered, already badly mauled. If the RAF were still able to intercept the Germans through gaining prior warning of their approach, then destroy their warning system! A lion, summed up Hitler, was no longer a danger when blinded. The attacks on the airfields were to go on; and once the RAF was beaten the British would be attacked without fear of opposition, which ought, he added, sarcastically, to appeal to the Luftwaffe who seemed so sadly lacking in the will to fight.

And this, though more tactfully, was how a few hours later Göring, still much chastened but now recovering some of his usual bombast, persuaded his reluctant air commanders to continue the costly attacks of the last few weeks. One more effort, he assured them, and the RAF would really be swept from the skies and the Luftwaffe could fly at will over Southern England as it had once roamed over Spain and Poland. The Luftwaffe generals were not convinced but they were well disciplined. The staff officers laboured all day over their maps and intelligence appreciations and that night the orders went out: knock out the radar stations, then the forward airfields, then the main fighter stations and sector and group headquarters. Every bomb and every bullet was to be aimed at an Air Force target.

The renewed attack on the radar chain took Fighter Command by surprise and soon ominous gaps were appearing on the plotting boards at 11 Group Headquarters at Uxbridge and at Fighter Command at Bentley Priory, Stanmore, as the flow of information dried up, as the masts and control buildings of the radar stations lay in ruins or were rendered impotent by bombs severing the power supply. Day after day, guided now only by reports from the Observer Corps or their commander's intuition, the defending fighters reached the required height or area only to find that the birds had already flown, leaving behind them another airfield knocked out. Reinforcements flown in from the squadrons in reserve in the north found themselves pounced upon by the waiting Messerschmitts or, even more tragically, had to watch from a slit trench their newly-arrived Spitfires and Hurricanes being blown to pieces on the runways. And, final proof that the RAF was losing the battle, the Stuka dive-bombers again flew far inland and got safely home.

The high-ranking officers who assembled at 0900 hours on Saturday 14 September at Hitler's advanced headquarters were in a very different mood from that which had prevailed nine days before. A radiant Göring reported that the RAF was now visibly crumbling, while Admiral Raeder, though more reluctantly, admitted that the collection and conversion for invasion purposes of transports, barges and, the worst bottleneck, tugs had gone better than he dared hope. Given good weather and no interference by the British fleet, he now believed the Navy could safely carry the Army across the Channel. Göring told him promptly that he need have no fears about the enemy Navy. Once the RAF was finally knocked out the bomber squadrons could turn their attention to attacking enemy ports and warships and soon not a motor-torpedo boat, let alone a battleship, would dare to stir in daylight.

It was now Field Marshal von Brauchitsch's turn. The Army, he confirmed, was ready, as it always had been. The actual assault would be made by Army Group A under Field Marshal von Rundstedt, whose armoured divisions had so successfully crossed the Meuse and broken through at Sedan, while for follow-up operations, such as the occupation of Devon and Cornwall, Army Group B, which had so speedily defeated Holland and Belgium, was trained and waiting. He planned to get 50,000 men ashore within the first two hours, building up within three days, two days before the British counter-attack was expected, to 125,000 and within two weeks to at least 220,000, rising if necessary to nearly half a million within six weeks. Most would be infantry, but the second wave, due to

Building a strongpoint, Trafalgar Square, May 1940

2 *Weapon training for Members of Parliament, July 1940*

3 *Assault training for Southern Railwaymen, June 1940*

Central London street scene, May 1940

Enemy aliens en route to internment, May 1940

6 *A roadblock in Southern England*

7 *Home Guards erecting a wire trap across a road*

nd 9 *Anti-air-landing obstructions, July 1940*

10 *A roadblock near the coast. Note the farm-cart and the ancient bathing machines*

11 *The removal of place names. A notice in the Bristol area, June 1940*

12 *A church notice board, Summer 1940*

13 *Anti-tank roadblock, July 19.*

14 *An anti-aircraft gun's crew taking post, 1940*

15 *Sea-bathing on the south coast, 1940 style*

go in as soon as there was room to unload their equipment, would include four Panzer divisions and two motorised divisions, while a parachute division, 10,000 strong, was to capture Folkestone and later Dover and to protect the landing area during the early stages of the attack.

It had long been agreed that *Sea Lion* should be launched on a night of bright moonlight, to make it easier for Raeder's inexperienced crews to keep station, and that the ideal landing time was when high tide on the principal beaches occurred just before dawn, so that the troops could land well up the beach, just as it was getting light, and the barges could be towed off again on an ebb tide. The last time when both these conditions would be met before the winter was approaching and now, to everyone's relief, the meteorologists were able to announce that it coincided with a promised spell of fine weather, with calm seas and good visibility, likely to begin on 23 September and to last at least a week.

All now depended on the Führer, to whom the success of the strategy he had ordered came as less of a surprise than to his subordinates. There was, he said brusquely, no need for further discussion. Operation *Sea Lion* would go ahead as planned and, so that the troops could make the crossing on the first possible night, S Day would be Tuesday 24 September.

Even while the admirals and field-marshals were dispersing to their cars and Göring was ostentatiously making for his private plane, the teleprinters were clattering out the long-drafted operation orders. Already in the timetable drawn up several months before it was S–10 and there was not a moment to be lost. Next day attacks on the British Isles rose to a new degree of fury as Göring, true to his promise, attacked every ship his airmen could find, while others dive-bombed the British coastal batteries already too short of ammunition, had the Germans but known it, to offer much effective opposition to a landing. The RAF was now ceasing to be a factor in the Germans' calculations and when at dawn on 21 September, S Day–3, the largest German force since 15 August crossed the enemy coast, hardly a plane rose to intercept them. A few Spitfires and Hurricanes, a few brave Blenheims and Defiants, flew across Southern England in search of Germans and, when they met them, fought until their ammunition was gone and, diving to escape, were brought down by one of the waiting horde of Messerschmitts or attacked as they came in to land. All day the 'hunter groups' of Junkers 88s ranged the skies of Britain at will looking for 'targets of opportunity', and that evening Air Chief Marshal Dowding, never the man to show his feelings, gruffly reported to the Prime Minister that 11 and 12 Groups of Fighter Command, defending Southern and Eastern England, had ceased for practical purposes to exist.

But two days later, on 23 September, the news was even worse. With air supremacy lost, the defences were, as Churchill had always known, fatally crippled. All round the British Isles, at Dover and Deal, Brighton and Newhaven, Seaford and Shoreham, the German bombers, almost at leisure, pounded the beach defences, while pitifully few of the reconnaisance aircraft, sent to photograph the invasion ports, ever returned. Even more serious, the Luftwaffe was rapidly threatening the Navy's control of the seas. Off the east and south-west coasts eight destroyers had already been sunk by enemy aircraft; sixteen had been sunk or badly damaged while in port, and dock installations and ammunition and fuel dumps had also suffered badly. With the squadrons formerly covering the north now drawn south, to be lost in the general holocaust, the Luftwaffe's units based in Norway and Denmark had seized their opportunity to strike at Scapa Flow. The battleship *Rodney* was for the moment crippled, unable to play any part in the coming invasion, the cruiser *Manchester* had been sunk, and four destroyers now lay on the bottom or awaiting major repairs. The mighty *Hood* herself, most powerful and famous ship in the whole Royal Navy, had been at sea but a U Boat had stalked her and, with one lucky shot, had cut her maximum speed to 14 knots. The Luftwaffe had also scattered mines, many of them magnetic, over all the approaches to the British Isles. Off the mouth of the Humber a magnetic mine had crippled the cruiser *Birmingham*, hurrying south to reinforce the anti-invasion defences, while off the east coast three destroyers had been mined in a channel swept clear only a few days before. The British public was not told all this bad news at once but enough was released for the day to become universally known as 'Black Monday'.

The Germans had another name for it, S—1, the evening the weathermen, so often wrong in the past, were proved triumphantly right. The seas were calm, the skies clear. It was, the German soldiers joked as they checked their equipment and moved towards the embarkation points, a lovely night for a sail. This, too, was the verdict of the German Navy. On the western flank of the invasion route the German minelayers had been busy all day putting down a defensive barrier of mines, guarded by all ten of the Navy's available destroyers and twenty small but powerful E Boats. On the eastern flank of the cross-Channel corridor another thirty E Boats protected a second defensive minefield, while a third minefield, designed this time to entrap enemy warships, had been laid under cover of darkness between the English coast and the Goodwin Sands.

Knowing Churchill's obsessional determination to sink any German capital ship whenever it ventured out of harbour, the German Admiralty had assigned two of their few powerful units an important, if unheroic, role in the invasion plans. On S—2 the battleship *Scheer* was already at sea, having sailed from Trondheim in Norway out into the Atlantic, followed by the cruiser *Hipper*, making for the gap between Iceland and the Faroes. Bait of this size proved, as Admiral Raeder had foreseen, irresistible to the Prime Minister, and the result provided the British with their one cheering item of news of the day. The aircraft carrier *Furious* and cruiser *Naiad* were sent after *Hipper* and, having slowed her down with air attacks, finally overhauled and sank her. The two ships then set off in pursuit of the *Scheer*, a worthy objective but one which drew them further and further from the narrow sea-lanes of the Channel where the real battle was so soon to be fought.

A second diversion was practised in the North Sea. On S—2 a force of five large liners and ten transports, escorted by four cruisers, left Stavanger on a course for Northumberland, designed to nourish any remaining fears the British might have on a landing in the largely unprotected northern counties. Once they had been met and challenged by the battle-cruiser *Repulse* and the cruiser *Southampton*, which rapidly destroyed the escorting cruisers, the transports turned back and the British ships were recalled to base, but not in time to escape attack by long-range torpedo bombers based on Norway. Once again the contest between air and sea power went in favour of the former, and both ships were sunk and several of the escorting destroyers damaged before, laden with wounded and survivors from the sunken ships, they reached port.

As darkness fell on S—1 day, fifteen empty transports slipped out of Cherbourg on a third mission of deception, to make a feint attack on Lyme Bay, all of the original plan for a landing in Dorset that had survived. But the thoughts of the Army commanders were now elsewhere, on the troops filing, silent and grim-faced, aboard the transports, and on the tanks and guns and crate upon crate of stores already piled in the holds or now being swung into position by dockside cranes. On a calm sea, and in bright moonlight, with not an English aircraft in the sky and only the sound of the ship's engines, an occasional order, uttered in an unnaturally subdued voice, and the distant 'neigh' of a horse protesting at the sudden motion, to break the silence, the vast fleet slipped its cables and stood out to sea.

Crossing the Channel that night under their own power were about 170 4000-ton steamships, carrying mainly the heavier stores. The troops, 'soft' vehicles and horses mainly travelled in 1200 river and canal barges, some of them self-propelled but most towed by a larger ship or by one of the 390 tugs and trawlers mustered for the purpose. The fleet was completed by a motley armada of 1000 motor-boats, fishing smacks and even sailing boats with auxiliary motors, whose task it would be to transship men, horses and equipment from the larger ships on to the enemy beaches. One force of three convoys of troopships set out from Dunkirk, Calais and Le Havre, preceded by minesweepers and towing behind it the smaller craft to be used during disembarkation. It was followed, from Dunkirk, Calais, Boulogne and Etaples, by a second force made up of eight convoys of fifty barges each, towed in pairs or, due to a last-minute shortage of tugs, in threes. The men aboard, had the sea been higher, would have had a rough passage, but once again, as so often during the past few days, fortune seemed to be on the side of the attackers.

The planners of Army Group A had divided the coastline on which they were to land into two sectors, the Western, from Rottingdean near Brighton to Hastings, being the responsibility of the Ninth Army, the Eastern, from St Leonards to Folkestone, being that of the Sixteenth Army. The two armies' immediate objective, after securing the initial foothold, was to push inland until they were entrenched along a line running roughly from Brighton to Uckfield, thence across the centre of Kent to Etchingham and Tenterden, then through Ashford to Canterbury and finally back towards the sea at Deal. A bridgehead on this scale, more than seventy miles across and fifteen deep, was, the Germans believed, needed to give them room in which to accumulate stores and reinforcements, to resist the inevitable counter-attack, and to prepare to break out towards the next objective, bounded by a line from Gosport on the Solent to Guildford and thence across country to Gravesend on the Thames.

For the British, planning in the dark without radar or reconnaissance aircraft, the first news of the approaching landing came half an hour after midnight from a motor torpedo boat stationed at Calais, which had discovered and sunk two minesweepers; and as the night wore on further reports reached the Admiralty of tugs and trawlers sighted towing barges. Everyone was eager to avoid another false alarm but at 4 am a special meeting of the Chiefs of Staff was called in Whitehall, the Commander-in-Chief, Home Forces, being summoned from his headquarters at St Paul's School, Hammersmith. The Prime Minister, who had given instructions that he was only to be awakened for news of invasion, had so far been allowed to sleep on, but was roused at 0435 hours when it was decided to send out the codeword 'Cromwell', which would ensure that the men on the coast, after standing-to at dawn, would remain on watch ready for an attack. It was also decided to authorise the local commanders in Southern and Eastern Commands to begin evacuation of the coastal area, but fortunately, everyone agreed, there were now few left in places like Folkestone and Hastings apart from members of the Home Guard.

'What about the church bells?' asked someone, producing the only laugh of the conference, and it was agreed that these could be rung when any area seemed directly threatened, but not before.

And then at 5.30 am, with the first signs of light already in the sky, came news which put an end to all uncertainty. 'Vast numbers' of parachutists, 'too large to count', it was reported, were coming down on the hills north and west of Folkestone. The Chiefs of Staff had heard more than enough of parachutists in the last few weeks. 'Probably only a platoon,' remarked one sceptical officer. 'Or a bomber crew baling out,' suggested another. But before long a further message proved them wrong. The force was now revealed as 'several thousand' strong and before long a 'most immediate' signal reported that the parachutists had, after a bitter fight, captured the small forward airfield of Lympne, on which, soon after dawn, small aircraft bringing Army and Luftwaffe liaison officers began to land, despite harassing fire from the British troops still dug in on the perimeter.

The lack of wind had made it easy for the airborne troops to descend precisely on their dropping-zone and the perfect weather conditions had also made the sea crossing far less hazardous than the Germans had feared. The Royal Navy, badly hit by its losses in the last few days and now impatiently held back while the Chiefs of Staff waited to see where the main German landing would fall, had so far hardly interfered at all. But the Germans, too, had had their problems, with no warships to spare for preliminary bombardment of the beach defences and as at 6 am, dead on schedule, the first barges touched down, the ramps in their bows collapsed with a bang and the tense but determined troops charged down on to the beach, they seemed to the officers on the transports anchored off-shore, watching through their binoculars, to be charging an impenetrable wall of barbed wire and iron posts. Already ragged salvoes of rifle-fire were coming from the pillboxes commanding the exits from the beaches and, as the first troops splashed their way through the shallows, the first machine-gun opened up, and as the leading troops moved higher up the beach and prepared to demolish the barricades, the first mines, planted just above high-water mark, began to explode and hurl sand, pebbles, metal and men into the air. Taking what shelter they could behind groynes or rocks, or frantically digging in to give themselves a little head-cover, the first men ashore waited for reinforcements, and especially for engineers to clear a way through the minefields and obstacles ahead, while rifles, machine-guns, grenade-throwers and even an occasional mortar poured down a heavy fire from the trenches and pillboxes commanding the shore below.

This was the scene on some beaches. On others, which there were not enough men to defend adequately, or where dive-bombing had blown a hole in the usual wire and concrete obstacles, units managed to get on to dry land almost unscathed and then deploy off the shore on to the promenade or road behind. Field-guns, horses, ammunition wagons, bicycles were ferried on to the beach and then led and heaved on to the sea-front, less because the assault troops needed them at this stage than because the captains of the ships concerned were eager to unload their cargo and get away.

While civilians elsewhere in the country were waking up and listening on the 8 am news to the first, very guarded, reports of the landings, Bomber Command was sent to try to mend the breaches in the island's defences. The crews' instructions were simple: to bomb any transports and barges they could find along the south coast and any concentrations of enemy forces, especially tanks, which had forced their way off the beach. It was a hard assignment. The Whitleys, Wellingtons and Hampdens, designed for high-level bombing after dark and, as bitter experience had already proved, ill-equipped to carry out a low-level, close-support role in daylight, did heroic work, often taking the Germans by surprise by coming in from the direction of the sea, flying low above the waves, and they did much to raise the morale of the defenders, but they were too few to do more anywhere than slow down the build-up of men and guns ashore. The Navy, also hastening to the rescue, had on the whole less success. Destroyers from Harwich and Sheerness, charging down at full speed towards the eastern flank of the invasion fleet, ran headlong into the newly-sown enemy minefield and suffered grievous losses. On the west the British were more fortunate. The cruiser *Newcastle* and a force of eleven destroyers made their way unscathed through the enemy minefield and did great havoc among the diversionary force steaming towards Lyme Bay, sinking six of the transports and three of the escorting destroyers. Interrogation of a rescued merchant seaman, although survivors were few, for the British captains were in no mood to linger with one wave of bombers only just beaten off and another probably approaching, revealed the news, intensely disappointing to the victorious sailors, that the ships had been empty. But to the British Chiefs of Staff when, much later, it reached them, the report was reassuring: the attack towards Weymouth was clearly only a feint. 'Our appreciation is', a junior officer at GHQ Home Forces recorded that night in the war diary, 'that any further landings that may occur will only be diversions.'

The 9 pm BBC news that Tuesday was cautiously optimistic. Some enemy units were ashore, they admitted, and Dover harbour had been conquered from the landward side by enemy parachute troops – that same

7th Parachute Division which had secured Lympne airfield that morning – but not till blockships had been sunk at the entrance. Many enemy troops had been killed as they came ashore and some were believed to have drowned in holes in the sea-bed, weighed down by their equipment. The evacuation of civilians from the affected towns was proceeding smoothly, an announcement heard with a derisive snort by more than one recent resident of Hythe and Sandgate who, like many thousand others, had been woken that morning by police pounding on their doors, forced to leave home with a single suitcase packed within the hour, and were now, after an uncomfortable journey in a slow and crowded train, huddled into school halls in Reading, an unwelcoming town already choked with evacuees. So far, said the announcer, civilians had obeyed the order to keep off the roads and any who found themselves in an area where military action was taking place – a BBC euphemism for getting caught in the middle of a battle – should take refuge in the nearest house and await further instructions.

After the news came a broadcast from the King, a brief, unemotional but stirring call to arms, intended primarily to let the nation know that, contrary to the stories that German radio had been putting out all day, he was still, as he had promised, 'with his people'. The national anthem followed and then a special announcement about future radio services. Henceforward, explained the BBC, the Forces Programme would disappear and all transmitters would carry the Home Service, which would broadcast frequent news bulletins, separated only by light music and other recorded programmes. If the government, which had asked the press to play down the initial success of the Germans in securing a number of beach-heads, had wished to divert attention from the subject by its orders to the BBC it could not have succeeded more completely. Next day the newspapers, recalling those weary, wireless-ridden days at the start of the war, with continuous records varied only by Sandy Macpherson on the theatre organ, devoted almost as much space to the coming entertainment famine as to the Germans who had just spent their first night on British soil.

German radio was that night surprisingly restrained, contenting itself, apart from dramatic accounts of 'our brave fellows leaping on to the beach', largely with repetitions of the first bulletin issued that day: 'Our troops are ashore at several points and moving inland.' The generals, still fearing some devastating British counter-stroke, had for once prevailed upon the Propaganda Ministry to be restrained and cautious. As von Rundstedt and his Chief of Staff at Army Group A headquarters, still on the French side of the Channel, reviewed the day's progress they agreed that, while the sea crossing had gone better than they had dared hope, the actual landing had met with far more stubborn resistance than they had expected. The outstanding success was the capture of the harbours at Dover and Folkestone, due to the surprise achieved by 7th Parachute Division, whose assault had gone with textbook precision. The same division landing behind the Royal Military Canal, running roughly parallel to the coast just inland, had not, however, achieved its objective of securing and holding a crossing for the 17th Infantry Division, arriving by sea. The division had suffered a heavy mauling, with a third of its troops becoming casualties even before the first units got off the beach, and when the survivors had managed to get across the A259 coast road, south-west of Hythe, and had even landed some tanks and anti-tank guns, they had found themselves hemmed in by the canal and unable to cross it. The situation on the division's left flank was not much better. Here 35th Division had successfully occupied Dymchurch and Littlestone and had managed to land tanks and artillery on the foreshore, but the network of dykes just inland, almost ignored by German Intelligence, was slowing up their advance. German troops who had forced their way into New Romney had been driven out again after fierce fighting and, though German patrols had penetrated as far as Lydd and Ivychurch, the main road between New Romney and Brenzett, a key factor in the defence system, was still in British hands.

Further left again, at Camber, a small beach-head had been secured by advance elements of the 7th Division on the right bank of the River Rother and two out of three battalions of amphibian tanks had safely got ashore, the rest succumbing to mechanical breakdowns or sinking as soon as they left their transports. They had, however, encountered an unforeseen obstacle, after turning off the Rye to Winchelsea road to move inland. The details were still not clear, but it seemed that a low-lying stretch of the road had been flooded with petrol and the leading Panzers had been engulfed in a sheet of flame, knocking them out and effectively blocking the way forward. The incident seemed, too, to have affected the men's morale, for the other tanks had hastily withdrawn under fire from anti-tank guns and not stopped till they reached the supposed safety of the beach. Their commander, knowing the ways of soldiers, suspected that already rumours of the new British secret weapon, to which increased terrors would be added in the telling, would be spreading all over the division.

But the main anxiety that night of General Busch, in command of the Sixteenth Army, was about the 1st Mountain Division whose commander had proved during training to be so curiously ignorant of the behaviour of the tides, and had now annoyed his superiors even more by getting himself killed just when he was most needed. Some battalions of his division had landed successfully on Winchelsea Beach and secured the Winchelsea–Guestling road, while a patrol had reached as far as Northiam, ten miles inland, but another battalion, after being put ashore on narrow beaches at Fairlight, had found the cliffs above them unscalable and become trapped between sea and shore, while everyone in the district who could fire a gun had been mustered on the cliffs above shooting at them, and, when their ammunition ran out, pelting them with stones.

Three miles away at Hastings, where formidable hills and cliffs and a Norman castle built by William I overlooked the section of the sea-shore on which the same ill-starred division had landed, the only exit secured from the beach had led into the narrow and easily defended streets of the Old Town, where men of the Devon Regiment and Somerset Light Infantry had deluged the troops struggling to get inland with intense rifle and machine-gun fire, and bombarded the vehicles massed on the shore with mortar fire. The way ahead here seemed for the moment barred.

To Field-Marshal von Rundstedt, considering the reports he had received from the Sixteenth Army, the situation on its front, apart from the capture of the ports, seemed far from hopeful. If this was the resistance on the coast, where the British had clearly thinned out their defences to provide reserves and where the Germans had achieved tactical surprise, what would it be like further inland? Happily, on the other wing of Army Group A's front, in the area from Brighton to Hastings, the report from General Strauss, Commander-in-Chief of the Ninth Army, was a good deal more encouraging. Assault troops of the 34th Division, supported by amphibian tanks, had got ashore on his right flank on either side of Bexhill with relatively light losses and had penetrated several miles into Sussex, while the 26th Division had successfully landed at Pevensey with only slight casualties. Bitter fighting had admittedly followed around the shacks and chalets along the Crumbles and there had been a determined attempt to halt the advance by men manning defences around the sewage farm at Langney, a mile further on, but they had eventually been killed and the division had pushed on to the outskirts of Hailsham, nearly six miles from the coast. Resistance was now clearly hardening again, but a reconnaissance patrol had managed to reach Hellingly, two miles ahead of the main positions, which augured well for events on the following day.

The 6th Division, coming ashore at Cuckmere Haven, had also learned at first hand the practical results of General Brooke's defensive strategy of the 'thin crust'. The division had suffered badly as it fought its way off the shore towards the Eastbourne–Seaford road near Exceat, but, once across the road, it had advanced with relatively little opposition through Litlington and Lullington as far as the Eastbourne–Lewes road at Wilmington, where it was now dug in. Its neighbour, the 8th Division, landing on either side of Bishopstone, had also had a good day, capturing Seaford and then pushing westwards to overrun the harbour at Newhaven with its cranes still largely intact. Other units had pushed up the valley of the Cuckmere river, through some of the most beautiful scenery in Sussex, though the Germans had little time to enjoy it, for though the main defence had withdrawn there was sniping from the woodlands overlooking the valley and from the bushes beside the river. One platoon, held up for several minutes by a particularly persistent sniper, eventually stalked and shot him. He proved to be an elderly grey-haired man in an ill-fitting uniform, armed with an ancient rifle with a red band painted round the barrel. Though clearly in pain, his only regret seemed to be that he had not killed even more men and he died cursing the Germans. His killers, after looking curiously at the first dead Englishman most of them had ever seen, rolled his body with their feet out of the way and into the shallow river alongside which they were advancing.

By nightfall they had reached Alfriston, another famous beauty-spot, recalling the photographs of historic English towns and villages they had already seen in their guide to Britain. Most of the inhabitants had been evacuated and the few remaining behind stayed silently in their houses, but the German commander, fearing treachery, ordered his men to spend the night in the open which, muttering protests under their breath, they prepared to do. They were more cheerful after those not on guard were allowed to go foraging in one of the abandoned inns, returning with a promising-looking barrel. One sip, however, was enough. What the publican had used to deny the Germans his beer they never discovered, but the taste and the whisper of 'poison' which passed from lip to lip was enough to make them settle for the contents of their water bottles, later refilled after one brave soldier had tried the water from a still-flowing tap from the supply in the empty houses. While they settled down for a peaceful night, broken only by guard duty, patrols were pushing on to Glynde and Ringmer and the commander, to his great relief, had established contact with the neighbouring 6th Division at Wilmington. Secure in the knowledge that his right flank was no longer in the air, and allowing himself a luxury denied his men, he spent a comfortable night in a bed in a hastily requisitioned house, with his batman on guard outside the door.

His opposite number to his left, the major-general commanding the 28th Division, which had landed on the extreme west of the invasion

front, slept less well, for his formation had faced the fiercest opposition
encountered anywhere by the Ninth Army. Coming ashore at Rottingdean, a suburb of Brighton, they had forced their way off the beach which,
except at this point, was everywhere commanded by steep cliffs, only after
a bitter battle. The narrow beach had seemed by midday to be littered with
dead or dying and, at the road junction just behind the beach, which
formed the centre of the village, there had been a hand-to-hand clash
with the defenders, a brief, untidy scuffle in which bayonets and even rifle
butts had been used, the whole scene, with men rising up and charging
forward with wild cries, and the aftermath, of bodies lying twisted and
bleeding in the roadway, recalling a scene from the first world war. The
general, with dreams of capturing Brighton, a name which was well known
in Germany, had tried to widen his front in that direction, but his men
had found the road along the cliffs blocked by barbed wire, anti-tank
obstacles and, worst of all, anti-tank guns, and by an enemy who was
clearly determined not to give an inch. Thwarted there, the division had
tried to break out in the opposite direction and link up with the units on
his right by securing the shabby bungalow town of Peacehaven, set on
cliffs too high to assault from the sea. Here also the first probing attack
had been thrown back so decisively that the battalion commander had
decided it would be folly to renew it with the depleted and weary companies
under his command.

But the day had not been wholly unsuccessful. The division had
occupied Falmer later that afternoon and was approaching Lewes when
he decided to halt it for the night, while by dusk a patrol had reached
Ditchling Beacon, the most conspicuous strategic feature for miles. The
cost, however, had been enormous, with one in every three of those who
had landed dead or wounded. There had been very few prisoners on either
side, the British refusing to give quarter and, even when outnumbered,
unwilling to surrender. The general, a professional, had long been sceptical about the tradition of units which fought to the last man but today he
had seen it in action. If every day was going to be the same, he reflected,
he would by Thursday night not have a division to command. But
such reflections were futile. Mentally the general turned his back on
the sea and on the immediate past; the future, and the way forward, lay
inland.

Chapter 6: Break-out

After the arrival of sufficient forces on English soil, the Army Group will attack and secure possession of the line Thames estuary–heights South of London–Portsmouth.

Instructions of the Commander-in-Chief, Army, to Army Group A,
30 August 1940

At dawn the counter-attacks began, as yet only in company or battalion strength: the major offensive which was to clear Kent and Sussex of the intruders was still being planned at GHQ. But, refreshed by a night's sleep, well dug in, and with morale high now that the hazards of the crossing and landing lay behind them, the Germans fought well. Only on the east of the invaded area near Hythe, where they were already in trouble due to the failure to cross the Royal Military Canal, did the attack have some success. The 28th Maori Battalion of the New Zealand Division, with their strange hats and even stranger war-cries, poured down on to the weakest point in the enemy line, that classically vulnerable spot where two formations met. Here the 17th Division, taken by surprise by these unfamiliar opponents and badly mauled on the previous day, rapidly gave ground, but the situation was restored by the airborne troops of the 7th Parachute Division, now serving as ordinary infantry, tough, resourceful soldiers, not easily dislodged and, though the New Zealanders drove a salient into the enemy front, they failed, as they had hoped, to break through to the sea.

Another attempt, later in the day, to recapture Folkestone harbour, defended by the parachutists of the same division, met an equal rebuff and the exhausted British troops, back where they had started, watched in fascinated horror as the British bombers sent to try and put the port out of action fell victim one after another to the anti-aircraft guns now mounted all round it and along the high ground of the Leas. By the time a squadron of Luftwaffe fighters, flown in that morning to Hawkinge landing ground, arrived on the scene, there were few targets left for them. A few hits had been scored, but the line of ships tied up in the docks and the convoys of vehicles driving away from them, made clear enough that the attack had failed in its main purpose. This failure had repercussions unknown to those who watched it, for it finally convinced the Chiefs of Staff, now meeting almost continuously in London, that in the absence of fighter cover orthodox bomber operations were almost futile and at 11 am the Chief of the Air Staff formally advised the Defence Committee of the War Cabinet that the RAF could no longer be considered an effective fighting force. Reluctantly the Air Ministry ordered that all aircraft from training units which could not be fitted with makeshift bomb-racks or gun mountings should be withdrawn to bases in Wales and Scotland. Those remnants of operational units still able to fly should attack the enemy at will, whenever opportunity offered, until, as was not said but tacitly admitted, they too were shot down.

For the Germans it was a day of consolidation, a day for digging in, setting up signal networks, choosing premises to serve as temporary head-quarters, preparing the wounded for shipment back to Germany, and burying the dead. By nightfall much had been done. Every formation had now established contact with its neighbours, so that the sixty-mile front was no longer held by separate units, but by a single fighting force. Some second-line troops had arrived, but most of the shipping which had re-turned to its home ports on the previous day was now being loaded with supplies for the units already ashore. That day many units, which had lived off cold combat rations on the previous day, had a hot meal for the first time since embarking on Monday night, the cooks having comman-deered the kitchens of abandoned restaurants of which the captured resorts offered a vast profusion.

The few British civilians left in the occupied area kept largely out of sight. So far the enemy commanders had been too busy with more urgent matters to impose the formal machinery of military government. There had been no formal requisitioning. Units had taken what they needed from the civilian population under the simplest and most effective author-ity of all, a machine-carbine or automatic rifle pointed at the owner of the goods in question. In the centre of Folkestone one man who had foolishly charged towards a German patrol, shouting abuse and waving his only weapon, a walking stick, had been shot and his body had been left where it had fallen—a warning to other would-be heroes; an elderly woman, flourishing a carving knife at the officer who had announced he proposed to billet himself in her house—why she had not been evacuated no one knew—had been disarmed, and had thereupon spat in his face, at which she had been knocked down by an escorting sergeant and told to behave herself. She was now wandering about the house, muttering darkly, but the Germans had decided to ignore her. 'Correctness', they knew, was the official policy towards civilians.

Already some Germans were discovering with surprise that the British, whom they had assumed to be little different from themselves, seemed to expect them to behave like barbarians and savages. A German Medical

Officer who had entered a small private nursing home at Hythe, revolver in hand for fear of enemy soldiers, to set up a casualty-clearing station had found that the nurses, left behind to look after a few patients too ill to be moved, had assumed that he had come to shoot them. One had yelled defiance at him, one had cringed and pleaded for her life, and the others had merely stood and stared at him sullenly, determined not to kow-tow to a German. This last group had seemed more embarrassed than relieved when he had explained that murder was not the German way, and soon British nurses and German orderlies were working together to unload the patients, and German wounded and the few captured British soldiers were occupying adjoining beds.

During the day German engineers and naval experts had inspected the port installations at Dover, Folkestone, Newhaven and Rye and had discovered with relief that, though the entrance of Rye harbour was totally blocked and Dover was unusable until the blockships at the entrance had been lifted, Newhaven would be ready for use in twenty-four hours and Folkestone in forty-eight. Thus even if the weather deteriorated there need be little fear of the task force being cut off from its bases and starved of supplies. By S+2 tanks, bridging equipment, anti-aircraft guns, heavy artillery and ammunition were all being unloaded at Folkestone and Newhaven, and further troops were still coming in across the captured beaches. By black-out time (far less rigorously observed by the Germans than by the British, it was noticed, but they of course had little fear of air attack) on Friday 27 September, the Germans had already well over 200,000 men encamped on English soil, with many thousands of lorries, bicycles and horses.

The use of horses had come as a surprise to the defenders and some squeamish soldiers had at first hesitated to shoot them, though many were killed and injured by mortar bombs, but the sight of the animals being harnessed to field guns and ammunition limbers, as in some scene from a first-world-war film, soon caused the defenders to overcome their reluctance. To animal-lovers far from the battle-front, however, such insensitivity seemed an outrage. Although using these noble animals to serve their evil purposes was yet one more proof of the wickedness of the Germans, 'Horsewoman' wrote to *The Times*, there was no reason to suppose that, even if they were German by birth (and many had no doubt been requisitioned in occupied countries and could be considered slave labour) they had wanted to take part in the invasion. Could not there be a special 'animals armistice' with the Germans being asked to hand the horses over for safe-keeping until the end of hostilities on the understanding the English would make no use of them? She was answered by a military correspondent writing from 'somewhere in Southern England' who remarked dryly that he found it as disagreeable being shelled by a horse-drawn gun as by any other type of artillery and, personally, he hoped if the Germans were going to hand over anything, he would prefer them to surrender their tanks. The correspondence provided, however, a little light relief at a grim time and was much referred to, usually under running headlines such as 'A horse laugh' and 'A mare's nest', in the popular papers.

By now most British troops in the forward area were very tired and ammunition for their artillery, which regularly pounded every German position as fast as it was identified, was running short. General Brooke and his advisers, while eager to stem the German build-up, were in a quandary. They had, they knew, only sufficient supplies for one major counter-attack and if it were launched prematurely, before the enemy's intentions were clear, there would be little in hand for a further effort. London, clearly, would be the target but would the thrust come from the Ninth Army, holding the coast from Rottingdean to St Leonards, or the Sixteenth Army, which controlled it from Hastings to Dover?

By now the lull which had followed the first day's hard fighting was coming to an end. The German commanders reported that night after night their patrols were making deep penetration into the countryside in front of them. The British were, it seemed, preparing to counter-attack in force and had largely withdrawn their troops to regroup and prepare. Although, von Rundstedt knew, the mere possession of ground was not necessarily an advantage, the existing lodgement area was undoubtedly too small to allow much freedom of manœuvre, and ever since August it had been agreed that Army Group A's 'initial task' was to reach a line a good deal further inland than that so far occupied. He accordingly ordered an advance, during the night of 29 September and the following day, of up to ten miles to occupy a new line running from Margate, on the coast on his east flank, through Canterbury, Ashford, Etchingham, Hadlow Down and Uckfield and then back towards the sea on the west flank near Falmer, since Brighton itself was still in British hands.

Up to now, although both sides had fought hard, the rules of war had not been too grossly violated. A few men trying to surrender after a hard battle had been shot, some houses from which missiles had been thrown had been set on fire by the Germans, and one vicar, who had tried to stop a unit roaring into his town by standing in the road with hand held up as though halting the traffic, had simply been run down. (He was in fact trying to warn them that in England it was the custom to drive on the left but this was never discovered.) On the whole the Germans, according to their own not too exacting lights, had behaved correctly. Too few civilians had been left in the coastal strip to offer serious resistance, and the Home Guard, despite all Hitler's threats, had when captured, though very few were, been treated as ordinary soldiers. The chief inconveniences suffered by the Germans in the towns they had occupied had been broken milk bottles and nails scattered at road junctions, with no clue to the culprits, and – an annoying and at first even frightening trick recommended earlier that summer in a British magazine – the removal of manhole and coalhole covers after dark. More than one member of the Wehrmacht had, as a result, slipped and broken his leg and a few, either exceptionally slim or exceptionally unfortunate, had found themselves suddenly and painfully precipitated into a cellar, usually more astonished than hurt, incidents which their comrades above ground had tended to find amusing rather than proof of the existence of British saboteurs.

During the move forward, however, it was different. Although the troops and Home Guard had largely withdrawn, occasional suicide squads still stayed behind, hiding in roadside coppices and behind walls, and leaping up to fling Molotov cocktails at every tank and lorry that came within range, although the Germans soon found the missiles were singularly ineffective, for they either failed to catch fire or burned out harmlessly yards away from their target, while more than one, the startled cries from cover revealed, had gone off prematurely. In one narrow street in Ashford a blanket had been hung on a clothes line stretched between windows on opposite sides of the street, apparently to blind any oncoming driver, but the soldier in the first lorry to reach it had simply stood up, torn it down and folded it up into a cushion for himself and his neighbour, making a gesture of thanks in case the donor were still watching. Such incidents apart, the real trouble came from road-blocks out in the country, which the troops encountered round every bend, but by now they had a well-developed technique for dealing with them. Some convoys were led by a heavy recovery vehicle, which easily pushed all but the most formidable aside, or by a truckload of engineers who leapt out and pulled to pieces any home-made barriers or blew up those which it would take too long to demolish. Roadblocks, both British and Germans were realising, were little use unless they were defended, and most of the British troops had now withdrawn, but occasionally Home Guards manning a slit trench refused to give in, and a section had to be despatched to deal with them with grenades and automatic weapons. Some pillboxes, too, which seemed unoccupied, came suddenly to life as the advancing Germans drew within range. But the men who had smashed through the Belgian forts were not to be held up by block-houses on which the cement was barely dry, or sandbag emplacements from which the sand was often already leaking or so unstable that a single shell nearby could set the whole unsteady edifice tumbling.

And so, stopping often, fighting occasionally, but mostly moving, the trucks spaced out in accordance with the usual convoy rules, the men marching in single file, with sections posted on alternate sides of the road in the march discipline common to every army, the Germans moved forward. The tank commanders cursed the narrow English roads, the infantry cursed the staff cars which roared past them spraying them with dust, and the British farm carts and tractors which trundled past, often forcing them into the ditch, not perhaps to the regret of the driver, who stoutly refused to let a mere invasion interfere with really important matters like preparing the fields for next year's crops. More than one stalwartly insular civilian narrowly escaped a collision when, driving as usual on the left, he found himself making straight for a head-on collision with a German Army driver keeping, as all over Europe, to his right. Already the Army Group commander had issued an order that the German rule of the road would be observed in 'Occupied Territory', as he rather grandiosely called the few square miles of Kent and Sussex so far surrendered by the British, but there had as yet been no opportunity to enforce the new law and for the moment the Germans relied on pressing ruthlessly on, leaving the few civilians still on the roads to get out of the way.

The infantry had largely been assigned the minor roads, leaving the 'A' roads, as the British called them, free for the tanks and heavier transport, and for many men it was little more than a pleasant walk through the autumn countryside. The day was fair, though cloudy, and the English landscape, they reflected, looked prosperous and not so very different to the countryside they knew at home.

Some units, however, had no time to spare for such frivolous thoughts, and outstanding among these was one battalion, described on the Germans' 'Order of Battle' as 'Elements of the SS "Das Vaterland" Division', but now attached to the 34th Infantry Division. The 'Waffen SS' were the military wing of the security service controlled by Heinrich Himmler, Minister of the Interior. Most of the SS were civilian policemen, though of a particularly brutal and vicious kind already notorious throughout Europe, but the SS had also contributed some divisions of regular troops to the Wehrmacht. They consisted of tough, crack battalions of dedicated Nazis, who rarely took prisoners and who were only too happy to undertake any 'pacification' operations that might be required in occupied territory. Killing was their trade, torture their recreation, brutality their hallmark, whether it was practised, as it was by their civilian brothers, in underground torture chambers or, as by the SS in military uniform, on the battlefield. No SS division had been assigned to take part in the invasion of England, but Himmler, with his rival Göring's Luftwaffe so deeply involved in the operation, had been anxious that his men, too, should play some part in it. The result was the SS battalion, now pushing forward through the lanes of mid-Sussex from Hellingly towards Horam.

By midday the battalion had already met more than its share of obstructions. The battalion commander, a lieutenant-colonel whose cruel face was made even harsher by duelling scars, was eager to show his efficiency by reaching the divisional objective precisely at the estimated time if not before. He gave short shrift to anyone, soldier or civilian, who got in his way. The Home Guards manning one roadblock, having surrendered on finding themselves surrounded, had been ordered to pull it down, barbed wire and all, with their bare hands and, having done so, had been shot out of hand. A little further on the battalion had suffered another annoyance, though a minor one. Three boys aged about twelve had ignored their mothers' orders to stay indoors while the Germans went by for it was a mild day and, the one good thing about the invasion from their point of view, the village school was closed. They had at first practised football and fought each other in the playing field adjoining the main road in the centre of the village and had clambered about the swings and slide intended for small children until, growing bored, they began to shout insults, in which the Germans could make out only the words 'Hitler' and 'Churchill', at the passing traffic. Finally, disappointed at the lack of response from the Germans, one boy had begun to throw stones at the lorries and the others, when these were ignored, followed his lead. One lucky throw struck a soldier sitting in a troop-carrying lorry smartly on the shoulder and just at that moment the truck halted, the line of traffic in front having stopped. The soldier who had been hit said not a word, but got to his feet in a leisurely, almost casual, way, selected a stick grenade from his belt and flung it at the little group. It exploded just above them, killing one outright, blinding another, and inflicting terrible injuries on the third. It took the villagers, summoned by the noise of the explosion and the resulting screams, a long time to get across the road to help the boys, for the convoy had moved on as suddenly as it had stopped. By that time the bright green of the grass was discoloured by a large red stain; the injured boy had bled to death.

Around midday the convoy stopped again and, while the officers were called forward to confer with the battalion commander, the men were given permission to take a short break. One jumping down from his truck and looking for a quiet place to relieve himself, wandered into the village churchyard and, having refastened his buttons, was looking with interest at the war memorial in one corner when a girl came in, carrying a large bunch of flowers and, not noticing him, made for a newly dug grave not far away. She was, he realised, crying, but she was also pretty. Suddenly she seemed to realise he was there – she must, he guessed, have seen the lorries outside – for she turned to him, white-faced and with a bitterness he had not seen on anyone's face since a Polish woman had shouted at him nearly a year before when he was dragging an old Jewess downstairs. That woman had been middle-aged and ugly, while this one was young and good-looking, but she gave him the same look of sheer disgust. She gestured towards the grave: 'My father!' she said. 'He went out on patrol with the Home Guard last Thursday and got shot. You killed him! You filthy Germans! He'd never hurt anybody in his life. And now we're all alone, mum and me!' The girl began to cry. It was the tears that did it. The soldier instinctively moved forward to console her, but she impatiently flung his arm off and shrank away from him as if nauseated by his mere touch. In a moment he was indifferent to her revulsion, being suddenly conscious only of desire, and seized hold of her roughly, pressing his rough uniform against her thin dress. She struggled violently at first, pounding him with her fists and hacking at his legs, and then began to cry again. Suddenly she went limp as if losing interest in the struggle, and he pushed her down on the grass verge beside the gravel path to the war memorial and raped her. It was not, he had to admit, looking back, very pleasurable and the look she gave him as he got to his feet made even him, a hardened SS man, wince, but at that moment the whistle sounded from the road and he turned and hurried back towards the truck. His last view of her was of her lying on the ground, her skirt still disarranged, the flowers she had been carrying to put on her father's grave lying scattered all round her, with great sobs bursting from her, her tears making even more unsightly a face badly bruised during the struggle. Two minutes later the advance had been resumed.

Due to the roadblocks, though many now were no more elaborate than a tree-trunk on a wheel which yielded easily to a wood-cutter's saw, and the frequent punctures, the result of the broken glass scattered everywhere on the roads nearer the coast, it was late afternoon before the battalion approached Horam. Before they could enter it they ran into one more hold-up, a flame-trap mounted in the bank at a bend, which suddenly shot a jet of evil-smelling burning liquid straight across the road and caught the leading troop carrier full on the bonnet. The men reacted swiftly. Without waiting for orders, the troops in the affected lorry leapt out and deployed alongside the road, shooting two men they saw running away, and the driver managed to put out the flames with an extinguisher. The vehicle, too badly damaged to use again that day, was manhandled through a gate into the nearest field and left for the breakdown unit at the rear of the convoy. Although no one had been hurt, the additional delay, including the time taken to allocate the men from the ruined lorry to other transport, infuriated the commanding colonel. His temper was not improved when he received orders to turn off the main A267 road, half a kilometre after passing through the town, down the minor road to the left leading towards the small village of Winter Hill, after passing through which he was to turn right again, down another secondary road leading into the main A272 from Uckfield to Burwash, which was, as he knew, the divisional objective. When he reached it he was to dig in, siting his companies to command the triangle of roads, like a river delta with its base towards him, immediately to his front. On his way he was to ensure that the surrounding area to his flanks was clear of enemy since it would lie directly behind the centre of the divisional position which was itself at the very heart of the whole front line.

The colonel recognised that he had been entrusted with a key point in the defences, likely to be an early target for an English counter-attack, but he looked with foreboding at the countryside between him and his objective. Unlike the broad open downland they had seen nearer the sea, this landscape was secretive and shut in, consisting of small fields interspersed with woodland. Everywhere there were small spinneys and coppices and many were close to the road, making it ideal for the small-scale ambushes in which the Home Guard specialised. The colonel knew by now the trouble that a few determined men could cause on these narrow country roads and, after the halt, he took up his usual position near the front line, not far behind the detachment of motor-cyclists who went ahead to ensure that the way was clear and to tempt any enemy lying in wait to reveal themselves prematurely.

At first, however, all went well. The colonel followed their progress carefully on a large-scale English map seized by some enterprising officer from a stationer's shop in Polegate, and the convoy had just crossed a tiny stream and was beginning to climb the slight rise leading to the village, when from round the bend in the road just ahead there came a sudden scream followed in rapid succession by the sound of two crashes. Almost before the order had been given the convoy stopped. The road was too narrow for the colonel's car to overtake those in front, but he leaped down and ran forward to investigate, following hard on the heels of the group of men, known in SS fashion as his 'bodyguard', who rode in the truck immediately ahead of his.

The scene which greeted his eyes made even the colonel, who had seen many gruesome sights, shudder. One motor cyclist lay sprawling beside his machine, obviously badly injured. The other's head, still in its steel helmet, lay near him but his motor-cycle, with its headless body still in the saddle, had roared on for several yards after he had been killed, before diving, the engine still at full throttle, into the ditch. The cause of the accident was not hard to find: a strong wire, probably cut from a roll used by a farmer for fencing his fields, had been stretched taut across the road between two trees, in a patch of shadow, just high enough above the ground to catch the neck of any unwary person coming fast round the corner. A car or lorry would probably have carried it away or broken it, a cyclist would not have been going fast enough to be seriously hurt, but to a motor-cyclist it was deadly, cutting through his neck like a cheese-slicer.

The moans of the injured man as he was carried away, and the sight of the dead man's helmet with his still bleeding head inside it lying in the road as if mocking the whole German army, strengthened the colonel's resolve. He had been ordered to pacify the countryside and pacify it he would. People who carried out acts of this kind must be taught a lesson. His company commanders, hastily called to an order group, were told to turn out their men and round up every civilian within a radius of two kilometres; men, women, children, old people, invalids, all were to be brought in and assembled in front of the church, the spire of which could be seen through the trees just ahead.

The people of Winter Hill had been expecting the Germans ever since the British Army had withdrawn, and when grim-faced soldiers in field-grey uniforms appeared outside their houses and cottages, battering on the doors with their rifle butts and bawling for them to come out, they were frightened, but not surprised. As, having turned the occupants out, the soldiers rampaged through each empty house, pulling curtains aside, thrusting their bayonets under beds and peering into cupboards, the residents assumed that the Germans were searching for British soldiers left behind during the retreat, or Home Guards waiting for darkness to attack them. But there was not a soldier, or a Home Guard, left within miles and the Germans' behaviour was in a way reassuring. This was the way British people expected the 'Huns' – the almost affectionate term 'Jerry' was heard less often now – to behave and these large, brutal and uncouth men were instantly recognisable for what they were, the Nazis seen in a score of war films. They even, as they yelled at the civilians, sounded uncannily like 'Fünf' in the radio programme *ITMA*. At any moment one expected Tommy Handley to make some devastating witticism that would put them in their place.

When the inhabitants were ordered to assemble in the churchyard, they assumed they were to be given a talk on how to behave by the German commander, who stood scowling by the churchyard gate, as each small group of new arrivals passed inside. He, too, looked remarkably like everyone's stereotype of a Nazi officer, and already the heartless brutality of the Germans was causing some of those assembled there to dread what was to come. Some men, rounded up from the fields, were driven in front of them by a group of Germans with prods from their rifles, like cattle going reluctantly to market, and one soldier casually jabbed a pregnant woman, who could only walk slowly, in the stomach with his rifle butt and laughed as she stumbled. When a blind man, led by his wife, temporarily became separated from her and blundered into the churchyard wall, the Germans clearly found this a fine joke, until an officer standing watching gestured impatiently to them to steer the blind man towards the gate. Once inside, lined up on the space between the graves and in front of the porch, the older women were mostly silent while the younger ones, many of them in aprons, having been interrupted while preparing the family tea, were fully occupied trying to calm the small children clinging terrified to their skirts, or to soothe the babies they were carrying. Two women were pushing prams, but most had cradled their infants in their arms. One baby was still fast asleep but most, infected by the prevailing atmosphere, were wailing rather than crying, a thin, infinitely dispiriting sound that more than anything else made the people realise that they were wholly at the mercy of the Germans now lined up on the roadway facing them. One woman, holding a small boy by the hand, was bleeding from a cut below the eye, and weeping, while the child, a pathetic figure in pyjamas, dressing gown and sandals, obviously hastily pulled on, still looked half-asleep. She had, she told everyone who would listen, told the Germans her son was ill in bed and could not be moved, but they had paid no attention, and one had threatened to stick a bayonet in him where he lay if she did not get him up and bring him to the churchyard.

There were very few men. Many were already in the Forces or in the Home Guard, but most of those who lived in the village were at work in Heathfield or Horam, for Winter Hill itself offered few opportunities for employment. The Germans had discovered half a dozen farm labourers, one of them still in his rubber boots and white overalls, who had been cycling to do the evening milking, which had to go on war or no war, a farmer, the proprietor of the village shop, the licensee of the nearby public house, a few old men, one deaf, who had arrived last of all and was asking loudly what was happening, and, most surprised of all, a Ministry of Food official, in dark suit and black shoes, who, rather late in the day, had been touring the district to check on emergency food supplies. Vaguely excited by the whole affair, and reflecting what a story he would have to tell the chaps when he finally got back to school, was a boy of fifteen, son of a local solicitor, having an unexpectedly prolonged holiday from his public school, which had delayed the start of its term because of the invasion threat.

The colonel, once it was clear that no more civilians were to be brought in, wasted little time. He gestured to one of his officers, who indicated to the men that they should move to one side of the churchyard; the fifteen-year-old boy, after a moment's hesitation, followed them. The women and children, alarmed at being separated from their menfolk, found themselves ordered to enter the church, a small, massive-walled building, but with ample room for the sixty people who filed inside it. There was a little delay at the door while one of the mothers wheeling a pram stopped to unstrap her baby and lift him in her arms, but the German NCO standing nearby barked an order and one of the soldiers motioned her aside and pushed the pram in through the narrow door and past the font into the nave. She turned to thank him, but he merely stared at her without speaking and gestured to the other mother with a pram also to push it inside.

The sight of a German, however grim-faced, pushing a pram had raised the women's spirits a little. 'They're going to keep us here out of the way during the fighting,' one suggested.

'That'll be it,' agreed another. 'I hope they get it over quick. My Jim's over at Horam and he'll be wanting his supper when he gets back, Germans or no Germans.'

'More likely going to loot our houses,' suggested a third. 'Won't do them much good. I hid all my valuables under the . . . no, I'm not going to say where . . . last Tuesday. I reckoned it wouldn't be long before they got here.'

'That's defeatist talk,' said another woman sharply. 'I've a good mind to report you.'

'Who to?' asked the other speaker, but before anyone could answer there came from outside the sound of a shouted order, followed by another order, and then a fusillade of shots, accompanied by a succession of sharp thuds as the bullets hit the outside wall of the church.

'Mum, Mum! The Army's come back,' shouted one boy and then, suddenly, the truth dawned.

'My God, they've shot all the men!' screamed one woman. 'My old man was out there. They've killed him, the bloody murderers!'

There was an outburst of talk and many of the women burst openly into tears; a few screamed, but everyone fell silent when the church door was thrown open and two German soldiers staggered in with a heavy crate, which they lowered into the middle of the aisle. One gestured to the women to move away towards the altar, while the other bent over the crate and began to run out from it a length of what looked like cord. Just before he reached the door he stopped and lit the fuse, then both men ran out and slammed the door behind them.

'They're going to blow us all up!' shouted someone and rushed to stamp out the fuse, but before she could reach it the crate exploded in a burst of flame which set the pews and fittings of the church on fire, and fatally burned anyone who came near it. Within minutes the building was filled with a thick, choking smoke that left everyone inside groping blindly – for their children, for a door, a window, for any way out – until with merciful rapidity most of them collapsed. When the screams and shouts from inside had ceased, the Germans threw open the door, brought in bales of straw dragged from a nearby barn, and strewed it all through the building and on the heaps of bodies, and set fire to it. Then, locking the door again, they climbed back into their trucks and continued their journey through the Sussex countryside, conscious of a job well done for Führer and Fatherland.

Much later, one man whose work had taken him several miles from Winter Hill that day arrived back, to be puzzled by his empty house and then, as he explored, by the deserted cottages nearby. Finally, the smoke still rising from the ruins and the steadily growing smell of burned human flesh had led him to the church, where, climbing over the bodies of his male neighbours, lying in a row outside, he had unlocked the church door and, after waiting for the smoke to clear, had gone inside. At first no one seemed to be alive, but then he heard a faint cry and discovered a baby which had evidently crawled under a pew and by some strange freak of ventilation had received enough air to save its life. A few minutes later, seated outside on a gravestone nursing the baby and trying to summon up resolution to go back inside, the same man had discovered another survivor, for a young girl, dress torn, face blackened and fingers bleeding from earlier efforts to escape, rose suddenly to her feet from a small mound of bodies lying below one window. When she had ceased shaking from shock, she managed to tell him what had happened. The Germans, she explained, had machine-gunned the few people who had not been burned to death or asphyxiated in the first few minutes and who had succeeded in reaching a window and climbing out, but when her chance came, they had been engrossed in shooting at a small baby which the woman beside her was trying to drop to safety and which provided them with an unusually interesting target. Both the mother and her child had been killed and the girl had fallen to the ground beside them, hardly appreciating herself that she had not been hit. When realisation had come, she had stayed where she was, hoping the Germans would take her for dead, and after a cursory glance at the other two bodies lying beside hers, and the bloodstains from their injuries on her dress, they had moved on without firing a final burst as they had done at anyone still moving in the church.

When, after a long delay, news of the Winter Hill massacre reached the government in London, via an 'auxiliary unit' of the underground resistance, the Cabinet debated long and earnestly whether to release the news, balancing the added impetus it would give the efforts of every man still fighting against the damage it might do to civilian morale. Eventually the decision was taken out of the government's hands, for news of the affair reached an American correspondent who, as a neutral, was able to get into the battle zone and confirm the rumours for himself. His despatch, which won him a Pulitzer Prize, was syndicated all over the United States and carried in full by every radio station. The German ambassador, driving to the State Department to receive a strongly-worded protest, was pelted with bricks when his car stopped by a building site, and was lucky to escape with his life. An SS lieutenant-colonel was too powerful a man to be relieved of his command but he was left in no doubt of his divisional commander's displeasure. Such conduct, it was hinted, might go unnoticed in Poland, but some show of decency was expected in England, at least until the British were finally beaten.

The day the news of the atrocity was released, Winston Churchill made one of his most vigorous broadcasts. The true nature of the beast was now disclosed in all its full and loathsome detail, he told his listeners. Mourning their murdered fellow-countrymen and punishing those who had committed this dastardly crime, which would have caused the name of Germany to stink in the nostrils of every decent human being throughout the world if – a Churchillian pause – it had not already done so, must come later. The need now was simply to kill any German whenever the chance occurred, even if it was the last service to one's country one lived to perform. The message of the hour was 'Take one with you!' Soon printed posters bearing this slogan in bright red letters appeared on hoardings all over unoccupied Britain. In the occupied zone there were no posters, but the same words were still to be seen, chalked after dark on pavements and walls, scribbled on menus in the few restaurants that were still open, traced in the mist on steamed-up windows and in the grime on unwashed cars, sometimes shortened to 'TıW', or simply to the letter 'T'.

If the SS officer responsible supposed that he had thereby crushed all resistance in his area, he was soon proved wrong. Two hours after Churchill's broadcast another of the battalion's motor-cyclists ran into the same trap which had precipitated the massacre of Winter Hill, but this time the wire had sagged and it merely flung him from his machine with a broken leg. As he lay there helpless, the unknown civilian who had sprung the trap removed the injured man's machine-pistol and ammunition and carefully poured over him the contents of a Molotov cocktail. When the next vehicle came down the road it found the rider, now burned to death, and his machine still blazing merrily by the roadside. Chalked on the road by the funeral pyre the Germans found the letters 'R.W.H.', which they took at first to be the initials of the unknown desperado or of some new guerrilla leader. An unfortunate field security sergeant spent a busy night studying a voters' list commandeered from the nearest post office and compiling a list of suspects from 'Hay' to 'Hyland'. It was not till morning, which revealed a rash of 'R.W.H.' signs chalked on walls and trees and even on the sides of German vehicles, that the Germans learned that the letters stood for 'Remember Winter Hill'.

The German advance on 30 September, of which the Winter Hill atrocity had been only one small incident, convinced the Commander-in-Chief, Home Forces, that he could delay his counter-attack no longer. Although the Germans' air superiority made it almost impossible to move his forces by day, delay would make the situation worse, not better, and on 1 October the decision was taken to move against the west of the occupied zone, now far too large to be dismissed as a bridgehead, since it was on this flank, General Brooke believed, that the break-out was most likely to occur. The immediate aim of the attack was to disrupt the German build-up, its secondary objective to recapture Newhaven, the major port serving the German Seventh Army, thus denying it to the enemy and splitting the German forces in two.

The offensive was carefully planned. Its chief striking force was to be 1st Armoured Division, which had been brought up to strength with tanks and supporting weapons, and which it was intended, after moving up to the area between Maresfield and Uckfield as its jumping-off point, should attack the German left flank and drive almost due south in the direction of Lewes. It would be supported on its left by the 42nd Division, whose start-line would be the A272 from Framfield to Blackboys, and still further to the left, between Blackboys and Heathfield and thus directly opposite the SS battalion whose commander was now the most hated man in Britain, would be the 1st Canadian Division. The infantry, it was intended, should advance roughly parallel to the armour, along the line of the railway from Heathfield to Horam and Polegate, and thence to Lewes, the key to the defence of Newhaven.

At 0500 on Wednesday 2 October, a fine, dry day, the advance began and almost at once the British were in contact with enemy outposts. By 0700 the first objectives had been reached and during the late afternoon, as the hitherto blue skies began to cloud over, the 1st Armoured Division reached the outskirts of Lewes. Soon after sunset, 1934 British Double Summer Time, the British commanders reckoned up their gains and losses. The infantry had lost 350 dead and 1250 wounded but they had advanced nearly three miles during the day, and were now dug in on a front five miles wide from Halland, via East Hoathly, to Horam. The armour, pulled back to the area around Spithurst and Isfield for the night, to avoid getting too far ahead of its supporting infantry, had advanced a similar distance for the loss of sixty tanks. The men's spirits were high, but they did not yet know of the naval disasters that had occurred that day. Two cruisers and a strong force of destroyers, bearing down from the North Sea towards the eastern invasion beaches, had almost all been sunk by mines or air attack, while in the west a powerful force led by the battle-ships *Nelson* and *Rodney* and the battle-cruiser *Hood* had, in a tremendous battle off Portland, sunk every German destroyer in sight, only itself to suffer heavy losses from air attack, including the sinking of the *Hood*.

At dawn on 3 October the British offensive was resumed and by midday armoured units were on the outskirts of Newhaven, while British infantry, not far behind, commanded the crossroads by Lewes Prison. But two hours later the German counter-attack began and, with the Luftwaffe sweeping down whenever a unit moved, the British were virtually im-mobilised and had to fight where they stood. At dusk the only alternative to being cut off was for the forward units to retreat, and retreat they did. By midnight, with nothing but heavy casualties to show for the offensive and the loss of 150 precious tanks, the three divisions were back on their start-lines and digging in. Next day Field Marshal Karl von Rundstedt crossed the Channel and set up his advanced headquarters in a hotel at St Leonards-on-Sea; the result of the invasion, his arrival suggested, was no longer in doubt.

The following day General Brooke recognised that to prepare another counter-attack he must make another withdrawal, this time to behind the strongest natural obstacle in the country. On 5 October VII Corps, facing the Germans all along the 'Sussex' line from Uckfield to Etchingham, was ordered to retreat behind the Thames, where other units had for several days past been assembling. Withdrawal, as the German commanders joked, was one operation at which the British generals were expert and as patrols, probing forward, again found only undefended territory in front of them, Army Group A was for the second time ordered to make a general advance. The new line would be very little short of the 'Supreme Command objective', laid down long ago by the *Sea Lion* planners, and ran from Portsmouth to Petersfield and thence to Dunsfold, Sevenoaks, Maidstone and Chatham, and the new advance gave the Germans possession of the former RAF airfields at West Malling and Tangmere, long since knocked out by bombing and, the greatest prize of all, Portsmouth, though this was only secured after a violent battle. As the smoke from burning stores of fuel drifted across the ruined docks and berths littered with wrecked or sinking ships – for here at least the work of demolition had been thoroughly done – the British commanders recognised reluctantly that they no longer had a mere 'bridgehead' or 'lodgement' to contend with. The whole of the south-east corner of England was now in enemy hands and, unless the Germans were soon driven out, the entire country must rapidly be at their mercy.

Chapter 7: Defeat

After gaining the first operational objective, the further task of the Army will be as follows: to defeat the enemy forces still holding out in Southern England.

Instructions of the Commander-in-Chief, Army,
30 August 1940

With most of Kent and Sussex and a substantial part of Hampshire safely in his hands, and winter already approaching, Field Marshal von Rundstedt decided that there was nothing to be said for delay. As the armoured and motorised divisions of his follow-up forces flowed in smoothly through the captured ports, from Dover to Portsmouth, already partly in operation again despite the recent demolitions, they were rapidly moved forward. Tunbridge Wells was reinforced with the 8th Motorised Division, and an even more formidable force, the 7th and 10th Panzer Divisions, was established around Petersfield, while, with little fear left of interference by the RAF, squadron after squadron of the Luftwaffe was flown into Britain to support the coming assault or transferred to bases just across the Channel. By mid-October, three weeks after S Day, more than 3000 aircraft were assembled in England or Northern France, half being earmarked for direct support of the Army, a role in which the German Air Force already excelled, and the rest being sent further afield to attack railways, bridges, fuel dumps and ordnance factories, and to disrupt the whole supply and communications network on which the defence depended.

The original *Sea Lion* instructions had been vague about the Army's long-term objectives. After the initial lodgement, Army Group A had been told, its task was 'to defeat the enemy forces still holding out in Southern England, to occupy London, to mop up the enemy in Southern England and to win the general line Maldon–Severn Estuary'. Further ahead than that the High Command's planners had not looked, promising merely that 'orders concerning further tasks will be issued at the proper time', though unhindered by false modesty they had conceded that 'if favourable circumstances allow the operation to be speeded up, our very mobile and flexible Command will be able to adapt itself to this favourable situation as quickly as in former operations'. The 'favourable situation' had now occurred and shortly before midnight on Monday 14 October, an ominous date for the British for it was the anniversary of the Battle of Hastings, the first German divisions began to close up towards the Thames.

The Germans now faced that 'opposed river-crossing' which they had anticipated ever since June but, unlike the Channel assault, it presented no particular terrors for them, and cautiously but confidently, the troops advanced to occupy the right bank of the river from Wallingford to Windsor. They had half-expected that the British, a sentimental race as everyone knew, might try to deny them the use of the latter town due to its long association with their royal family, but advanced patrols reported that the streets were empty of troops although Windsor bridge had been blown up.

It had already been decided that the main crossing would be made elsewhere and shortly after midnight the inhabitants of Streatley, Pangbourne and Wallingford, already roused by the noise of German transport rattling through their streets, finally gave up the attempt to sleep as the German barrage opened up with a roar against the British positions on the far bank. Two hours later, with the glare of burning houses reflected in the surface of the river, and the darkness lit every few seconds by the flash of exploding shells or the thin lines of tracer bullets, curving with apparent slowness towards their targets, the assault troops began to paddle across, some in collapsible rubber boats brought from Germany, the rest in rowing boats, motor launches and even punts hastily collected from boathouses up and down the river or unearthed from hiding places beneath the bank. Some boats, while being towed to the assembly points, had sunk, from holes concealed beneath the planking, and others, where a slow leak had been more carefully concealed, began to fill with water as they crossed the river. But the Thames was, by Continental standards, not a major obstacle; a few of the leading infantry only just managed to scramble ashore, soaked and cold in the chilly air of an early October night, and a very few, whose craft had drifted into a patch of darkness and whose shouts went unheard above the noise of the barrage, were drowned, their bodies drifting slowly downstream to start false rumours wherever they came ashore that the Germans had suffered a resounding defeat.

The German plan was for the three infantry divisions to secure a bridgehead for the two Panzer divisions to cross the river, and engineers of the 7th Panzer Division had gone ashore with the leading elements of the infantry at Pangbourne to build three temporary bridges, two of them strong enough for tanks. Within hours one was ready, but the exit from the rest was, the engineers reported, blocked by rubble which would have to be cleared in daylight. But the commander of the 7th Panzer Division, Major-General Erwin Rommel, was not the man to accept delay if he could help it. Two tank battalions were ordered across by the one available bridge and told to go forward without waiting for the rest of the division.

Behind the Thames, in addition to the regular forces now forming the British strategic reserve, there had assembled the remnants of a vast variety of units overtaken by the German advance. The headquarters staff of Aldershot barracks, many of them more accustomed to handling brooms than rifles, sergeant-majors without barrack squares, mechanics without workshops, sailors without ships and airmen without aircraft – everyone who had become separated from his unit, or been caught up in the great retreat as the Germans swept across Southern England, had somehow found his way towards the Thames and reported to the posts set up on the Berkshire bank to deal with just such stragglers. The men had been sent to hastily-formed training units; some, hoping to justify the old remark about the Battle of Waterloo, had even had a crash course in the use of cover and basic weapon training on the playing fields of Eton. There was no lack of instructors, for half the barracks in Southern England were now in German hands, though some, accustomed to the leisurely procedures of more normal times, proved unable to adjust to a world where a man who had barely seen a rifle before had to be turned into a soldier in a day. But this, of course, was just the problem the old LDV had faced back in May and June and, to their ill-concealed delight, some Home Guards now found themselves teaching the basic military skills to members of the regular forces who up to now had fought their war with a screwdriver or typewriter or a carving knife, for among what General Brooke had named his 'Irregulars' were many RAF ground crew, several units of the Catering Corps, dislodged from their barracks on Salisbury Plain, and the 12th Training Battalion (Clerks), from Aldershot, speedily nicknamed by their little more military comrades 'the Fighting Twelfth'.

While the officers and NCOs of units which had survived Dunkirk and even the great withdrawal from the coast and the Uckfield to Etchingham line struggled to weld this ill-assorted army of civilians in uniform into some sort of fighting force, one small group among them needed little such instruction, having already learned the grammar of their trade and making up in fighting spirit what they lacked in military experience. These were the Sandhurst cadets, several hundred strong, who, when their seniors had been sent to fill the gaps in the regiments which had borne the brunt of the fighting in Kent and Sussex, had reluctantly surrendered to the Germans without a struggle (though not without planting a number of lethal booby-traps) the hitherto sacred buildings of the Royal Military Academy and made their way in good order towards the west. Already they knew well enough that in a straight-encounter battle the Germans, with their overwhelming air power, were likely to have the best of it, but ambushes were another matter, and while the Germans had been forming up for their assault the cadets, after an intelligent appraisal of the most likely area for a crossing, had been busy laying an extensive minefield just where the tanks of Rommel's leading battalions were now beginning to deploy to left and right to take the defenders of the river line in the rear. The result was the most heroic action of the whole campaign. The cadets were armed only with small arms and grenades, but as one tank after another ground suddenly to a halt, its tracks blown off, or its way ahead barred by a wrecked neighbour, they leapt upon it, pounding on the roof, thrusting grenades through any opening they could find and greeting with furious volleys any Germans who, as the stranded tanks began to 'brew up', climbed out and ran for cover. In an hour the two tank battalions had ceased to be an effective fighting force, and by the time the German infantry arrived to rescue the survivors 200 cadets lay dead or seriously wounded and the rest were stumbling away, battered, bleeding but, most of all, exultant, supporting their walking wounded. Too tired to get far, they sought refuge in a barn and there that night were captured, but not before the story of their exploit had thrilled a public desperate for good news.

But this mishap was insufficient to halt the German advance. On the left of the front the engineers of 10th Panzer Division, assisted by pioneers and engineers, had already rebuilt the bridge linking Goring to Streatley and, to speed up the build-up on the far bank, had built another temporary bridge close by and a second at Wallingford. By the early hours of the morning the whole of 10th Panzer Division was across the river, being followed by elements of 7th and 8th Panzer Divisions, so that by nightfall on 15 October they and their supporting infantry controlled the whole area of Oxfordshire enclosed in the bend of the Thames, nearly fifteen miles across, from Wallingford to Henley, with other units established along both sides of the river as far as Windsor. So far the main forces had barely come into contact, for the British troops had made full use of the breathing space of the last few days and everywhere the infantry were well dug in but, with only meagre artillery support, and with their positions dive-bombed the instant the defenders revealed them, the enemy armour was advancing almost at will.

Now, the British realised, was the moment for a supreme effort, and from the headquarters of Home Forces went out an appeal to the RAF for every aircraft that could stagger into the air to be loaded with whatever bombs it could carry and sent against the German river crossings. This was the RAF's equivalent of the 'irregulars' now fighting on the ground and the result was an epic as glorious as any in British history. From still operational bases in Wales and Scotland, halting to refuel at unbombed airfields in the Midlands, the last machines in the British reserves flew south; from factory landing strips, with test pilots at the controls, new aircraft just off the production lines, prototypes not yet in production, and unfamiliar types still on the secret list rose up, some of them a little uncertainly, into the autumn sky; from supply and storage units, from which the civilian pilots of Air Transport Auxiliary delivered new and repaired machines to the squadrons and where now men and women eagerly competed to be given an aircraft to make what, they well knew, might be their last flight, brand-new planes which had never been in action and battered old veterans hardly fit to fly soared upwards towards the battle. From all over the British Isles an extraordinary variety of machines made their way towards the middle reaches of the Thames, briefed with the simple instructions that any troops or tanks crossing the river, and any vehicles or concentrations on the right bank, could be attacked at will. Those on the ground looking up as raggedly, and at long intervals, the fleet of aircraft passed overhead, as once Drake's little ships had stood out of Plymouth Sound to harry the Spaniards all the way up the Channel, could hardly believe their eyes at the number or variety of machines that, by a supreme effort, had this day been brought into action.

There were battered Blenheims, already damaged in many a sortie against the invasion beaches and far too slow to escape the Messerschmitts; long, slim Fairey Battles, fatally slow and ill-protected, which had suffered such appalling casualties in France; Wellingtons and Hampdens and Whitleys from Bomber Command in the black paint they wore for night bombing; twin-seater Defiants with their high turrets, long-since withdrawn from daylight operations as no match for the German fighters; single-engined Harvards with their yellow Training Command paint still on their wings, flown by instructors or their most advanced pupils, and easily identified from afar by the ugly, raucous grinding noise of their engines; flimsy Tiger Moths piloted by cheerful young men who had only just done their first solo; ancient Gloster Gladiator biplanes dragged from the hangar where they were awaiting breaking up or despatch to an RAF museum – all passed overhead in a gallant, ungainly procession, like a history of the RAF through the ages at an air display. Only after the most heated argument were a group of enthusiasts who wanted to load up with bombs the vast but derelict airship R100, lying idle in her hangars at Cardington since the disaster to her sister ship the R101, persuaded that to make her airworthy would take too long and that, if they did get her into the air, the brisk wind would make her almost unmanœuvrable for an inexperienced crew.

But they were almost the only would-be aviators to be frustrated that day. Every plane that could get off the ground, every man and woman with a pilot's licence – and a substantial number who had not – was got into the air for the RAF's last stand. All those concerned knew well enough that only the few operational aircraft were likely to do much damage to the enemy, but the urge to strike some sort of blow against the apparently invincible Germans was irresistible and dedicated fitters and armourers had managed to give almost all a weapon of some kind. Many had machine-guns, hastily fixed to a temporary mounting, to be fired from an open cockpit, some had a 50-lb bomb slung behind the cockpit or beneath the wings and controlled by improvised release gear; a very few had no more than a determined pilot armed with a tommy-gun or even a bag of grenades like a pioneer of air warfare in 1914, useless against enemy aircraft but sufficient perhaps to kill a few Germans on the ground. All those at the controls that October day knew only too well that their chances of coming back were slight. ('Just as well,' one unpromising pupil at an elementary flying training unit had told his instructor, as they made for their separate aircraft, 'I never was much good at landings.') But Churchill's 'Take one with you!' appeal had not been made in vain. None of those now waiting anxiously for the first signs of enemy fighters as the familiar soft and green landscape of Southern England, which had rarely looked more worth protecting than on this clear autumn day, slid beneath them, was given to heroic gestures. If asked they might, a little shamefacedly, have confessed that they would rather die than live in a country ruled by a foreign enemy, but they were not asked. Instead they talked of 'having a go' and joked, rather tensely, of giving Hitler and Göring a lesson they wouldn't forget in a hurry.

The resulting attacks, with ancient biplanes roaring out of the sky just above their heads, firing a single machine-gun, or dropping a solitary bomb while heavy bombers bombarded the temporary bridges from several thousand feet, briefly threw the Germans into confusion. The very lack of planning, due to the vastly differing speeds of the attacking aircraft and the fact that many had not been ordered to fly at all, was more disruptive than a better coordinated and more predictable attack. No sooner had one Battle or Whitley or Swordfish flown away, firing as it went, or been shot down by ground fire, than some other unfamiliar aircraft would appear in the distance, making an equally heroic attack. By the time the slower machines arrived the Luftwaffe, summoned by half a dozen indignant commanders who had been told that no danger of attack from the air existed, was waiting for them and the massacre began. One Tiger Moth, spiralling down after some impressive aerobatics by a flying instructor in which it had out-manœuvred a Messerschmitt 110, only to be easily overtaken and shot down as it flew away, crashed on to the temporary wooden bridge at Marlow and briefly set it on fire. But the flames were rapidly put out, and though elsewhere some gutted lorries, a few dead soldiers and a cluster of craters round the approaches to the bridges showed that the attack had not been wholly in vain, by late afternoon the enemy reinforcements were once again pouring across them.

While the RAF had been making its final gallant stand in the skies above them, the last major land battle of the invasion, later known to historians as the Battle of the Chilterns, was being fought out on the ground. With the Germans' crushing superiority in armour aided by the desperate British shortage of both tanks and anti-tank guns, the result was never really in doubt, but the German infantry found the opposition facing them far tougher than their comrades of the armoured divisions. As darkness began to fall, they were exhausted. Soft-hearted British civilians in the Buckinghamshire villages, watching from behind their curtains as the enemy columns passed, felt almost sorry for the young Germans, many of them no more than twenty, who marched sullenly forward like automatons, too far gone to sing or even talk, or, when ordered to halt, fell to the ground where they stood.

As one division after another signalled its position to him as the advance halted for the night, von Rundstedt realised that, though their reports were couched in the cautious, formal terms which the German Army enjoined upon its officers, he had achieved a great victory, even though the casualties were heavier than he had expected. The time had come to move forward, nearer to the front, and, while his signallers were conveying the news of his success to von Brauchitsch, the rest of the headquarters staff were busily packing up for the move to the riverside hotel at Maidenhead earmarked for their use. Before the convoy of staff cars and command vehicles could set off, von Rundstedt received a far-from-welcome reply to his signal. The Commander-in-Chief, Army, had decided that he should now take command in England, as von Rundstedt's Army Group A would soon be reinforced by General Busch's Army Group B, brought over from France to occupy the rest of the country, while the troops already there carried out mopping-up operations. For the present his headquarters were to be in Sussex in a beautiful country house at Glyndebourne, recommended (though this von Rundstedt was not told) by a music-lover on his staff with a passion for Mozart.

That evening was also a time of frenzied activity in Whitehall, as the small key sections of the few ministries still left prepared to withdraw to the north, the way westward now being blocked. The Civil Servants left behind, not always with much regret, selected for destruction the files of minutes and reports that might assist the Germans and would now go un-read for ever, before settling down to sleep in the ministries' air-raid shelters and in beds lining basement corridors. Soon after midnight the Commander-in-Chief, Home Forces, who had spent most of the day in the secret war room beneath Whitehall, went in search of the Prime Minister and found him standing, preoccupied and unspeaking, in the Cabinet Room. The next German move, General Sir Alan Brooke warned him, was likely to be to cut off London from the north and he must formally advise the Prime Minister that he could not guarantee to hold the railway line linking London with the Midlands for more than the next twelve hours, although he hoped the line which ran further east, from King's Cross to York and Edinburgh, might remain open a little longer.

Already the Cabinet had agreed on the action to be taken in this eventu-ality. The governments-in-exile from the countries overrun by Germany, who had already fled once from the Germans, must, everyone agreed, cross the Atlantic to refuge in Canada, and with them must go the ambassa-dors already accredited to them and the royal families of Norway and Holland. 'But,' insisted Churchill, 'the British government stays in the British Isles', although he had already ordered a few ministers, much against their will, to leave with the foreign governments, to provide the nucleus, if necessary, of a British government-in-exile. A number, whose departments were already evacuated to Lancashire or Wales or the West Country, had now gone to join them and some, whose departments would cease to be necessary when the Germans arrived, had begged for and been granted permission to attach themselves to the Palace of Westminster Home Guard, or had left to organise resistance in their constituencies. Their last decision, duly recorded in the Cabinet minutes which were even now being carried to safety in Canada, was to reaffirm that there would be no capitulation. The pledge of 'No surrender' given by him in the House of Commons could not be broken under any circumstances, for not merely—the Prime Minister's voice swelled with indignation—would it be dishonourable in the extreme, but it would expose members of the 'Auxiliary Units' still fighting to the risk of being shot as partisans. The time might come when an armistice must be sought, but it would not be by this government. As for himself, it was useless for the general to try to persuade him, as others had done, to go to Canada, or even to some other part of the country. 'The enemy has already laid impious hands upon Chartwell,' explained Churchill, 'the place closest, after Westminster, to my heart, an act of impertinence for which in due course he will be made to pay a heavy price.' Now, beyond question, his place was here, at the heart of the Empire, where he hoped to die like a hussar and an English gentleman.

'What about His Majesty?' asked the Commander-in-Chief. King George had wished, explained the Prime Minister, to put himself at the head of an underground resistance movement, like King Alfred leading the Saxons against the invading Danes. But reluctantly they had decided the risks were too great. So long as the King was known to be free, on friendly soil, the illegality of any puppet government set up in the British Isles would be apparent, while the events which might follow the King's capture were almost too appalling to contemplate. The barbarian invaders, direct descendants of the Huns of old, might try to bargain his life for concessions by the British government-in-exile or exhibit him in chains in the enemy capital. Already arrangements had been made for the royal household, with the other groups he had mentioned, to leave the country and the moment to put these plans into action had arrived.

Prompt at 11.30 the following morning, Wednesday 16 October, the first of the special trains pulled out of Liverpool Street station, routed, to avoid the advancing Germans, via Cambridge and York and thence to Edinburgh and Glasgow. The King, in admiral's uniform, was clearly deeply moved as he climbed aboard with his wife and daughters, escorted by the station-master resplendent in frock-coat and top-hat. For security reasons the Chiefs of Staff had insisted that no publicity should attend his departure but one concession had been made to the King's desire not to leave his country without some ceremonial, and from the footplate of the engine flew a small royal standard. The Prime Minister, who had come to see his sovereign leave, was in tears as the train slowly steamed out of the station, then, turning to the group of ministers, police and railway staff, who stood watching it disappear in the distance, he pulled himself to attention and took off his hat. Without a sign being given the little group struck up the national anthem, its words echoing oddly beneath the high roof of the now empty platform.

Despite the precautions, the news that the King was travelling north spread ahead of him, after the train had been briefly held up at Cambridge and someone had recognised the slim, dark-haired figure looking sadly from a window. For the rest of his way north, the King's journey resembled a triumphal progress rather than a flight into exile. Everywhere, at small wayside halts and from little rows of houses backing on to the railway line, Union Jacks flew, many of them at half mast, and crowds waved farewell, though there was little cheering. At Edinburgh a civic reception awaited the royal train at the station and, though the King refused an invitation to drive through the streets to bid farewell to his Scottish capital, the Scots were not to be cheated of their moment of emotion. As the train pulled away, a band of Scots pipers, in kilts and full regalia, burst into the sad strains of 'Will ye no' come back again?', the words being taken up by the waiting crowds, until the great volume of sound drowned even the noise of the departing carriages. Then, sadly, the citizens of Edinburgh went home to look to their shelters, or reported at the offices set up on the outskirts of the city, where volunteers for digging defence-works were being enrolled.

That night the party from London embarked at Greenock in two waiting cruisers. Already in the Clyde were two other cruisers, twenty-five destroyers and the aircraft carrier *Furious*, almost the sole survivors of the once mighty Home Fleet, and as darkness fell the whole convoy set sail on the first stage of its voyage, making for Iceland where the destroyers were to refuel. It went unharmed. The Germans' thoughts were all on the closing battle in the south, and they had no ships left to pursue it and no aircraft with the range needed to harass it. A week later the whole force was met by ships of the Royal Canadian Navy, escorting it on the last stage of its journey to the West Indies. That night, while the swastikas were already flying over much of the British Isles, the same small, smoke-stained, slightly torn Royal Standard that had travelled with the royal party from London was hoisted over Government House, Nassau.

With the King gone, a strange silence fell over London. Those commanders and ministers who had not, on Churchill's orders, left with the King had done all they could. From within the massive walls of the Citadel fronting the Mall the Admiralty had issued its orders to the surviving units of the fleet. The five surviving British submarines were proceeding independently to Halifax to serve in a combined Commonwealth Fleet now being formed, and all other British squadrons anywhere in the world, except in the Mediterranean, where the fate of Malta and Gibraltar had not yet been decided, were to join them at the earliest opportunity. Orders had been given for the four large aircraft carriers, five battleships and many smaller craft now under construction in British yards to be destroyed. Some particularly precious items, likely to be invaluable in the long struggle ahead, had also been ordered to Canada, among them the prototype jet engines, on which development had recently begun, a mass of heavily guarded equipment escorted by key scientists and technicians from the radar research establishment in Swanage, and, their contents and purpose known only to a few, mysterious crates of chemicals and instru-

ments from a secluded basement at Imperial College, London, and a research establishment in the Midlands, accompanied by a small group of
physicists and chemical engineers. Already the Foreign Office had warned
British missions overseas that, after a certain signal had been sent to them
from London, the codebooks would be destroyed and further orders pur-
porting to come from the Foreign Secretary should be disregarded.
British heads of mission must use their discretion as to how to behave in
what the Foreign Office, with typical understatement, called 'the exceptionally difficult situation now developing', but, as a last resort, could put
their staff and papers under the protection of the nearest United States
embassy or legation. Nearer home the Regional Commissioners had been
warned that once communications with London had been cut they must
take over the administration of their areas, as planned before the war,
avoiding useless sacrifices but not hesitating to use their life-and-death
powers when necessary.

With the British apparently decisively beaten in the Battle of the
Chilterns and his superior, von Brauchitsch, already in England and
showing increasing signs, like every Commander-in-Chief, of wishing
himself to take over the conduct of operations, von Rundstedt saw no
reason for delay. On 16 October he allowed his forces, who had suffered
heavily in the previous day's fighting, to rest and regroup, a lull taken
advantage of by many patriotic British citizens to carry out the instructions
given in *If the Invader Comes*, to attempt to deny the Germans anything
useful to them. Everywhere in the south of England, and even farther
afield, factory workers were smashing their machines or setting fire to
their factories, while more than one fire brigade found itself suddenly
called to a serious blaze at a garage, where the desire to prevent the
Germans acquiring any petrol had led to underground storage tanks
being set on fire. There were a few incidents in newly occupied areas,
where panicky sentries opened fire at cyclists who failed to stop or
even at passers-by who stared at them too aggressively, but in most places
the streets were quiet and the population stayed indoors, as if occupiers
and occupied had tacitly agreed to ignore each other's existence. Few
civilians were any longer in much doubt, however, about what the end
would be and when the BBC announced that its services would cease to be
broadcast on the normal wavelengths, and that henceforward the population would be informed of what was happening through a network of
small, local stations, many with a radius of only a few miles, this was taken
as proof that not merely Broadcasting House, but, far more important,
the great transmitters at Droitwich and Daventry and elsewhere would
soon be in enemy hands. It certainly, a few cynical citizens eager to find

something to smile at even in this dark moment agreed, made the recent BBC series, *Napoleon couldn't do it*, look rather silly.

On 17 October von Rundstedt resumed his advance, sending his forces on a great left hook round London, and severing its connections, as General Brooke had foreseen, with the north, for every road and railway from Windsor, twenty-three miles to the west, to Chelmsford in central Essex, thirty-two miles to the north-east, was now in German hands. This was as far ahead as the *Sea Lion* planners had looked and Phase II of the operation, devised by von Rundstedt's staff since their arrival in England, now began. Its aim was to dominate the Midlands up to and including Liverpool and Manchester by a show of strength, and with six divisions available, four from those landed in the early stages of the operation and two from the follow-up troops landed since then, there was no shortage of men for the purpose. Two main thrust lines were drawn on the headquarters map, one running towards Liverpool, via Oxford and Birmingham, the other towards Sheffield, via Northampton and Nottingham, the two most formidable formations, the 8th and 4th Panzer Divisions, being earmarked for Liverpool and Manchester, while the infantry divisions were also to occupy Derby, Rugby and Coventry. Five days later, on 23 October, Phase III of the operation to occupy the British Isles began. To dominate the northernmost counties of England and to seize Scotland where British forces were few but where nature, at least in the Highlands, favoured the defence, von Rundstedt assigned no fewer than two armoured divisions, two motorised divisions and two infantry divisions, plus his solitary parachute division, its reputation high after its brilliant success in capturing Folkestone and securing the right flank of the original invasion. The parachutists, he decided, should drop in the lowlands of Glasgow and Edinburgh, for both of which the Scots could be expected to fight hard, while the ground forces would continue along their existing axes, one force pressing on from Manchester to Blackburn, Carlisle and thence to Glasgow, where it would relieve the parachute troops, the other advancing from Sheffield to Leeds, Darlington, Newcastle and Edinburgh. With the cities behind them secure, 7th Parachute Division would be stationed along the line from the Clyde to the Forth, ready to move if necessary into Stirling, Perth, Inverness and the Highlands, but the Germans had no intention of tying down a large force in these thinly populated areas if they could avoid it.

Simultaneously with the drive to the north would come the main offensive to the south, for which two armoured divisions and three infantry divisions were available. Here, too, the forces available would be divided into two, one group taking the southerly route from Salisbury to

Exeter and thence to Plymouth and Falmouth, the other moving further north, towards Bath, Bristol and Gloucester. The two Panzer divisions were destined here, also, to occupy the major ports and largest cities, Plymouth and Bristol, for which the remaining British forces might be expected to fight hardest, while other towns tentatively selected for garrisoning included Stroud, Totnes and Truro. For the occupation of Wales and Northern Ireland von Rundstedt had at this stage made no plans. They must wait, he had decided, till the rest of the British Isles was secure, producing, he hoped, a wholesale capitulation which would give him those troublesome areas, the one mountainous and the other only accessible by sea, without a fight.

But here von Rundstedt had, in the German proverb, reckoned without his host. There was, either then or later, to be no general capitulation. On Friday 18 October, a gloomy day of lowering skies and poor visibility, for which the British would have been grateful a week earlier, the advances towards the north which formed Phase II of von Rundstedt's plans began, meeting as little opposition as he had expected, for most of the fighting formations had already been drawn south. All day the tanks and lorries and company after company of infantry moved closer to London, and one after another the headquarters from which until recently the RAF had fought its battle fell into their hands. Bomber Command at High Wycombe, Coastal Command at Northwood and—the finest prize of all —Fighter Command at Bentley Priory near Stanmore, echoed to the footsteps of German soldiers. As the Germans had foreseen, nothing of value had been left. Telephone cables were ripped out, plotting boards and screens stood blank and empty, and only a blackboard on one wall, on which were chalked details of the last mission of some squadron now destroyed, recalled the recent conflict. The buildings were deserted except at Bentley Priory where the Germans found one pilot officer, with his arm in a sling, wandering rather aimlessly about. He had, he admitted, somehow been overlooked when the last lorries left. When formally called on by a somewhat pompous Luftwaffe colonel to surrender the headquarters, he laughed aloud. There were, he explained, no headquarters left and, even had there been, a mere pilot officer had no right to surrender as much as a drawing pin.

The government had long planned to conduct the defence of the country, if Central London were threatened, from an emergency underground headquarters at Dollis Hill in north-west London, but the German decision to advance from that direction instead of, as anticipated, from the south across Westminster Bridge (admirably commanded by a machine-gun sited in Mr Speaker's dining-room and manned by an enthusiastic group of Home Guard MPs) caused this plan to be abandoned. The Dollis Hill headquarters was overrun long before the Germans drove into London down the Edgware Road and Haverstock Hill, but the unit which captured it proved only a little more fortunate than their comrades at Fighter and Bomber Command, finding it manned by a few telephonists and clerks and a distinctly disgruntled junior officer left in charge in case it should be needed after all. When asked what had happened to the Prime Minister and the Commander-in-Chief, he replied, with perfect truth, that so far as he knew they were, like himself, in their usual places.

October 19 was another misty morning, but the skies over London were clear enough for the Luftwaffe to launch one of those sudden raids against undefended targets which Hitler was fond of calling 'terror attacks', the target, according to German radio, being 'the government quarter' around Charing Cross. Several ministries were hit, and some Civil Servants, putting the final touches to the destruction of government records, killed. When the bombers had gone and the dust from the wrecked buildings had settled, the smoke still rose from a great pile of burning files in the middle of Horse Guards Parade and another, smaller one, in the garden of No 10 Downing Street. At first there was a strange quiet, recalling to more than one listener the two minutes' silence which descended upon Whitehall every Armistice Day, and one watcher on the roof of the Admiralty claimed he could hear the cries of the seagulls on the river a hundred yards away and even the flapping of the wings of the pigeons in Trafalgar Square, which had risen in a great white cloud when the bombs fell nearby but had already returned to their usual haunts.

Towards midday, when the sound of gunfire was heard in the distance, followed by the rattle of small arms and the sudden loud 'plop' of distant mortar bombs and grenades, the signallers still busily operating the tele-printers and morse keys within the massive red walls of the Citadel over-looking the Mall, and in the underground Cabinet Office headquarters stretching from Storey's Gate, near Parliament Square, almost to Downing Street, sent their final messages and began to destroy their equipment. While one officer, also following previous instructions, began to gather up the maps in the war room for burning, the Prime Minister led the small team of men manning it—the women had, on his insistence, already been sent to rejoin their units—up into the grey October daylight. He was dressed in his favourite dark blue siren suit, with a massive revolver in a holster strapped to it, and paused briefly to address his staff. They had done their duty nobly, he told them, and they must not think they had failed. This was the end of a chapter, but some of them, though not him-self, would live to see the start of a different story. Those who wished to try to escape and carry on the fight elsewhere must feel free to do so. For himself he proposed to stay and fight it out here and any who cared to remain were welcome to join him. 'We have,' he remarked with a flash of his old humour, 'a distinguished commander. I refer not to myself, though I once did the state some service on the battlefield, but to the Commander-in-Chief, Home Forces, who has, I regret to say, defied my orders to leave the country and is still here beside me, as he has been through all the last anxious days.'

From their right there came the sound of machine-gun fire. The clerks from London District headquarters now manning the sandbag emplacement under Admiralty Arch had opened up on an enemy patrol advancing down the Mall from the direction of Buckingham Palace, and the Germans scattered and took cover in St James's Park, preparing to resume their advance.

'It is, I think, Prime Minister,' said General Brooke, with a slight smile, 'a case of action this day.' He led the little group towards a sandbag barricade at the top of the steps leading from Downing Street into the park, where already several soldiers were absorbed in aiming their rifles and firing at the Germans now crawling forward below. At a gesture from the general, another soldier set up a Bren gun and Prime Minister and Commander-in-Chief settled down behind it, the one to fire it, the other to pass up more magazines as each one was emptied. As he took aim, Winston Churchill seemed to several of those watching him to look suddenly younger. The cares and anxieties of the past months had fallen from him. In spirit he was again the subaltern who had charged the dervishes on horseback at Omdurman, or the battalion commander touring the trenches on the Western Front. When in a brief pause in the battle one of his private secretaries, looking absurdly out of place in his dark jacket and striped trousers, recalled the former occasion to him, the Prime Minister, while keeping his eyes on the field of fire ahead, shook his head. 'Gordon selling his life dearly on the steps of the residency at Khartoum would be a more appropriate parallel,' he suggested.

'Yes, sir,' agreed the Civil Servant. 'They beat us then, too, but we won in the end.'

Later that afternoon, with the Germans already in Trafalgar Square and advancing down Whitehall to take their position in the rear, the enemy unit advancing across St James's Park made their final charge. Several of those in the Downing Street position were already dead, among them the Commander-in-Chief, and at last the Bren ceased its chatter, its last magazine emptied. Churchill reluctantly abandoned the machine-gun, drew his pistol and with great satisfaction, for it was a notoriously inaccurate weapon, shot dead the first German to reach the foot of the steps. As two more rushed forward, covered by a third in the distance, Winston Churchill moved out of the shelter of the sandbags, as if personally to bar the way up Downing Street. A German NCO, running up to find the cause of the unexpected hold-up, recognised him and shouted to the soldiers not to shoot, but he was too late. A burst of bullets from a machine-carbine caught the Prime Minister full in the chest. He died instantly, his back to Downing Street, his face towards the enemy, his pistol still in his hand.

The sound of various minor engagements still being fought on the south bank across the river, as the Germans attacked the units posted there from the rear, could still be heard as the general in command of the leading division arrived at Downing Street in search of someone to surrender the city to him. He found awaiting him, however, only a somewhat sheepish group of senior officers, captured after a defence of the War Office, all denying with every appearance of sincerity that they were in any position to capitulate. With the King gone—if German radio were to be believed—the Chiefs of Staff nowhere to be found, and the Prime Minister and C-in-C dead, no one, they suggested, not without satisfaction, had authority to surrender.

Finally in his room overlooking Horse Guards Parade, where he had withdrawn to await events, a solitary brigadier was discovered who agreed, reluctantly and in the interests of saving life, to make a formal request for a cease-fire on behalf of the troops in London. But, he pointed out, he had no authority over troops in other parts of the country. After prolonged negotiations, a compromise was arrived at. Other commands could be notified of the fall of London, but the signal should be marked 'For information only'. Whether local commanders then chose to capitulate, or to fight on, must be left to them.

The announcement of the surrender of London, followed by the news of the Prime Minister's death and then, belatedly, the revelation that the King had left the country, caused those British still fighting to lose heart. Was there now any point in getting oneself killed? Would it not be better to look after one's family and secretly prepare for the day when the Germans could be driven out? Through mile after mile of the Midlands next day the German lorries rolled forward with barely a road mined or a shot fired, while in their secret hideouts, dug into lonely hillsides or hidden in isolated woodlands, the men of the 'Auxiliary Units', the nucleus of Britain's resistance army, listened unspeaking to the faint voice on their radio. Henceforward, they knew, it was up to them.

The fictional part of the book ends here. The remaining chapters describe not merely what might *have happened, but what* probably would *have happened since they are based on the known plans of the Germans, on the way in which when faced with similar problems, they behaved in other countries, and on an assessment of the likely course of events by those in a position then or now to judge what would have occurred.*

Chapter 8: Wanted: a Quisling

The Ordinances of the Military Commander shall have the force of law and on publication shall be recognised as such . . . by the authorities of the occupied country.

German Occupation Ordinances, *1940*

By September 1940 the Germans had already had extensive experience of imposing their rule upon conquered countries. An unimaginative, law-abiding, somewhat pedantic people, they placed in all the activities of life great emphasis on 'going by the book' and 'the book' concerning the occupation of Great Britain, or England as the Germans usually described it, was already a very substantial volume. In addition to the private documents prepared by the Security Service, and the detailed 'shopping lists' already drawn up by the 'Defence Economic Staff for England', who were to seize the country's resources for German use, the Army, which was responsible for maintaining order, had an impressive paper armoury of its own. On 9 September General Halder had drafted on behalf of von Brauchitsch an elaborate set of *Orders concerning Organisation and Function of Military Government in England* which, with appendices containing internal directives and public proclamations, ran to nearly twenty foolscap pages, but also in draft were scores of regulations or *Ordinances* on a vast variety of subjects which, when collected together in the following year, formed a book ninety pages long.

On first moving in the local commander would usually proclaim martial law, which gave him unlimited powers, including the right to shoot civilians after the most cursory trial. Soldiers in every army, however, dislike entanglement with non-military concerns and the stage of martial law was likely to be succeeded before long by ordinary occupation, with the Army, while retaining the right to deal with any signs of 'armed resurgency', working through the existing civil authorities who were required to enforce the large and daily growing body of occupation regulations. The Germans, in every country they occupied, tried to rule through an existing peacetime government, as in Denmark or the Channel Islands, or one which had come into existence specially to treat with them, as in France, or through a puppet regime, as in Norway, and it was here that the first difficulties in England were likely to arise. The King, the official ruler of Great Britain, would, by the time the first German staff cars drove into the courtyard of Buckingham Palace, have been safely beyond the Germans' reach and if, as also seems likely, the members of the British government were either dead or in hiding, or had escaped overseas, the Germans would have been hard put to it to sign a cease-fire, much less negotiate a full-scale armistice agreement.

They had faced a similar problem once before, in Norway, but here a puppet prime minister in the shape of a name soon to become notorious, Major Vidkun Quisling, had been ready to hand. Quisling, a former Minister of War, had been leader of the extreme Norwegian Nationalist Party and had been active for years in encouraging friendship with Germany. He had helped to plot the invasion of his country, and when the Germans did arrive in April 1940 had, to the consternation and fury of his countrymen, announced on the radio that he had now formed a pro-German government, though many officials refused to serve under him, and the King and properly elected government of Norway later fled to London.[1] Did Great Britain possess a potential Quisling? It seems unlikely. The British Cabinet anxiously considering this question on 22 May 1940, at the height of the Fifth Column scare, were unable to point to any individual who seemed ripe for treason. Two officers of MI5 who had been studying the British Union of Fascists had failed to discover any evidence that it was engaging in subversive activities, although they did conclude that a quarter to a third of its members would 'be willing, if ordered, to go to any lengths'. The Cabinet decided on that occasion that the existing Defence Regulation 18B should be amended to give the Home Secretary power to order the detention without trial of anyone belonging to 'an organisation having hostile associations subject to foreign control', but on 21 November, with the immediate danger past, the Cabinet was informed that though 750 known Fascists were now under arrest, two thirds of these were not dangerous and could be released. This decision was almost certainly correct. Many Fascists, though undoubtedly anti-Jewish, opposed to the war, and sympathetic to the ideals and methods of Nazism, would have claimed that it was only a patriotic desire to see their own country restored to her former place in the world, and to free her from alien influences, that had carried them into the Blackshirt movement. The parallel with Quisling, who was actively pro-German and had plotted his country's downfall, was therefore false.

The leading British Fascist, Sir Oswald Mosley, was still only forty-three in September 1940 and must have seemed to the Germans (wrongly it will be seen) an excellent candidate to rule the country for them. Mosley, born into a wealthy and well-known family, had had a classic upper-class education at a preparatory school, Winchester and Sandhurst, and showed

[1] After the war Quisling was shot for treason.

many of the attributes the Germans most admired, from skill in fencing to physical courage; he served both as an airman and as a cavalry officer during the first world war, and was wounded in action. After the war he became a very successful young Conservative MP and, after 'crossing the floor', a highly promising Labour minister until he had resigned in disgust at the government's failure to tackle either unemployment or the country's long-term economic problems. Mosley, like many British politicians, had met both Hitler and Mussolini and he had made no secret before the war of his desire for peace with Germany, even at the price of returning the former German colonies. After war had broken out he had advised his followers to obey the law, while still hoping for a negotiated peace, taking the line that it was pointless Britain giving guarantees to a country like Poland which she could not protect. Many people between September 1939 and April 1940 still hoped for peace (not perhaps excluding the Prime Minister, Neville Chamberlain), but Mosley always insisted that, while Britain was mad to fight for other countries, she had every right to defend herself. If the country were invaded, he told public meetings at this period, 'we would immediately stop our peace campaign and fight the enemy', and on 9 May 1940 the British Union of Fascists officially declared that 'every one of us would resist the foreign invader with all that is in us'.

But the government was not impressed. On 22 May the Cabinet decided, as already mentioned, on a wholesale round-up of Fascists and German sympathisers, and the Home Secretary advised his colleagues that Sir Oswald Mosley, 'though a most mischievous person, was too clever to put himself in the wrong by giving treasonable orders'. The next day Mosley was arrested, along with many of his followers, and two other public figures, a former extreme right-wing Conservative MP, and an ex-admiral deeply involved in the highly-dubious Anglo-German friendship organisation, *The Link*. No other individuals of any standing were considered dangerous enough to detain. Misguided Fascists, admirers of Hitler, even some anti-Semitic thugs, there undoubtedly were in Britain, but Quislings there were not.

In making plain the illegality of any regime set up by the Germans in Britain, the establishment of a British government-in-exile responsible to the man described in the Coronation service three years before as 'your undoubted King . . . head of the Commonwealth', would have been of crucial importance. In time of peace the sovereign might have been a mere figurehead, a convenient focus for sentiment and loyalty; in the hour of defeat he would have been the symbol of all his subjects' will to resist oppression and achieve ultimate victory. The British government would undoubtedly have done all it could to send the royal family to safety, and the obvious refuge for His Majesty was Canada, nearest, oldest and most powerful of the white dominions. Australia and New Zealand were far weaker and too far away to be able to influence events in Europe, as well as already preoccupied with the threat from Japan, while South Africa, apart from being 6000 miles by sea from England, was less whole-heartedly committed to the allied cause.

Yet, distressing though it would have been to the beleaguered British had they known the fact—and indeed to many Canadians—the Canadian government, both Canadian historians and those closely involved at the time now admit, was not at all anxious that King George should set up his court within its borders. Canada had by 1940 established herself as a world power in her own right, a position which would inevitably have been jeopardised had the government from London, or its shattered rem-nants, set up its headquarters in Ottawa. Although Canada had been a self-governing dominion since 1867, she had in 1914 automatically be-come involved as soon as Great Britain had declared war on Germany, and there had been ample evidence of what a Canadian observer later described as 'the attitude of rush over to help the motherland, where Britain goes we go'. By 1919 the relationship had already begun to change. The Canadian government had insisted on being a party to the Treaty of Versailles in their own right and were not content to allow Lloyd George to sign it on their behalf. In 1939 Canada had freely chosen to join Great Britain in the struggle against Hitler, but she could, had she wished, have stayed aloof. A Canadian division had been sent to England and its mem-bers would, had Britain fallen, have become prisoners of war, but it had served under its own commanders. There were many in Canada who, while still deeply attached to the motherland, recognised that economically Canada's future was linked to the United States and that, politically and militarily, too, the goodwill of her immensely powerful neighbour on the North American mainland must be 'the decisive factor in all her planning.

The Canadians might wish to rescue the homeland from German oppression, but with only one fully-trained division left in Canada, with conscription only just introduced, with only a small Navy of their own, and few aircraft that could fly the Atlantic even one way, and none at all that could fly to Britain and back without refuelling, there was little they could do alone. The Canadian Prime Minister, Mackenzie King, although intensely loyal to the British crown and, like most of his colleagues, full of admiration for the British Prime Minister and the British people's stand against Hitler, had to recognise, too, that there were divisions within his own country. A sizeable minority of Canadians spoke French as their native language and still felt some loyalty to France, and now that France had made peace the temptation to profess willingness to fight for their own country, but not for a distant, occupied island, was clearly more powerful.

Mackenzie King's government had another reason, too, to regard with mixed feelings the possibility that Winston Churchill and his surviving colleagues might arrive in Ottawa to set up a government-in-exile. As Mr M. J. Coldwell, then deputy leader of the Canadian opposition party, the Co-operative and Commonwealth Federation, has recently pointed out, 'If members of the British Cabinet had come we would still have expected our own government to continue as the extreme authority in this country', but if the King, the official head of the Commonwealth, and Winston Churchill, by far its most forceful and most important minister, had both been resident close by, the relationship would obviously have required enormous diplomacy on both sides. By upbringing and instinct Winston Churchill was essentially a Victorian, who thought in strictly imperial terms, rather than self-governing dominions. As Mr Coldwell says, he 'often referred to the overseas countries as though they were possessions of Britain'. The British government, had it come to Canada, would, he points out, have been 'in exactly the same position that the governments of Norway and Denmark and Holland were in Britain, they were governments in exile and they had no part in the government of the country in which they found themselves. . . . We had through the years obtained our freedom from the domination of Downing Street. We had no desire to return to it.' The relationship between the Canadian government and this forceful figure, chafing at his position as a Prime Minister without a country and a Minister of Defence without an army, was bound to be uneasy. With the King there as well, it could rapidly have become intolerable. A large old house not far from the Parliament Buildings in Ottawa, known as Earnscliffe, was, many Canadians believe, earmarked for the British government's use. As for King George VI and his family, if they had arrived in Canada, 'they would', believes Mr Coldwell, 'have been received right royally and have been treated with the utmost respect and consideration, but we were glad they didn't come'.

There was, finally, a more powerful reason, even more difficult to acknowledge in public, why the royal family would probably not have gone to Canada. The liberation of the British Isles rested ultimately on the willingness of the United States to become involved in the war, and with isolationism still rampant, and a presidential election only, in

September 1940, two months ahead, the American government was anxious to prevent any development which might provide fuel for the anti-colonial feeling that was never far below the surface in parts of the United States. Although the Prince of Wales had been rapturously received there before the war, as had George VI when he visited briefly in 1939, the United States had gained independence from British rule only 164 years before, a short period in the history of national prejudice. Divided on much else, the Americans were united on one point, that they did not want a monarchy, and in 1867 when Canada had become self-governing the term originally contemplated of 'kingdom of Canada' had actually been altered to 'dominion' out of deference to American anti-royalist sentiment. At a meeting as early as 25 May, while the British Expeditionary Force was still fighting in France, President Roosevelt and his Secretary of State, Cordell Hull, had already discussed with Mackenzie King what should become of the British sovereign if Britain were defeated. Roosevelt, according to a Canadian historian, 'started to say that the King might come to Canada. He hesitated and Mr Hughes [Cordell Hull] intervened to point out that this would have an adverse political effect in the United States. They agreed that it would be used by political opponents of the administration to accuse Mr Roberts [President Roosevelt] of "establishing monarchy on the North American continent". They further agreed in suggesting that the King might take refuge temporarily at, say, Bermuda without arousing republican sentiment in the United States.'

And this, it seems probable, is what would have happened. There was already in the Bahamas one former British sovereign, King Edward VIII, now Duke of Windsor, compelled to abdicate in 1936 and appointed Commander-in-Chief and Governor of the Islands in August 1940 after his escape from France a few weeks earlier—an undemanding post which kept him safely out of reach of the Germans, who might have tried to use him as a hostage. In the Autumn of 1940, therefore, by a curious quirk of fate, King George VI might have found himself living as his own elder brother's subject, unless he had taken over the Duke's appointment from him, which seems unlikely, for the title of 'King-Emperor and Governor of the Bahama Islands' sounds distinctly incongruous. However this constitutional problem was resolved, his court, though not the headquarters of the British government, would, it seems likely, have been set up at Government House, Nassau, a long, low, white building, built in 1801 in the heyday of the 'colonial' style of architecture. Mount Fitzwilliam, on which it stood, was manifestly not Constitution Hill; George Street, which led up to it, was not the Mall. But the gardens at least were magnificent, filled with vegetation far more lush and exotic than anything which Central London could provide.

And as the King tried to wile away the years of exile, wandering up and down those immaculate paths, between their beautifully kept lawns and flower-beds, or perhaps filling in long hours on the superb course of the Nassau golf club, which would certainly have offered him honorary membership, what would have been happening in London? The Canadians, like many people in Britain, believed that the Germans would have tried to set up a new government under Sir Oswald Mosley, though Mosley himself believes that, before he could have been approached, some undercover security agency might have arranged for him to be killed. In fact, he insists, he planned, had the Germans arrived, to escape from prison to become a resistance fighter. 'I had', he has said, 'had marksman standard in the Army. I would have put on my old Army uniform and fought to a finish and no doubt have been killed, which would have settled the problem.' Had he still been in Brixton it seems inevitable that the Germans would have arrived to offer him at the very least some senior position in a new administration, but his answer, Mosley says, would have been clear. 'While there was a single German soldier on British soil, I would play no part whatever, refuse to do anything at all. . . . When you've withdrawn, if and when you do withdraw from Britain leaving British people, British soil and British Commonwealth intact, then, and not before, by commission of the crown and by election of the people, I will, if I am asked to, form a government.' Rather than accept office on any other terms, he insists he would have committed suicide and ultimately, he believes, the Germans would have recognised him as an uncompromising opponent, so that he might have found himself back in Brixton, with German gaolers instead of British ones.

If the one man whom his countrymen certainly, and the Germans possibly, had in mind for the post had refused to head a British government, who could von Brauchitsch have found to act as the indispensable link between his military government and the existing Civil Service and local authority machine? Mosley himself, who had known personally almost every politician of any consequence in the inter-war period, and had moved in those fashionable circles where pro-German sentiment was most conspicuous, never, he says, came across anyone who looked remotely like a collaborator. Certainly if potential traitors there were they were to be found among the upper classes rather than lower down the social scale. It was in London society that Hitler's ambassador, von Ribbentrop, a man detested by most other people who met him and ultimately hanged for his crimes, was dined and lionised, and it was in comfortable country houses by the Thames and in the Home Counties that pro-German sentiment, masquerading as a desire to do justice to Germany, and the gangrene of appeasement spread fastest. In every country enslaved by the Germans it was the rich who found it easiest to come to terms with occupation, not least because Hitler had destroyed the spectre of Communism and provided a stable order of society where strikes and demonstrations were banned. Somewhere among the noble families which feared a revolution and which had fawned upon von Ribbentrop or been entertained by Göring at his hunting lodge, there may have been someone ready to persuade himself that it was his duty to interpose himself between the invaders and the British people and become head of a 'caretaker' government, which would in time have become permanent, but if there were the Germans had not identified him. Their 'White List' of thirty-nine 'English people friendly towards Germany', compiled in Munich in September 1940, which will be discussed in more detail later, contained not a single well-known name and none of those mentioned had anything approaching the qualifications needed by a Quisling. Sixteen, indeed, were women, which to Hitler, a firm believer in the doctrine that women's interests should be confined to 'children, church and kitchen', would have disqualified them from the start.

Yet in the opinion of Sir Alexander Cadogan, at that time Permanent Secretary of the Foreign Office, who was himself on the German 'Black List', there was an obvious candidate for head of a pro-German government. On 20 May 1940 Cadogan had a chance encounter with Sir Samuel Hoare, a former Foreign Secretary, who had been appointed British Ambassador in Madrid, where it was assumed, rightly, that his reputation as an arch-appeaser would make him highly acceptable to France. Sir Alexander deduced from a remark of Lady Hoare's that she was already anticipating Britain's defeat and later that day confided to his diary: 'The quicker we get them out of the country the better. But I'd sooner send them to a penal settlement. He'll be the Quisling of England when Germany conquers us and I am dead.'

Cadogan's opinions, despite his high position, were often erratic, but it seems at least possible that Hoare had been sent to Spain partly to get him out of the way. And it would certainly have been logical for the Germans to look towards him if Britain had been beaten, for he had been, with the then French Foreign Minister, Laval, the architect of the Hoare-Laval pact in 1935, which had proposed to reward Mussolini's aggression in Abyssinia by giving him a large part of the country, a plan which caused such an outcry in Britain that Hoare had been forced to resign. His old ally, Laval, was now deputy prime minister and the most powerful member of a collaborationist government in France. That Hoare, if asked to fulfil the same role in England, would have agreed is, of course, uncertain, but that he would have been asked seems far from unlikely. Failing him, the Germans would have had to scrape a long way down the barrel to find a figure even remotely credible – some senile old general, perhaps, or a still-ambitious retired senior Civil Servant – who allowed himself to be persuaded that it was his duty to his fellow countrymen to take over the government as a first step towards enabling life to return to normal. Failing any such figure they might have been driven to ruling direct through a 'Reichs Kommissar', a combination of viceroy, ambassador and governor, who would have issued orders to the Civil Service through his own officials, who would, in practice, have been departmental ministers.

Captured documents make clear that the Germans, like the British government, had made the mistake of identifying 'pro-Fascist' with 'anti-British' and they greatly overestimated the number of likely collaborators. A note drawn up on 26 August referred to 'the release of Englishmen detained since the beginning of the war on the ground of "friendship with Germany" ', and suggested that 'after checking these political prisoners with the aid of Home Office files', it would be desirable to 'attach some of them immediately to certain Search Commissions [Mosley supporters]'. The same writer advised the first arrivals in Britain to investigate the prospects of 'collaboration with English anti-Churchill groups'. But by September 1940, apart from the Communists and some right-wing Conservative MPs who had struggled to keep Chamberlain in office, there *were* no 'anti-Churchill groups'. In seeking a civilian ruler for Great Britain the Germans would therefore have been forced back on some senior Nazi or diplomatic official who already knew England. Von Ribbentrop would have been the obvious choice and, though it would have been a form of demotion for the German to become 'Protector' of the British Isles, he might have felt it acceptable, since it would have enabled him to live in Buckingham Palace, which he had last entered as a not-over-welcome guest, and lord it over his former British acquaintances. Another name sometimes mentioned is that of Ernst Bohle, a thirty-five-year-old Under Secretary in the Ministry of Foreign Affairs, who had specialised in Nazi activities overseas and had been promised by Hitler the post of German Ambassador in London when the British made peace. The truth is, however, that despite the elaborate preparations for the military side of the occupation, no real plans for its replacement by a civil administration had been made.

What would have been the first signs for a British civilian after the fighting had stopped, or peace had been signed, that he was now living

under an entirely new form of government? Visible evidence would have
been the arrival of the German infantry in the main streets of his town
moving cautiously at first in the middle of the road, rifles ready to respond
to any sudden shot from a window or rooftop. Then, gaining confidence,
the men would have moved along the pavements, kicking open the doors
of shops and houses and venturing inside, occasionally returning loaded
with a clock or ornament or some other article too tempting to resist.
After the infantry would come the motor-cycle detachments, their side-
cars loaded with route signs pointing the way ahead for later units, which
would be nailed up at cross-roads and fastened to lamp-posts. Soon there
would be military policemen, large, grim figures silently directing the
traffic and ignoring the few civilians in the streets and the curious groups
of children gathering to watch. Within hours anyone walking through
the town would see German sentries posted outside the police station, the
Post Office and the telephone exchange and many other buildings, all of
them displaying notices in German, some neatly painted beforehand,
ready for this occasion, some hastily scrawled in chalk with pasted beside
them a standard printed notice, in German and English, forbidding entry
to civilians. The Town Hall would by now probably have been taken
over as a German headquarters, though before long the fighting formations would move out to make room for the officers of the military
government. At least one hotel would have become a divisional head-
headquarters or officers' mess, while schools and church halls would be
requisitioned as canteens or barracks for German other ranks. The largest
cinema would before long be showing only German films, to German
soldiers, while pioneers might be busy in the local park wiring off a large
area to serve as a temporary 'cage' for captured British prisoners. Everywhere, in car parks, by the side of roads, in the main square, and on the
verges of quiet, tree-lined suburban estates would be parked German
tanks and lorries, waiting to be redirected into more permanent quarters
as the first confusion of military victory was followed by the tidy pattern
of long-term occupation. By now, too, the queues would be forming outside the Town Hall, the public library and parish halls, as the public
waited to obtain the new identity card required by the Germans, or one of
the numerous passes necessary for travel after dark or outside the district.
(The buildings, and the clerks already used for distributing ration books,
would perhaps have been taken over for the purpose.)

The other unmistakable sign of defeat would have been the German
soldiers, swaggering along the streets as if expecting the local population
to get out of their way, or behaving with studied, unsmiling politeness,
relieved by an occasional attempt to talk to a small child in a shop. This

would probably end with a small voice, hastily 'shushed' into silence, asking piercingly, 'But, mummy, *why* is it naughty to talk to that man?'

The Germans have always been great posters of notices and soon after their arrival in any area walls and hoardings would have carried this *Proclamation to the People of England*, signed by Field Marshal von Brauchitsch, the Commander-in-Chief of the German Army, the style of which admirably reflects the German attitude to the British people, at once 'correct' and arrogant:

1. English territory occupied by German troops will be placed under military government.
2. Military commanders will issue decrees necessary for the protection of the troops and the maintenance of general law and order.
3. Troops will respect property and persons if the population behaves according to instructions.
4. English authorities may continue to function if they maintain a correct attitude.
5. All thoughtless actions, sabotage of any kind, and any passive or active opposition to the German armed forces will incur the most severe retaliatory measures.
6. I warn all civilians that if they undertake active operations against the German forces, they will be condemned to death inexorably.
7. The decrees of the German military authorities must be observed; any disobedience will be severely punished.

Other posters would have appeared at the same time calling for the surrender of firearms, warning against helping anyone escaping from the Germans into unoccupied territory or taking part in any form of public demonstration without prior permission, and imposing a black-out. This would, of course, have been no new hardship and, if experience in Europe was any guide, would probably have been less rigorous than the one the British had already imposed on themselves, especially as police and wardens would no doubt have shouted 'Put that light out!' less zealously now that they did so on German orders. Although 'assembling in the street, circulation of pamphlets, holding of public meetings and processions without previous authorisation . . . or any other demonstration hostile to Germany' became illegal under pain of court-martial, as did any 'incitement to stop work' or 'stopping work maliciously', the Germans were anxious that so far as possible normal life should continue. 'All businesses, trade undertakings and banks are to remain open', ran one order. 'If they are closed down without justification the persons responsible will be punished. Producers of and dealers in goods required in everyday life are to continue in their occupations and distribute goods to the consumer.' Nor were the Germans willing to allow any section of the population to exploit the situation to obtain higher pay or charge higher prices. 'The raising of wages, prices and remuneration of any kind above the level of the day of the occupation is forbidden unless exceptions have been expressly authorised', ordered another regulation.

The main immediate change that the shopkeeper was likely to notice was that German money, as well as sterling, now became legal tender, the rate of exchange being fixed at 9·60 Reichsmarks to the pound, i.e. at just over two shillings to the Reichsmark in existing currency, or 10p in to-day's money, a fair enough level at that time. Perhaps prompted by bitter experience elsewhere, the Germans warned that there should not be one price for the locals and another for the gentlemen from Deutschland. 'All merchants, manufacturers and retailers', laid down Article 7 of Part III of the Occupation *Ordinances*, 'are forbidden to sell any member of the German forces or to any German official any commodity or article of any sort whatsoever at a higher price than that paid by others'; although the troops were, in fact, officially discouraged from doing much private shopping.

Both the Army Commander-in-Chief's 'Most Secret' orders, collected together in German War Office File Number 3000/40 'Military Government (England): General', and the detailed collection of *Ordinances* to be enforced later, refer to the existence in Britain of both an 'occupied' and an 'unoccupied' zone, as in France. Willingness to leave a large part of the country in French hands had proved a powerful bargaining factor in June 1940, though the agreement was torn up in 1942 and the whole country overrun. The Germans had perhaps some such intention in mind in the British Isles, but no map was ever prepared showing the proposed demarcation lines and, with no formal capitulation and no Vichy-type regime, it seems likely that they would have been forced to occupy the whole country, at least in the legal sense. The *Sea Lion* plans, as already mentioned, looked no further ahead than a point in the campaign where German forces occupied the central band of the country from Hampshire to mid-Essex, and made no mention at all of Wales, Scotland or Ireland. The Gestapo's blueprints for occupation did envisage a Scottish office, and they advised that 'It is essential that Ireland be also occupied', though only on the grounds that 'the shortest distance from England to Ireland is twenty kilometres and therefore many Englishmen would try to escape by motor-boat'. Wales was apparently regarded as part of England; the only reference to its existence on the part of either Army or Gestapo was a regulation that 'no language other than German, Italian, Spanish, French, Dutch or English may be used in correspondence by post. Dialects are not permitted.'

Probably in practice German forces would have been stationed in South

Wales and Southern Scotland, at least during the initial months of deportations and requisitioning, when resistance was to be expected. Later the troops here might have been thinned out (for the Germans Britain always meant England and England meant London) and the mountainous, thinly populated areas of Snowdonia and the Highlands would probably have been almost permanently ungarrisoned, perhaps with occasional 'sweeps' to round up any resistance men who might be lurking there. What would have happened to Ireland is even more speculative. With the rest of Britain beaten, Ulster offered little real threat to the Germans and it was perhaps in more danger from its neighbour to the south, which had consistently refused to cooperate with the British government during the summer and had maintained towards Germany a policy of benevolent neutrality. Apart from occasions when it suited them, the Germans were not the people to bother about such niceties as the difference between Northern Ireland and the Irish Republic. It seems likely that in the long term, especially if, as the Gestapo anticipated, refugees from the mainland fled across the Irish Sea, or British saboteurs used Ulster as a base, the Germans would have occupied both countries. To imagine that they would have stopped at the Border merely because the government of Eire had been careful not to offend is clearly naive.

Once the British people had come to accept the presence of German troops they might not have proved particularly obtrusive. The absolute maximum that the *Sea Lion* planners had contemplated landing to secure the country had been about half a million men and, once the war had been won and Hitler's thoughts were turning, as they very soon were, towards Russia, the best of the fighting troops among these, say, half, might well have been withdrawn. 250,000 men, though a formidable body en masse, would not have been particularly conspicuous once spread over the country—certainly less so than the million and a half British soldiers who had been stationed there before the invasion or the million or more Americans who were to pass through it in 1944 alone. In many places it might well have been possible to go for months without ever seeing a German.

The military structure through which the Germans planned to rule the British Isles consisted of the two armies of Army Group A, which was to make the actual assault, General Busch's Sixteenth Army and General Strauss's Ninth Army, and these names, like that of the Army Group Commander, Field-Marshal von Rundstedt and the Commander-in-Chief, Army, General von Brauchitsch, would rapidly have become familiar to the British civilian. So too, very probably, would those of General von Bock, commanding Army Group B and General von Reichenau, commanding the only Army so far assigned to it, the Sixth, if this, as planned, was brought in to occupy the south-west. The power to issue occupation regulations was delegated to the Army commanders and in some cases to corps commanders, a corps normally consisting of two divisions, and as there were altogether ten corps in Army Group A and three in Army Group B, there would have been, beside the three Army commanders, thirteen different rulers governing the British Isles.

The Germans planned, too, to bring across the Channel as soon as victory was won a substantial number of administrative troops to man what in military jargon was called 'the lines of communication area', which meant setting up supply depots and communications networks, base workshops and hospitals, and the whole elaborate machinery needed to keep a large army fed and ready for action. These were to be responsible for military government outside the areas controlled by the fighting troops, and the Germans had worked out in detail the establishment each local commander needed, which included a section of 'Secret Field Police' and 'I local defence battalion on bicycles', a mode of transport for which, like the horse, the Germans had a great respect.

The German military occupation machine was rounded off by 'The Defence Economic Staff for England', whose role will be discussed later, and by the Central Security Office, or RSHA, whose most feared arm was the Gestapo. The sign that they had arrived, and that no man's life was now safe, would have been the appearance of a new poster in a type that was a compromise between familiar British and German Gothic:

Dieses Haus darf nur mit Genehmigung des Befehlshabers der Sicherheitspolizei für Grossbritannien betreten werden.

No entrance without permission of the Chief-in Command of the German Secret Police for Great Britain.

Chapter 9: The Merseyside spies

Your task is to combat . . . all anti-German organisations, institutions, opposition and opposition groups which can be seized in England . . . to prevent the removal of all available material, and to centralise and safeguard it for future exploitation.

Instructions to the Representative of the Chief of the Security Police in Great Britain, 17 September 1940

After the wild beast had killed his prey the jackals arrived to dismember it. The Army's duty was to defeat the enemy and prevent a military rebellion, the economic staff's to strip the captured country bare of its resources. The Security Service had a darker, more evil, task to perform— to stamp out any organisations that had harmed Germany in the past or might do so in the future, to root out all undercover opposition, and to impose upon the vanquished, by persuasion or terror, not merely German rule but Nazi culture.

The Reich Central Security Office, or *Reichssicherheitshaumptamt* (RSHA), had been set up only in 1939, when the Criminal Police (i.e. the CID wing of the German Police), the Security Service of the Nazi Party (*Sicherheitsdienst* or SD) and the Secret State Police (*Geheime Staatspolizei*) had been merged into one organisation. The whole of this was often referred to by those outside by the name of this last body, the Gestapo, which specialised in tracking down and interrogating suspected enemies of the regime. The Security Service, while ready enough to call on its Gestapo colleagues when necessary, was largely an intelligence organisation, collecting material of the kind which in Britain might have been assembled by the Special Branch of the Police and by the intelligence departments of the three services. The German system, with no one trusting the man in the next office and with a large number of little overlapping empires, while well calculated to make internal treason difficult, was not likely to promote efficiency in dealings with the world outside. The unclassified material collected for the use of the Armed Forces when they reached Great Britain, described in an earlier chapter, was not unimpressive, especially considering the speed with which it had been got together, but the secret documents prepared by the Security Service for their own use and their internal memoranda give a different picture. At least five different sections at headquarters in Berlin were involved and clearly a good deal of readily available information simply slipped through the net. It is clear, too, that various sections had private filing systems of their own, and that card indexes of potential suspects had also blossomed in profusion. A conference called by one Section in Berlin in March 1941, six months after the target date for *Sea Lion*, while eager to make plain that 'in calling this meeting, Section VI did not in any way wish to arrogate to itself the central direction of the planning in regard to England', revealed how desperate was the need for coordination. Despite the lack of up-to-date information on conditions in the British Isles, it was reported, 'it frequently happened that diplomats, journalists, etc., arriving in the Reich from London could not be questioned because the Foreign Ministry did not report their arrival . . . to the HQ of State Security', while the meeting ended with the chairman, a senior SS officer, remarking with pained surprise that 'when studying personnel records, he had been struck by the large number of staff proposed who neither knew English nor had ever been in England or abroad or been concerned therewith'. Considering that much of their work involved studying the British press this must have been a formidable handicap.

The same meeting reaffirmed that responsibility for all Security Service planning for England rested on 'SS Standartenführer Professor Six', of Section II. He had been appointed at the suggestion, or at least with the approval, of Göring, following the setting up within the Security Service of a special headquarters entrusted with requisitioning 'the entire results of British aeronautical development and research' and for seizing particularly valuable items such as machine tools. Since this came within Göring's special sphere of interest he seems to have used the opportunity to steal a march on his rival Himmler in the obscure backstairs power-struggle that was for ever in progress around Hitler, and to have moved into one area, security in occupied territories, which really belonged to the Minister of the Interior.

On 17 September a formal memorandum was addressed to Dr Six, nominating him Chief of the Security Police in Great Britain on Göring's authority, and informing him that 'Reichs-Marshal Minister-President Göring' had 'decided . . . that the Security Police . . . will commence their activities simultaneously with the military invasion in order to seize and combat effectively the numerous important organisations and societies in England which are hostile to Germany. . . . Your task is to combat, with the requisite means, all anti-German organisations, institutions, opposition, and opposition groups which can be seized in England, to prevent the removal of all available material, and to centralise and safeguard it for future exploitation. I designate the capital, London, as the location of your headquarters as Representative of the Chief of the Security Police and SD, and I authorise you to set up small action groups

(*Einsatzgruppen*) in other parts of Great Britain as the situation dictates and the necessity arises.'

These 'Action Groups' consisted of small units of utterly ruthless Nazis who descended suddenly upon an area, tortured and executed known enemies of the regime, and tried to paralyse all opposition before it could begin by taking into 'protective custody', without trial, any leading local figures whose arrest might strike terror into the hearts of their potential followers. They later gained an evil reputation in Russia, where many murders were laid at their door and where their equipment ultimately included mobile extermination centres. One of those convicted at the war crimes trials at Nuremberg in 1948 of participation in these massacres—though he escaped with a light sentence and was released long before it expired in 1952—was the man whom Göring had chosen to become security overlord of occupied Britain, Dr Franz Six.

Six possibly appealed to Göring because of his interest, of which he had perhaps already revealed some signs, in acquiring the art treasures of other countries for the Reich, a subject in which the Reichs-Marshal took a personal interest, for many of the finest paintings and works of art looted from France and Holland later turned up in the private collection at his resplendent hunting lodge, Karinhall, where so many susceptible English aristocrats had been entertained before the war. Six's defence of his later activities in Russia was that he had gone there to place Smolensk Cathedral and other historic churches under his protection, because they contained various gold crowns and other precious objects, and England, with its magnificent cathedrals, offered the prospect of an even richer harvest. Possibly Six owed his appointment to some private understanding with Göring to keep the pick of the crop for him, for though he wrote excellent English, he had up to this time shown no particular interest in that country.

The mere title of 'SS Colonel Professor Dr Six' was sinister-sounding enough, but the reality of contact with the man would have been far worse. Six was only thirty-one, but he was already head of the Enemy Information Department (Amt II) of the Security Office when in the first week of September 1940 he was called back from his Action Group, busy in France, to take charge of some forty officers who were to cross to England and attach themselves to divisional and Army headquarters there as soon as the fighting was over, but he had already had a long and impeccable career of service to the Nazi cause. Like many of the most ardent Nazis he was a self-made man who had achieved academic distinction, or at least impressive paper qualifications, despite financial hardship and, one suspects, a somewhat repellent personality. He came from a working-class back-

ground in an industrial town and his education had been interrupted by
the need to earn his living and to him, as to many frustrated young men
of his generation, Nazism had clearly come like a revelation, to be em-
braced with the fervour of a religious conversion. Six had joined the Nazi
Party when he began to read history and political science at Heidelberg,
and he seems to have taken little part in the traditional amusements of
German student life in that beautiful old city. His time was divided between his miserable lodgings and the lecture-room, and the Nazi meetings
he attended were no doubt oases of colour and excitement in his drab life.
In 1934, the year after Hitler became Chancellor of Germany, he obtained
his doctorate of philosophy and took an academic post at the University
of Leipzig, where he became an even more active Nazi, which perhaps
helped him in 1937 to become a professor at a remarkably early age. In
1939, with war clearly approaching, he was made head of a new faculty of
political science at the University of Berlin, designed to give leading Nazis
the theoretical knowledge of the Nazi philosophy, and of other countries,
that those who had come up the hard way had so far had no chance to
acquire, and Six seems to have made a success of it. On the outbreak of war
he was placed in charge of the cultural branch of the Foreign Office, and
became even more deeply involved in the RSHA, which sent him to
France after it fell, and from which he was called back to Berlin to prepare
for the invasion of England. When in due course Operation *Sea Lion* was
cancelled, Six was found a congenial job as head of Section VII of RSHA,
a small department which carried out basic research into such Nazi obses-
sions as freemasonry and the Christian religion, one of those agreeable
'soft options' which the enterprising academic can often find in time of
war, and then followed his dubious activities in Russia. He spent much
of the last year of the war back in Germany trying to organise an all-
European anti-Jewish Congress, a somewhat unnecessary undertaking,
one might have thought, considering that Six's colleagues had by now
murdered almost every Jew in Europe. At the end of the war Six disappeared, but was eventually caught and sent to gaol. He last emerged
from obscurity in 1961 when he volunteered to appear on behalf of the
mass-murderer Adolf Eichmann at his trial in Israel, an offer prudently
withdrawn when the Israelis refused to promise that the witness might not
also find himself in the dock.

This was the man on whose whims and prejudices the fate of every
individual in the British Isles would have rested in the autumn of 1940,
had Britain fallen, and his name would soon have become as familiar to
the vanquished as those of his hero and superior, Hitler. Six's appearance
in those days was a gift to the cartoonists for he was short and bald, with

ears that stuck out, and heavy pebble spectacles that inadequately concealed a pronounced squint, but it seems unlikely that, except in the underground press, anyone would have dared to caricature him.

The Gestapo planned to set up, in addition to Six's own headquarters in London, provincial offices in Birmingham, Bristol, Liverpool, Manchester and either Edinburgh or Glasgow, and despite some glaring deficiencies, already indicated, they had prepared for the proud day when they finally hung up their long black raincoats on the hat-stand of requisitioned British offices with meticulous care. Some of their plans for London have survived and will be mentioned later, but the thoroughness with which the occupation had been planned is demonstrated even better by the preparations they had made for the takeover of Liverpool. Besides the more obvious forms of intelligence work and espionage, such as the assembling of useful documents on public sale like the Automobile Association *Handbook* and the *Police Almanack* and the photographing of the whole British coastline by the German airline, *Lufthansa*, during its regular peacetime flights, the Germans, even before the Nazis came to power, had collected every scrap of information that came their way from German residents in Great Britain. They had been helped by the gullibility and good nature of many English people who, in the 1920s and 1930s, genuinely believed that Germany had had a raw deal in 1919 and that the best way to avoid the horrors of another war was to entertain Germans in their own homes. This was the policy that had earlier in 1940 yielded such rich dividends in Norway. Many well-meaning Norwegians in 1919 and the years that followed had generously given shelter to German children suffering from the after-effects of the allied blockade, and others had helped to entertain visiting German lecturers, singers and artistes. They were rewarded in 1940 by seeing the children they had cared for, and the visitors they had applauded, returning as part of the occupation forces, when their knowledge of Norwegian proved invaluable in interrogating captured resistance men. People in England having, unlike the Norwegians, suffered already in one war caused by Germany, had on the whole been more hesitant about extending the hand of friendship, but a substantial number had done so and in Liverpool, as in many places, schools had organised exchange visits in the 1930s, enabling German children to stay in private homes. One Liverpool woman, eleven in 1939, still remembers the firm refusal of her father, an ex-serviceman, to have one to stay before the war on the grounds that 'Once a German always a German'. When, in 1940, the family were bombed out by 'the bloody Huns', he blamed the accuracy of the attacks on Liverpool on these former visitors who had, he believed, taken back to Germany with them maps and photographs of the docks. He was very probably right. Another popular belief in Merseyside and elsewhere was that the pilot of one low-flying enemy aircraft had been identified as a German apprentice who had worked at a local factory before the war. The truth of this was more doubtful, but it could have happened, for many Germans repaid their hosts by spying on them.

Liverpool, due to its importance as the chief transatlantic port and, later, to its selection as one of the Security Service's provincial headquarters, seems to have received particularly thorough attention, although similar dossiers were no doubt compiled on other centres. The university, practising the tradition that learning overrode national barriers, was an obvious target and the official *Austauschdienst*, or student exchange service, provided a steady flow of young Germans allegedly eager to drink at this fountain of British culture. The head of one department, which regularly exchanged first-year students, discovered that among those sent to him was 'a thug of a Nazi who started putting up notices without permission and snooping on the other German students in search of forbidden literature'. In the summer of 1938 the Professor of German, an active member of the Liverpool committee for helping German refugees, returned unexpectedly to his office to find a German exchange student engrossed in the contents of his roll-top desk, in search of information about these unfortunate fellow-countrymen, and the university, though discreetly, since officially Germany was still a friendly power, ended the exchange agreement.

But some spies at Liverpool, especially in earlier years, went undetected. Among them was a future SS leader, Rudolf Thyrolf, who arrived in Liverpool in 1929 to spend the coming academic year there while the Nazis were still bawling and bludgeoning their way to power. Thyrolf, however much he neglected his academic work, did not waste his three terms in England. While other foreign students drank with friends, or laboured at their notebooks, his sharp eye was everywhere and his ear was attuned even in the lecture room to any hint of friendship or hostility towards Germany. On 5 September 1940, with invasion believed to be only days away, his big moment arrived. Now an officer (*Hauptsturmführer*) in the SS in Dresden, he submitted to his superiors in Berlin a long report marked 'Very Urgent!', on which its recipient, suitably impressed one hopes, duly minuted 'Pass to Liverpool Commando leader'.

The material on the organisation of the university which Thyrolf had compiled, useful though it was, could have been garnered from any good reference book, but his impressions of the teaching staff were likely to be of real value to a Gestapo officer arriving in a new town, and in 1940

Thyrolf's reactions, which the intervening decade had not mellowed, might well have served as the death-warrant of some harmless academic. One professor, for example, was described as 'in his outlook . . . a typical Englishman, although one can never quite rid oneself of the feeling that he is not of pure Aryan descent. . . . A cunning and dishonest man.' Another departmental head was 'to judge by his appearance . . . probably of Jewish origin. . . . In his lectures he often put forward a Socialist-Marxist point of view.' After such dubious personalities it was a relief to turn to a professor who 'was . . . a great admirer of German culture' and another member of the Liverpool faculty who was also 'very fond of Germany, where he went for his holidays, and he had his children taught German', but unhappily 'wielded little influence . . . and had few listeners'. On the Vice-Chancellor of his time, Professor Hetherington, Thyrolf reserved judgment, though he paid the Scots an unexpected compliment: 'Hetherington is of Scottish origin. He was therefore regarded as clever and businesslike.'

Thyrolf had devoted less attention to his fellow students but he had not found them impressive. 'The student body was largely made up of the sons and daughters of ordinary middle-class families from the immediate neighbourhood of Liverpool', he reported. 'Hard work was the rule in Liverpool, not so much to acquire deeper knowledge as to pass the examinations in the shortest possible time.'

A constant anxiety in many quarters in Britain in 1940 was that those Germans not so far interned would, when the time came, prove loyal to their native country, however vehemently they professed at the moment to oppose it. The Cabinet was told on 10 May, the day that Britain woke up to its danger, that, in addition to 164,000 non-enemy aliens belonging to countries with which Britain was not yet at war, and at that stage of course including Italians, there were 73,000 German citizens in Britain who had not yet been interned. The government feared that each of these was a potential fifth columnist or, at best, a potential collaborator after Germany had won. The Germans running restaurants in Soho, forming brass bands in Birmingham and managing butchers' shops in Sheffield might indeed be harmless or even actively helping the war effort *while Britain stayed uninvaded*. Once she was occupied and part of Greater Germany, German citizenship, except of course by the Jews, would be resumed and deeper-rooted loyalties than those attaching them to their adopted country might triumph. This at least was what the British government believed and it was also what the German government expected, for one intelligence survey after another identified German nationals in England as future supporters. It was not, as some people supposed, to show sympathy with Nazism to acknowledge that ties of birth and blood were among the most compelling known to mankind, surviving time, distance and even persecution. The whole history of Germany in the 1920s and of Britain in 1940 had shown that loyalty to one's country was by no means an out-of-date conception. It could convert Mosley from a sympathiser with Germany to a would-be guerilla fighter against her; and equally it could cause nice, amiable Mr Miller at the pork butcher's shop to become again Herr Müller, who was a German first and an Englishman second.

Certainly Rudolf Thyrolf, writing in September 1940, devoted a good deal of space to the German community in Liverpool. Before 1914, he recalled, there had been several thousand Germans in the city, including more than 1000 butchers, the classic trade of Germans in England, just as catering, and especially ice-cream vending, was that of the Italians, but by 1930 few were left and 'those who retained their nationality were the exception', while 'only in very few cases did their children speak a word of German'. However, after 1919 'new immigrants carried the banner of the German spirit in Liverpool', the banner flying most strongly around the German Literary Society, whose officers were naturalised Germans, the German Church, which had regular 'German evenings' during the week, and the Consulate General, which, however, 'at any rate up to 1930 did not play a leading role on behalf of German nationalism'.

No Gestapo intelligence report would have been complete without a reference to those legendary enemies, the Jews, the Communists and the Freemasons. In Liverpool, reported Thyrolf with obvious regret—he had, he reminded his superiors, 'been an active anti-Semite since 1923'— 'the position . . . in 1930 was the same as in the rest of Great Britain. . . . Jews everywhere in business and culture, among the teaching staff at the university and in the student body. I got to know a young Jew who wanted to be an officer. This was quite possible. There was no sign of an anti-Semitic movement, although I was particularly on the look-out for it. Only occasionally did one hear a student say, "I can't stand Jews".' The position about Communism was a little more hopeful, for though 'invitations to Communist meetings were often seen chalked on the roadway or on walls . . . these small groups exerted no influence', but Thyrolf's one good contact, a trades union official who was learning German and who had visited him in Germany in 1936, had proved uncooperative after 'I had a violent personal argument with him . . . about the Spanish Civil War, which threatened to bring our friendship to an end'. Freemasonry, however, was a real danger. 'English freemasonry gives the impression of being a much stronger movement than in Germany. One met them more often and more openly. . . . I knew a number of students who were masons at twenty. It was nothing out of the ordinary to be asked by fellow-students whether one was a freemason. A freemasons' lodge met in the Students Club, the main hall of which was decorated with Masonic emblems.'

Thyrolf had also looked into a number of other suspect organisations. Rotary, because of its international associations, had always troubled the Germans and the intrepid Nazi had penetrated the very heart of the citadel and attended a rotary club lunch; he attached his invitation, carefully preserved, to his report, a curious proof of his bona fides as a spy. Another document which duly found its place in the Gestapo archives was his invitation to attend a social and dance 'to meet members of the University of Liverpool International Society. . . . Book day return ticket to Town Green, 1/4', but this occasion, too, had proved disappointing, the society being 'fundamentally very nationalistic', i.e. not pro-German. As for the League of Nations Union, that supporter of Germany's old enemy, the League, it had done nothing more alarming than 'holding evening dances'.

Thyrolf was not the only person eager, if England were to be occupied, to get into the act. Other enterprising underlings did their best to cash in on their knowledge of the country and pulled what strings they could to exploit it. Gestapo headquarters seem to have called in August for volunteers to serve there, for on the 22nd its Munich office signalled Section III, responsible for the collection of material on England, in Berlin, that Professor Haushofer had recommended his son, a lecturer in the Faculty of Foreign Affairs in Berlin, as being a useful source of information and 'through all his connections and his knowledge, fully in the picture on personalities and institutions'. He would, Sturmbannführer Dr Spengler of Section III was assured, be available in due course for interview in Berlin, but he was at present inaccessible, being 'on a mountain slope near Partenkirchen'. A month later, on 23 September, the Security Service's Dortmund office teleprinted Berlin that a keen local Nazi, Dr Büchsenschütz, had given in his name. He had, it was explained, escaped call-up into the Forces because the President of Westphalia had wished to retain him as a headmaster, but the call of duty could no longer be denied and 'Party Member Büchsenschütz' had offered to put his 'complete written and spoken command of English' and his personal knowledge of the country, at the disposal of the Reichsführer SS.

What, one wonders, would have happened if Dr Six's henchmen, perhaps including Thyrolf, who would have been a natural choice for a post on Merseyside, had one evening stepped from a train at Lime Street station or driven up in their Mercedes, or a captured Rolls, to the Adelphi Hotel, a likely choice as the German officers' mess, or the Liver Building, whose modern offices would surely have been taken over by one of the German departments swarming into the city? The Germans, the papers show, had some hopes that the large number of Irish in the city, many of them working in the docks, would have been well disposed towards them, but they seem likely in fact to have found the docks in ruins for one professor in the university learned from an extra-mural class of dock-workers that a plan existed to destroy all the cranes, warehouses and other installations. The Germans themselves deduced from the multi-racial nature of the city, and particularly from the presence of so many Irishmen, that they would find a large number of sympathisers in Liverpool, but one man who had himself worked in the docks from seventeen until the age of forty, and is now a retired official of the dockers' trade union, is convinced that the German port authorities would have been in for a disagreeable surprise. Dock work, he points out, lends itself to sabotage. 'A skilled man, of course, strives to ensure that the cargo will not shift, but the same skilled man . . . forced to work for people he loathed, would equally be able to use his skill to put what is known as a "Glasgow Face" on the cargo, so that to anybody looking at it, it appeared absolutely stable and secure, but under the stress of bad weather conditions . . . would shift.' Fragile articles, he believes, would deliberately have been packed dangerously close to cases of heavy machinery, and liquid cargoes, then still largely carried in casks, would have been stowed 'in such a way that to anybody looking at them they would appear perfectly stable, but they would not be stable at all as soon as the ship got into heavy weather'. This ex-doc-worker suspects, too, that 'as many of the dockers had a background of years of work in shipyards, or of experience as firemen or greasers in the engine room at sea', they would also, whenever they got the chance, have known 'just where to go and what to do' to damage the ship's engines and machinery.

More open resistance in Liverpool, however, as everywhere else, would probably not have lasted long once the Germans had taken over. 'It's nice to think we might have been heroes, but I'm sure we would have done just what we were told to do', believes one of those who held a key position on the five- or six-strong Emergency Committee, which met daily at the Town Hall, and the thought of responsibility for the unprotected civilians in their care clearly weighed heavily upon all those in authority. Sir Joseph Cleary, a future Lord Mayor of Liverpool and then a member of the council, also has no illusions about the council being able to defy the Germans. 'I suppose,' he believes, 'the council would have had to suffer or tolerate German occupation . . . knowing victory would come. . . . We would need a structure of government, we would need our social services, we would need the city, in that context we would have gone on controlling the city to the best of our ability in the interest of the citizens. But I still feel that come what may and no matter what the risk might have been, I could not have carried out policies which would have meant the deporting or executing of Jews or any other minority.'

Another member of the council at that time, and also a future Lord Mayor, Harry Livermore, would have escaped the agonising official dilemmas of his colleagues but would have had far worse difficulties of his own, for he was a Jew. Although he is sure that local people 'would have helped as much as they could', as experience in other countries made clear it was difficult to hide wanted people for long, and 'if the Nazis got here,' he is convinced, 'I was as good as dead.'

Chapter 10:
Whatever happened to Nelson?

The Sector has been notified by people who know England of the following cultural items, the safeguarding of which would in their opinion be in Germany's interests.

Memorandum addressed to Section III of the
Security Service, 11 November 1940

Anyone who had not visited Central London for several weeks after the arrival of the Germans and who now walked down the Strand or Charing Cross Road towards Trafalgar Square would have been troubled as he approached it by the sense of something missing. Not merely would the sandbagged machine-gun emplacements and debris of the recent battle, and the placards exhorting the public to 'Lend to Defend the Right to be Free', have gone, but in the middle of the square would have been a stretch of newly paved terrace occupied by the pigeons—and nothing else. Nelson's Column, 170 feet high and erected in 1843 at a cost of £50,000 raised by public subscription, would have gone, leaving nothing behind it but a scar in the ground. With it would probably have vanished the four great bronze lions which had once flanked its base, designed by Sir Edwin Landseer and representing the very epitome of Victorian security and taste, and the fountains in which revellers had splashed on Bonfire Night, Boat Race Night, Mafeking Night, Armistice Day 1918 and many another national occasion. For Hitler, desiring some visible proof of his victory over the British and delighted to be reminded that he had succeeded where Napoleon, thanks to Nelson, had failed, planned to remove the whole edifice to his own capital.

The suggestion occurs in a document bluntly entitled 'Plans for England', prepared within Department III of the Security Service on 26 August 1940. 'There is no symbol of the British victory in the World War corresponding to the French monument near Compiègne', wrote its author persuasively. 'On the other hand, ever since the Battle of Trafalgar, the Nelson Column represents for England a symbol of British naval might and world domination. It would be an impressive way of underlining the German victory if the Nelson Column were to be transferred to Berlin.' It seems only too probable that the idea would have appealed to Hitler and that, by Christmas 1940, despite the formidable engineering problems involved, Nelson would have no longer looked down Whitehall towards the Houses of Parliament but over the tops of the lime trees in Unter den Linden towards the Reichstag and Hitler's Chancellery.

The same Londoner who had gazed aghast at a Trafalgar Square without Nelson would probably have been conscious of a flurry of activity around the National Gallery, with heavy pantechnicons, driven by British drivers but escorted by lorry-loads of German troops, pulling up one after another to be loaded with heavily crated objects, and then driven off towards Victoria for transport to the Continent. The same helpful Gestapo department which had earmarked Nelson's Column for removal had also prepared lists of art treasures which Germany should take into its 'protection'. 'Special team required for British Museum', it advised, in a style of telegraphic urgency. The immediate targets should be the National Gallery in London and the Ashmolean Museum in Oxford, and the first concern should be to retrieve a 'selection of Germanic works of art in the widest sense of the term, also Rubens and Rembrandt, etc.'. Since Rubens, though born in Germany, had lived most of his life in Flanders and Rembrandt was a Dutchman, this was certainly interpreting 'Germanic' in a very wide sense, though it does throw some light on the curious German desire to establish a moral claim, however dubious, to property which they were in fact stealing by armed robbery. The same strange reasoning presumably prompted another suggestion. It went almost without saying, Department III implied, that items associated with the painter Holbein and the great musician Handel should be sent back to Germany, but so too should the 'works, products, etc.' of such lesser-known figures (at least to the British public) as 'the astronomer Herschel of Hanover, buried at Greenwich' and 'the orientalist Max Muller, buried in Oxford'.

The inability of the Germans to see themselves as others saw them, namely as the greatest thieves in the history of Christendom, was revealed in another suggestion in the same paper, that Germany should set herself up as the policeman of Europe and 'for reasons of external policy' organise the 'return of stolen works of art and scientific articles to their original owners' (possibly Elgin Marbles to Greece, mummies to Egypt, others things to Japan, South America, France, etc.) – where they would presumably have filled some of the gaps left by items already plundered by the Germans themselves.

The list of sources of loot drawn up in August was, the Security Service realised, by no means up to their usual comprehensive standard and other offices throughout Germany were invited to put up suggestions, just as they had been asked to recommend people with special knowledge of

Great Britain. The Brunswick office responded with a will, submitting a 'shopping list' of art and literary treasures worth millions of pounds, 'the safeguarding of which . . . would be in Germany's interests'. Gestapo headquarters had already agreed that a 'special team' was required for the British Museum, and the informants in Brunswick recommended that, to begin with, it should not merely seize 'Gutenberg's 42-line Bible and Gutenberg's 36-line Bible', both, of course, almost priceless, but 'many early printed books' from the King's Library (a section of the Museum), and 'a very large and world-famous collection of old manuscripts of the Greek, Roman, Byzantine, German, French, Italian, Flemish and English schools', from 'the manuscript salon' and 'the Grouville [i.e. Greville] Library'. The plunderers would round off their day's work by seizing those few items to which Germany could perhaps lay some slight claim, such as the 'famous collection of autographs, including letters from Bismarck, Kaiser Wilhelm I and Kaiser Friedrich III'.

The cultural locusts from Berlin then proposed to move on to Trafalgar Square, stopping at the National Gallery to seize all the Rembrandts, a painter for whom Hitler seems to have had a special admiration, before travelling on across London to 'the South Kensington Museum', meaning the Victoria and Albert, where the curators were to be called on to surrender 'sculptures by Leonardo da Vinci [and] early printed books and famous prints of the Kelmscott Press and the Doves Press'. Surprisingly, no mention was made of the Tate Gallery, perhaps because the Nazis officially considered most modern art decadent, or of other major treasuries of art, such as the Wallace Collection, perhaps because it did not occur to anyone in Brunswick to suggest them. No doubt other Gestapo officers, whose replies to the appeal from Berlin have not survived, would have filled in this and other gaps.

In fact few of the items listed by the Germans were where they believed them to be, since the most precious items from the great museums and galleries had been evacuated at the outbreak of war to various country houses, a quarry in Wales and other safe spots, but it would not have taken the Germans long to discover these hiding places and unless, which seems unthinkable, their custodians had preferred to destroy them rather than see them leave the country, the fact that they were already crated and stacked would merely have made their removal easier. No doubt, too, since the Gestapo instructions said that the National Gallery and other buildings were to be stripped, something would have been removed from them, even if only the single picture displayed each month to remind the British public of the riches it was missing, or the much-criticised examples of British modern art acquired under the Chantry

Bequest and lying undisplayed in the basement beneath the Tate, an action which might have saved future curators some embarrassment. On items worth seizing outside London, the Brunswick office of the Gestapo was less well informed. It recommended the 'Reference Library, Piccadilly, Manchester', as 'one of England's most famous libraries' and hence worth serious scrutiny by the Germans' bibliophilic task force, while other teams of experts, it suggested, ought to visit 'the Archaeological Museum, Cambridge, and the Ashmolean Museum, Oxford', where 'antiquities are preserved which, judging from their character, are from Lower Saxony'. These presumably were also to be restored to their native earth, several thousand years after first being interred in it.

But it was not only the art galleries which would have echoed to the heavy tread of uniformed Gestapo officers and the softer and perhaps even more sinister footsteps of their civilian-suited advisers. Victims of their own propaganda, the Nazis believed that London was the centre of a whole network of anti-German conspiracies, which it was the duty of the Security Service to root out. The most urgent task lay at the Home Office which contained records 'on all foreigners in England', including 'Irish Nationalists, Moscow agents, German emigrants such as Brüning, Hanfstängl, etc.', as well as 'political prisoners . . . detained since the beginning of the war on the ground of friendship with Germany', but the officers in charge of the search there were also warned to look out for evidence of 'the beginnings of an English Gestapo, only recently established by Anderson'. This notoriously humourless and solidly Conservative ex-Civil Servant, promoted by Chamberlain to the post of Home Secretary, would surely have been surprised to learn that 'personnel attach great importance to the apprehension of Minister Anderson, a real rogue'. Other Gestapo men would meanwhile have been busy at the nearby Foreign Office in search of 'Vansittart, the Head of the Intelligence Service', Sir Robert (later Lord) Vansittart, the leading anti-Nazi in the diplomatic service, whom, due to his opposition to appeasement, Chamberlain had 'kicked upstairs' to be his Chief Diplomatic Adviser in 1938 and then ignored, 'his brother-in-law, Sir Eric Phipps, previously Ambassador in Berlin . . . his private secretary, Norton, a younger man (possibly recruited? [i.e., to the British Secret Service])' and 'Leeper, racial expert, carried out propaganda', also 'Deputy Secretary of State Cadogan'. All these public servants were no doubt patriotic Englishmen but their supposed connection with the intelligence service seems questionable. The future Sir Reginald Leeper had indeed worked in the Intelligence Bureau of the Department of Information in 1917, but had had a conventional diplomatic career since and a few years later, in 1944, was to incur the wrath of the left in Britain, as an alleged right-winger, during the anti-royalist revolution in Greece, while if Sir Alexander Cadogan was involved in espionage no hint of the fact appears in his otherwise remarkably indiscreet diary. The man in the greatest immediate danger of all appears to have been the author and former diplomat, Harold (later Sir Harold) Nicolson, then a backbench MP who, while others in London society and the House of Commons were losing their heads about von Ribbentrop and his friends, had firmly kept his. Nicolson was under no illusions what his fate would be if the Germans landed, and had indeed written to his wife on 26 May that he had secured a 'bare bodkin' in the shape of poison, with which to kill himself rather than be captured. The Gestapo had, of course, no knowledge of this and seem to have imagined that he would obligingly have given them the benefit of his expert advice. He was, noted the author of a paper modestly entitled 'Tips for Operations against England' on 6 September, 'one of the most knowledgeable Englishmen to get hold of in this connection', as he had taken 'part in the Versailles negotiations' and more recently been 'a contact point for Anglo-American propaganda'.

More surprising were some of the Gestapo's other immediate targets. They included Sir Nevile Henderson, who as British Ambassador in Berlin until the outbreak of war had been the weak and willing tool of Chamberlain's appeasement policies, and 'Benett of the Royal Institute', presumably the 'Royal Institute of International Affairs', a body of which most Englishmen had never heard but one to which, as will be seen, the Germans attributed enormous influence. 'Important as a contact point', the same memorandum advised, 'is an otherwise unknown Stock Exchange jobber, Anderson, [with a] house in Portman Square'. The Gestapo clearly considered this house, which otherwise makes no appearance in the history of the period, a centre of anti-Nazi intrigue. The leading opponent of Hitler, Brüning, had, they believed, lived there at one time and contacted there not merely the ever-dangerous Vansittart, but also 'Dr Michael' of the *Münchener Neueste Nachrichten*, a South German newspaper, 'who had been an émigré in London since 1935'. The Gestapo had an obviously well-founded fear that all these enemies of the Reich might not wait tamely to be captured. It was, they advised, 'advisable to get hold quickly of pictures of all Englishmen to be arrested', and once they were caught there was an obvious source of information to be exploited. 'When arresting Englishmen', the future staff of the London office were told, 'it is important to apprehend their servants. Every distinguished Englishman has a valet, often an ex-regular soldier, who is usually exceptionally well informed on the private and official affairs of his master.'

Apart from Jewish organisations and individuals, who featured prominently in all Gestapo documents, the Germans had assembled a strange list of bodies and private citizens whom they considered a particular threat. Under the heading 'Opponents of Germany', part of it read:

The Friends of the Basque Children Society [i.e. child refugees from the Spanish Civil War].

The National Joint Committee for Spanish Relict [i.e. Relief] Welsh Section.

The Society of Friends (Quakers) (degot [i.e. depot] Barclays Bank).

The Quakers finance Cadburys chocolate through Sir Walter Layton, influence on the *News Chronicle.*

United Dominions Trust Ltd, City Bankers, published a memorandum last Summer directed against 'The Link'.

The Salvation Army spread over 54 stateless countries.

Brigadier-General E. L. Spears, MP for Carlisle, a most bitter opponent of the Munich Agreement, is chairman of the British Bata Shoe Company.

Sir Frederick Marquis, clothing director of Lewis Ltd, together with Lt Colonel S. S. G. Aham and R. A. Z. Cohan.

Sir Edward Spears, as he later became, was perhaps singled out for early arrest because he had been a key figure in Anglo-French liaison in both world wars, and enjoyed the particular confidence of the Prime Minister. Sir Frederick Marquis's (the future Lord Woolton's) appearance on the list was also predictable. He had attracted nation-wide attention, and what he called a 'rocket' from Neville Chamberlain, when in 1938 he had announced that, as a protest against German persecution of the Jews, his stores would no longer stock German goods.

The Germans were suspicious, for no obvious reason, of the 'British Engineers Association' and the British Electrical and Allied Manufacturers Association, apparently believing that their international affiliations had been used for anti-German propaganda, but the real centre of such activities, they were convinced, was the Royal Institute of International Affairs, 'which', it was said, 'possesses comprehensive scientific and political material on Colonial affairs and also copious material on international historical and political matters. This Institute served the Foreign Office as a source of records for the production of political memoranda, White Papers and the like. Especially in the case of peace negotiations, it played a preparatory role. It also indicated the course to be followed in strategic matters. . . . Before making important political decisions, English politicians made use of the unofficial preparatory work of the

Institute. There is hardly one English politician who does not rely on the work of the Royal Institute. This Institute must therefore be particularly carefully secured.'

With the supposedly dangerous Institute safely under control, the Gestapo could turn their attention to other potential enemies. Second on the list for immediate closure came the 'Academic Assistance Council' or 'Emergency Association of German Scientists Overseas', which helped anti-Nazis to escape from German universities and found them work elsewhere. After these former victims had been recaptured, it would be the turn of all those British citizens connected with the 'Central Committee of National Patriotic Associations' which, according to the Gestapo, had laboured hard to discredit Germany both in England and overseas. 'It is linked', their researcher reported, 'to many cultural societies and associations in all neutral countries and occasionally supplies them with material and speakers.' Surprisingly, however, no more recent example of its activities was provided than that during the first world war 'it distributed 850,000 leaflets to school children and 900,000 to workers in important industrial centres'.

Because learning had in their own country become a mere tool of the state, and the Security Service was itself full of former academics, the Germans were obsessed with the belief that the universities in Britain, and bodies linked to them, were actively working against Hitler. Little seems likely to have slipped through their net, for among the 'tasks of SD Units in Great Britain' was included the 'seizure of the historical, biological, scientific, theosophical, philosophical, medical and colonial institutions, most of which were entrusted with tasks for the political government offices', and 'particular attention', it was suggested, 'should be paid to the colonial scientific institutes, with their scientific records on the founding of the British empire. These institutes . . . also hold documents for the study of non-British colonial possessions. The chemical institutes working for the British Army should also be dealt with rapidly, together with the bacteriological institutes . . . which are working for the Army'. Hardly less urgent was the paying off of some old scores by the 'seizure of scientific societies and clubs', since 'they are the source of reports put out against Germany . . . that since 1933 German science has been visibly on the downward path. . . . In contrast to the university institutes which must be investigated by experts', wrote the author of this document, perhaps smarting under the recollection of some personal insult, 'the urgent matter here is the apprehension of the leading personalities.' Finally the Security Service commanders were to take over 'British academic foreign institutes', such as 'the Institut Français' in Kensington, which 'represent

focal points of British cultural propaganda, directed abroad'. The procedure in every case was to be the same. 'First the institutes listed above will
be closed, sealed and guarded without warning', then 'the Examination
and Evaluation Commando will . . . start work, and will subject the
records to preliminary sifting and evaluation, and sort it for transfer to
the Reich'. The resulting work would have kept many Security Service
officials happily occupied for months; whether they would have unearthed a single document remotely useful to the German war effort
seems more doubtful.

As the encouragement given to its various departments to nominate
people to serve in England had shown, the Gestapo was a body that
looked after its own and it did not intend that its members should lack for
any essentials while engaged in unmasking the undercover influences
which had caused so many people to dislike the Germans. (That the
Germans' own recent behaviour might have had something to do with
their unpopularity does not seem to have occurred to them.) An early
step, one inter-office minute advised, should be to equip each Search
Group with a 'portable typewriter, car and driver', these last being particularly important as 'everything is very scattered in the country'. Another
essential was a secretary and 'those from Hamburg firms are recommended,
as they can do English shorthand and typing', particularly Fräulein F,
who had formerly worked for one Munich official now recommended for
employment in London. Nor were the first arrivals in London destined to
be uncomfortable. 'The take-over commandos', advised the same document, should 'find accommodation, not in hotels, but in the premises of
the "Clubs" ', which 'are concentrated in a few of the most fashionable
streets in the West End of London, mainly in Pall Mall and near the
German Embassy. . . . In addition the club quarter is close to the government buildings (Foreign Office, Downing Street). They offer every
facility for residential purposes and for SD type of work, reference works,
lists of members, etc. Members are drawn from specific cultural and business circles (for example, leading members of the church frequent
the Athenaeum Club). To a large extent the members live on the
premises.'

Among the clubs singled out for urgent attention and the first to suffer
'possible occupation' was to be the Carlton in Pall Mall, described as 'the
most important Conservative Club', which numbered among its members
'Chamberlain, Eden, Halifax, the Earl of Derby, Samuel Hoare, Isidor
Salmon, etc.', the last-named being apparently included to show the
unreliability of the membership committee on racial matters. Further
down Pall Mall the Athenaeum was also to be taken over, its leading

figures including, it was said, 'Chamberlain and Churchill'; while not far away, in Hamilton Place at the bottom of Park Lane, 'the Bachelors, member, among others, Duff Cooper', an old enemy of the Nazis, was also destined to be seized, as was Brooks's, in St John Street, although it had been a hot-head of appeasement, its members including, according to the Gestapo, 'Sir John Anderson, Lord Halifax and Lord Runciman (Czechoslovakia)' – he had led the fruitless negotiations preceding the Munich agreement in 1938. Finally, a little out of place in such distinguished company, the Germans had marked down for closure the PEN Club, the leading literary society serving 'poets, essayists and novelists'. Its premises were far less palatial than those of the other clubs mentioned but the Germans apparently considered that its members made up in influence what they lacked in wealth.

Just as the valets of the leading politicians were expected to act as informants on their employers, so in the clubs another source of tittle-tattle lay ready to hand. 'The club porters', the Gestapo Commandos were advised, 'are often well informed on the private lives of the members.' In this belief the Germans were no doubt right, though nobody seems to have told them that club servants also had a reputation for being the most discreet people in the world. Assuredly the arrival of armed Germans in the hallowed hallways of the Carlton or the Reform would have been ill-received, as a cartoon which had appeared in the *Daily Express* on 10 August 1940 had suggested. 'Waiter', an elderly gentleman, in dark jacket and striped trousers, seated in a club armchair, was saying, as two rather abashed-looking German soldiers waited by the doorway, 'just go and ask those fellows if they're members.'

West End clubmen, displaced from their usual haunts, would no doubt have found a refuge as temporary members in the quarters of clubs which had escaped the Gestapo's attention, the German occupation of their own premises being treated as an extended form of the annual closure for cleaning, but less fortunate would have been some university staff and undergraduates. 'The English universities and colleges', recommended the same official who had urged the seizure of the clubs, 'Oxford, Cambridge, Eton, Harrow, etc., are exceptionally suitable for accommodating SS troops, [offering] large sports grounds, dormitories and community rooms [and a] favourable location.'

The Germans had a particular score to settle with Oxford, which they regarded as a centre of British propaganda between 1914 and 1918 and which 'before the present war started', according to a Gestapo minute, 'began in spring 1939 to work on a new series of Oxford pamphlets against Germany'. The titles of some which had given especial offence—*Mein*

Kampf, The Revision of Versailles, The Law of Force in International Relations—followed with the names of their respective authors, who were clearly marked down for early attention. But Oxford was not the only academic institution on the Nazi black list. Cambridge, despite an excellent record in taking in refugee scientists and even, if the famous Leslie Howard film, *Pimpernel Smith*, were to be believed, in snatching them from under the Nazis' noses, was not mentioned, but the vigilant watchers in Berlin had noted that London University also worked 'closely with the Ministry of Information' (the Ministry had in fact taken over its buildings when the University was evacuated) and that 'Bristol University, of which Churchill is the patron, was also increasingly involved in political activities and drawn into cooperation for propaganda purposes'.

Almost the only place in Great Britain to earn a good mark was Birmingham. 'Good propaganda material in German is published there', the Commando earmarked for the Midlands was told, and it was advised on no account to fail to turn for help (like many more welcome visitors in the past) to 'the Information Bureau of the City of Birmingham in the Council House, a very valuable institute of which little public notice is taken', although it possessed 'vast quantities of statistics' on all matters concerning the city.

Although the immediate aim of the Gestapo swoops was to identify, and appropriately reward, former friends and past enemies of Germany, they had, too, a long-term political aim, to turn up evidence which would embarrass the recent British government and its allies. 'The most pressing task', read one set of instructions prepared within Section III on 26 August, 'is to take possession of the files of the English government and to evaluate them quickly in the light of German foreign policy. The relevant individual tasks in order of importance are:

(a) Clarification of Anglo-American relations with a view to exposing Roosevelt. This group should make every effort to find documentary evidence of Roosevelt's interventionalist policy towards the European war. Question: How has Roosevelt, by giving assurances, etc., contributed to England's stubborn attitude towards the Reich? This material would have to be evaluated immediately for press and propaganda purposes, and possibly fed into the hands of the isolationists. This Group could be based on the Foreign Office.

(b) The obtaining of material on English and American intentions vis-à-vis South America with a view to wrecking Roosevelt's plans for the South American countries.

(c) The obtaining of material for inciting Arabs, Egyptians and Indians.

(d) The clarification of Anglo-Russian relations. Main question: Is Stalin out to swindle us? In this connection, particular importance when making arrests should

Invasion barges, as seen by the RAF

*Oil defences being tried out
the south coast*

19 *The defenders. Winston
Churchill and General Sir Alan
Brooke on the south coast*

*German storm troops
der training*

20 *The attackers. Hitler with
General von Brauchitsch and
Admiral Raeder, on their way
to an invasion conference,
June 1940*

21 *An invasion barge, during an exercise at Calais*

22 *Embarkation exercise at Dieppe, September 1940*

23 *A cliff-scaling exercise on the French co*

24 and 25 *A German p[...]
and a Pan*z*er break-thro[...]
British artist's impressi[...]

26 and 27 *Opposite: A* [...]
crossing exercise, with [...]
boats and German mote[...]
troops on mano[...]

28 *Attack: A pontoon bridge in use in Luxemburg, May 1940*

29 *Defeat: German troops occupying Luxemburg*

be attached to those Englishmen who conducted the Treaty negotiations in Moscow at the time. (Strang, etc.[1])

(e) Clarification of the negotiations of the Balkan countries with England.

The Gestapo posed for its investigators a number of unanswered questions, which confirm that much of its information on Great Britain was sadly out of date. 'Is the Société des Amis de l'Espagne still connected with the Anglo-Spanish Society?' it asked. 'Is the Society Asiatique in Paris still connected with the Royal Asiatic Society, London?' and what was the status of the School of Oriental Studies, a notorious centre of pro-British propaganda during the first world war? These anxieties perhaps reflected a growing interest in Nazi circles about the Far East, possibly even some foreknowledge of the Japanese attack on British possessions there which came a year later. Another Gestapo document dating from this period had referred to the large number of Japanese in England and 'the possibility of Japanese espionage in England via the embassies'. The number of Japanese in the British Isles was, in fact, small —only 2300 at the last census in 1931—but they included one group making a vital contribution to the British livestock industry by practising the arcane craft of chicken-sexing, in which few Englishmen were qualified. Perhaps the Gestapo were unaware of this little-known fact of English agricultural life. Or perhaps, since they proposed to loot most of the country's food, they felt that this tiny Asiatic task force would soon have its own unique contribution to make to the breakfast and dinner tables of the Third Reich.

---

[1] A British mission led by a relatively junior Foreign Office career diplomat (Sir) William Strang had visited Moscow from April to July 1939 to try to secure an Anglo-Russian treaty. Its failure was followed by the Russo-German treaty, the announcement of which on 21 August 1939 had been the prelude to the outbreak of war. Hitler decided in July 1940 to attack Russia and did so on 22 June 1941.

Chapter 11:
To laugh at the Führer
is forbidden

All publications . . . of a nature to prejudice . . . the dignity of the troops of occupation are forbidden.
                                    Ordinance *of the German Occupation Authorities, 1940*

If there was one skill on which the Germans prided themselves besides the waging of war, it was the spreading of propaganda, and the first essential listed in a memorandum sent to Dr Six on 27 September on 'Immediate steps to be taken in the cultural-political sector on the occupation of England' was 'The closure of the Ministry of Information and its dependent organisations'. This was to be followed by 'the closure of the press agencies and information offices (Reuter, Associated Press, Exchange, Central News, etc.) . . . closure of the press archives and libraries of the Ministry and of Parliament' and of the 'newspapers and editorial offices' themselves. Once life was beginning to get back to normal the Germans would surely have reopened at least some of the newspapers, as they did in other countries, since the press was necessary for pro-Nazi propaganda and to inform the population of their lords and masters' latest demands. As they possessed far too few people with an adequate understanding of Great Britain, or even of the English language, to have replaced even the senior editorial staff of the 900 national, regional and local newspapers, what would probably have happened is that only one or two newspapers with a particularly 'bad', i.e. anti-Nazi, record, such as the *News Chronicle*, would have been shut down. The rest would have been allowed to reappear under strict censorship, and on the understanding they would be closed down the instant they failed to toe the Goebbels line. For some papers this would not have meant too drastic a change in policy—*The Times*, for example, when Nazism might still have been crushed, had consistently played down news of German atrocities against the Jews. Most journalists were resigned to having at some time to write against their own convictions, and even against the national interest, when their proprietors required. No doubt they would have resisted the Germans as far as they could but, like everyone else, reporters and feature-writers had their livings to earn and their liberty, such as it was, to preserve.

What seems likely to have happened is that all newspapers would, as far as they were able, have published German orders and communiqués 'straight', without comment, filling the rest of the paper with news of a non-political kind. The quality papers could still have carried 'society' news, including reports of official receptions given by prominent Germans, the popular press could still have filled its columns with gossip about actors and actresses, 'human interest' stories about children and pets, cookery and domestic hints, letters to the editor (strictly avoiding criticism of the Germans) and competitions. Much of the feature material already appearing in British papers, on how to rear your own rabbits or chickens, or to make clothes last longer, would, as the Germans stripped the country bare, have become even more necessary than before. The citizen would soon have needed to know how to repair his own shoes or service his own bicycle merely to survive, and suggestions for games to play, or books to read, in the black-out would have been even more welcome in the Occupied Winter of 1940 than in the Phoney War of 1939. Much space, too, would no doubt have been filled with advertising of the type with which the British public was already beginning to become familiar: 'Go easy with the . . .' or 'If you're lucky enough to find a tin make it last', though companies would have to tone down the promises, common by 1943 and 1944, that ample supplies would again be available on a day not too far ahead. Campaigns like 'Dig for Victory' or 'Watch your fuel target' could have continued, though sometimes under different slogans, and as the newspapers, already much smaller than pre-war, would have shrunk even further, space would still have been at a premium. In the Channel Islands, late in the war, the daily newspapers had shrunk to a single four-page sheet, published on alternate days, despite the arrival of reels of Finnish newsprint, addressed to a Bristol newspaper, which the Germans had somehow acquired. The British Isles, like Jersey and Guernsey, would during an Occupation have had access again to Scandinavian supplies, if the Germans were willing to make shipping available, though cut off from the other main source, Canada.

For the local press the adjustment to Occupation would have been even easier. Most local newspapers had rarely referred to national events and the activities which provided their staple raw material—local court cases, obituaries, weddings, school prize-givings—would have continued, while, if Channel Islands' experience is any guide, one major space-filler would have expanded, in the 'For Sale' and 'Exchange' columns of small advertisements. So long as an editor was discreet he could probably have survived, perhaps soothing his conscience by producing for private circulation an underground newspaper of the type which landed at least one

Channel Islands journalist in gaol. No doubt, too, there would have been minor gestures of defiance, like that of the *Guernsey Star*, which printed German-inspired news in its fifth column, and in the bars where journalists foregathered many stories would have been exchanged about the Germans' ignorance, as when they insisted on a headline in the same newspaper marking the start of the cricket season, 'King Willow returns', being deleted as an illegal, if veiled, reference to the monarchy.

Experience on Jersey provides similar examples of how the Germans exercised control over the local press. When the Jersey *Evening Post* carried a household hint about tightening up a loose hammerhead, the chief censor, a German major, demanded that it be taken out. The item appeared, he pointed out, alongside the words 'Be prepared', in an advertisement advising customers to stock up with 'winter woollies' at a local store, and the two together were clearly an incitement to the population to arm themselves to attack the Occupation forces during the dark nights. The editor had his revenge, however, when the same officer suggested that they might be photographed together. Overcoming his reluctance to be shown in the company of a German, the editor eventually agreed, carrying the photograph next day over the caption '*The Evening Post* is now subject to strict censorship'. This particular censor was an archetypal German officer complete with monocle—the unfortunate editor had sometimes to wait to have his proofs passed while an underling was sent for this vital piece of equipment—and he could not read English, every word that appeared in the paper having to be translated for him.

About the most blatant German propaganda stories not much could be done and they were probably in any case self-defeating, but a far greater problem in the Channel Islands was presented by German attempts to enforce the publication of material reflecting on loyal local residents. On one occasion the Jersey *Evening Post* was ordered to print a report attacking a local doctor who, it was said, after giving first aid to a woman and children injured in a minefield, had refused to drive them to hospital, the German account describing him as 'a disgrace to his profession' who 'ought to be struck off'. The true facts were that, having very little petrol and being on his way to visit other patients, he had suggested that a German doctor, who was also on the scene and had unlimited fuel, should transport the injured family instead. Although the editor was threatened with denunciation to the commandant of the island 'for having refused to take the word of a German officer', he stuck to his guns and was eventually allowed to publish a 'straight' account of the accident.

Despite the seriousness with which they took themselves, the Germans not infrequently provided local newspapers' readers with light relief. One local resident used to cut out particularly absurd items of German news and anti-British stories and paste them in a scrapbook, claiming that they made a good substitute for *Punch*, now unobtainable, though this was doing them more than justice. One such 'joke' declared that 'if you take off an Englishman's dinner jacket, you'll find underneath the same barbarian on whose neck Caesar placed his foot 2000 years ago', while in the same column appeared an extract from a speech promising that 'victory will be German as sure as the sun revolves round the earth', a claim which the delighted population pointed out the Germans had got the wrong way round.

The censors who in turn ruled over the destinies of the *Guernsey Star* and the Guernsey *Evening Press* were also ill-equipped for their demanding job. One of them, who arrived early in 1941, had formerly worked, though in a fairly low-grade post, in a German news agency in London, and spoke excellent English, but he was, in the eyes of one local journalist, a 'cissy' who 'pomaded and powdered himself' and after leaving Guernsey he was found guilty of Black Market offences and embezzlement and sent to gaol. His successor, who needed an interpreter, was far worse, a German Count who had been a founder-member of the Nazi Party and was a dedicated anti-Semite: he even banned the playing on the island of music by composers with Jewish grandparents. He had been badly wounded in North Africa but ignored medical orders not to drink, becoming when intoxicated 'a raving maniac', who wrecked his room and threatened to shoot anyone who came near him. He itched to be in action again, but could only demonstrate his loyalty to his beloved Führer by carrying out his duties as a censor with unintelligent ferocity.

Under these two men the press on Guernsey suffered a long series of acts of interference. Only months after the Germans' arrival they insisted on the editor of the *Star* being replaced because he had run as a front-page lead an appeal to the public to cooperate with the Germans in catching troops who broke into private property, his defence, that he had been ordered to give prominence to official announcements, being rejected. A little later an excellent story, worthy of a place in any London newspaper, about motor vehicles in the shape of Germans' cars and motor-cycles having appeared on Sark for the first time in history, was killed on German orders, and the paper was forbidden to mention that the German Civil Commandant on Sark had been blown up by one of his own land mines. The Germans prevented publication of letters of thanks from local children to a French charitable organisation which had sent them biscuits, an unheard-of luxury by 1942, and cut a whole page containing details of the island's annual budget, since this revealed that six months of Occupation had already cost the citizens of Guernsey £100,000. All this, and the suppression of reports of crimes involving Germans, or the motor accidents in which they were constantly involved, was understandable, but what seemed monstrous to the journalist forced to endure it was the deliberate falsification of a 1941 Christmas message contributed by a local clergyman. The Nazi censor refused to let him either print it as it stood or drop it altogether, so that the parishioners of St Stephen's church were surprised to read, over their vicar's name, that 'the recognition that Christ was born into the world to save the world, and bring peace on earth, is the need of Britain and her Jewish and Bolshevik allies'.

The regulations which the Germans had prepared for use in occupied Britain went even further than those actually enforced in the Channel Islands. One of the orders drafted for issue by the German Commander-in-Chief on arrival warned that 'any insult to the German armed forces or their commanders' was punishable by court-martial, and the Occupation *Ordinances* were even more specific, warning that 'no person shall by word, act, or gesture, conduct himself in a manner insulting to the troops of occupation or to the military colours or insignia'. It was also laid down that 'persons of the occupied country, wearing uniform or belonging to the police, fire brigade, customs and forestry service, shall salute the German colours and officers'. Since British firemen and customs officials were not accustomed to saluting British officers, or the Union Jack, let alone the Swastika, it seems likely that the Germans would either not have enforced the demand or have had to submit to some distinctly unorthodox greetings.

Similarly rigid rules applied to the press, where 'malicious and insulting utterances' ranked with the publication of 'information which may be detrimental to the German Reich', and the *Ordinances* were even more far-reaching:

All newspapers, publications, printed matters . . . writings, pictures, with or without words, music with words or explanation and cinematographic films which are intended for public distribution and are of a nature to prejudice public order or endanger the security or the dignity of the troops of occupation are forbidden and may be seized by order of the Military Commander by the representative of the county. In the case of a daily publication, the representative of the county may order its exclusion from his area for a period of three days. If such publication is published in that area, he may order its suspension for the same period. The action taken will be reported to the Military Commander who . . . may order that any periodical publication which shall offend against this article shall be suspended or excluded from the occupied territory for a period not exceeding three months . . . [and it] may, in the event of a subsequent offence, be suspended or excluded . . . for an indefinite period.

A three-day suspension would have cost a daily newspaper dear, a three-month one would have been sufficient to ruin any but the very richest, but this was only the start, for the military authorities could also order the closing for up to three months of any shop which, however innocently, had offered the paper for sale, or any library which had put it on display. The ordinary newsagent could hardly have been blamed had he played for safety and ceased stocking a newspaper with a reputation for sailing too close to the wind, while all those concerned in newspaper production had the greatest incentive of all not to fall foul of the law for, in addition to the paper being put out of business, not merely the author of an offending article but the 'editors, publishers or printers' who had handled it could 'also be prosecuted and convicted for their participation in such a publication or for their negligence'.

Nor was this the end of the hazards confronting an editor, for he was required to display in his columns any official announcement 'in such a manner as may be specified', although the space would be paid for. The Germans also arrogated to themselves a power for which many a mis-represented British politician or government department must often have sighed in vain. If any incorrect statement should appear, space had to be provided to carry a correction free.

Perhaps misled by the shady past of their own leaders, the Germans apparently believed that they had only to kick hard enough at the doors of British cupboards for sufficient skeletons to tumble out, not merely to discredit the aristocracy—everyone knew already what *they* were like—but even respectable trade union officials of impeccable working-class background. 'Documents' should be unearthed by the Gestapo when it reached England, urged a note prepared in Berlin on 26 August, 'for internal political propaganda in England. The aim: hastening of internal collapse by "exposure" of the English upper circles, including the ambi-tious Labour leaders [for example, by] (publication of their share-holdings, estates, etc., e.g. Sir Stafford Cripps' seat, "Goodfellow" in Filkins). Basis: Paper by Giselher Wirsing, *100 Families Rule the Empire* . . . Pillorying of prosperous trade-union leaders, such as Sir Walter Citrine and others.' Another suggestion, following 'discussions with people from Berlin, Munich, etc., who are knowledgeable about England' was put forward a few days later. 'Equip some groups with cameras', advised its author, 'as photographic reporting [is] important for propa-ganda. [Contrast] slums and distressed area of London, luxurious country seats and castles of the plutocratic Labour leaders, etc.'—though no addresses were given for these mythical residences. And if the present generation proved scandal-proof at least their ancestors' reputations could be besmirched, material, it was suggested, being sought in the Public Record Office, but 'above all [in] the family records, scattered over the stately homes of England and Scotland, e.g. papers belonging to the Chamberlains'. Curiously, although the Marlboroughs, like most ducal families, had had their share of scandals, no mention was made of Winston Churchill or his forbears.

Far more important to the British public than the press during the summer of 1940 had been the BBC which, during the war, enjoyed a prestige never equalled before or since, and the Security Services placed the taking-over of transmitters and broadcasting studios higher up their 'cultural commandos'' list of duties than seizing the newspaper offices. Also, while journalists, subject to good behaviour, could retain their jobs, the appointment of 'all radio announcers and all men and women holding a responsible position in the broadcasting system' was subject to German approval, and they could 'be removed from office . . . if such action seems advisable for any reasons, or when such official fails or refuses to conform to the Orders of the Military Commander'. If they had any more detailed plans for the BBC, these have not come to light; nor have BBC plans to cope with a German take-over. Presumably the British government would in the closing stages of a successful invasion have done its best to destroy both studios and transmitters, but before long it seems likely that some form of state broadcasting service would have been back on the air, with a German censor vetting every script; live broadcasting was in 1940 still the rule, though a few programmes were recorded on transmission for repeating later.

One man then serving in the BBC was Frank Gillard, an ex-school-master who was soon to become nationally known as a war correspondent and later rose to be Director of Sound Broadcasting. 'The BBC would still have been there, but under German direction', he believes, 'and many of the old familiar BBC voices . . . would still have been speaking to us. Great pressure would have been brought on many of the leading broadcasters and they might have had to make the agonising decision between collaboration with the Germans and suffering persecution, or even elimination – and perhaps their families, too. The Germans would have had it pretty much their own way, and it would have been very difficult indeed to resist them.' He recalls colleagues remarking to him in 1940 that if the Germans arrived at Broadcasting House—whether in Bristol, where much of the BBC was then evacuated, or in London—they saw no option except to do what they were told.

This was a rational attitude. Perhaps in the early days a few heroes might have shouted patriotic slogans into the microphone before the censor sitting in the central continuity suite or the studio control cubicle could take them off the air, but such gestures would have served little purpose. Once the country had been overrun, covert resistance was likely to be far more effective than open opposition, which, in this case, apart from removing one loyal Briton from the scene, might perhaps have led to broadcasting being closed down altogether for several days or weeks. This would have been a far greater deprivation to the British public than to the Germans, who would no doubt already have appropriated the best wavelengths for their own use, perhaps converting the second programme launched earlier in the year into the German Forces programme, with its own announcers and material, like the American Forces Network of later in the war.

The BBC would, Frank Gillard believes, have been the main instrument for making the population accept Occupation. 'The Germans' aim', he considers, 'would have been to brainwash us into a docile, utterly subservient nation, deeply aware of our faults, deeply contrite for them, and entirely responsive to the new leadership which the Germans were giving us. I once asked the editor of a totalitarian newspaper for his definition of news. And his answer was, "News is that which enables the will of the government to prevail". And that's exactly the principle on which the Germans would have worked. Every word, every line, every article that reached us would have been designed to serve their purposes. The old familiar newspapers and magazines and journals would have appeared just as they had done previously and authenticity would have been given to them, I think, by the fact that many of the old journalists would have continued to work for them, some perhaps because they genuinely believed in the German principles. After all we did have journalists before the war who wrote in praise of Hitler and Mussolini. Others would have worked for the Germans because they felt that the country had been through enough trials and tribulations already, and they felt it was their duty now to try and help us settle in the new regime. There would still have been the BBC—but under totally new control and totally new management. . . . It would all have been smoothly done, insidiously done and deadly deadly dangerous.'

One of the first *Orders* to be issued by the Military Government was for the surrender of all wireless transmitters, and the prospects that any effective alternative to the German-controlled BBC could have been put on the air from illegal transmitters seem extremely slight. Despite Hollywood films like *Freedom Radio*, in which heroic resistance men (and, this being Hollywood, attractive women) broadcast stirring calls to defy the invader, from under the very noses of the Nazi detector vans, no 'under-

ground' broadcasting occurred in the Channel Islands or, on any significant scale, in any occupied country. Frank Gillard believes that 'we would
in Britain have seen the springing up of clandestine broadcasting stations
using small mobile lash-up transmitters, moved from place to place, but
my own belief is that, brave as the effort would have been, it would not
have been very effective, because the range of these stations is only
limited, their appearance on the air would have been only spasmodic and
the Germans could easily have controlled them. A powerful occupying
force, if it's ruthless enough and determined enough, can suppress underground newspapers and underground broadcasting. In the course of the
war the only use of underground radio in Europe I encountered was in
Holland, where the resistance workers at Eindhoven built a high-
powered broadcasting transmitter in different parts of the big Philips
factory and on the day of their liberation they brought all these different
sections together and joined them up and went on the air to speak to their
fellow countrymen. But they couldn't possibly have brought that transmitter into operation before the Germans had been cleared out.' If there
had been underground stations 'coming on the air sporadically and then
going off again', they would, Frank Gillard is convinced, have amounted
to 'little more than a gesture of resistance'.

It has sometimes been supposed that the Germans would immediately
have seized all the radio receivers, usually known then as 'wireless sets',
in the country, but no such intention is mentioned in the Military Government *Orders* and such an act seems highly unlikely. All receivers were
indeed impounded in the Channel Islands in November 1940, but this
was a mass punishment due, one Guernsey man believed at the time, 'to
local people telling English-speaking Germans our news, who pass it on
to their pals', and the sets were returned after only six weeks, on Christmas Eve, 'the pleasantest Christmas gift imaginable'. They were seized
again, this time for good, in June 1942, after which possession of a set
could land one, at the very least, in gaol for three months. The reason for
the seizure, however, was that the BBC had announced that it would be
giving people in the occupied countries instructions over the air on how
to harass the Germans in preparation for the Second Front, which Hitler
had always anticipated might begin in the Islands.

The situation in England if the Germans had occupied the British Isles
in 1940 would have been totally different, for they would then have won
the war and the BBC would have been under Nazi control. Many sets
could, of course, pick up foreign stations and some even America—
'twiddling the knob' and boasting of the results had been a popular prewar hobby—but reception, in the face of German jamming, would have

been poor, even if 'free' British transmitters were set up in Malta and Gibraltar. On the whole, therefore, it seems likely that the value to the Germans of having at their command such a powerful medium of propaganda, reaching the whole population, would have outweighed the knowledge that a minority would, if sets were not called in, listen to foreign stations. Later, if an attack by Commonwealth and American Forces had become a real possibility, the Germans might have confiscated sets, as in Jersey and Guernsey, though it would have been a formidable job, for apart from nearly nine million officially licensed there were probably at least another half-million licence evaders, of whose ownership of a set no record existed.

As with the press, the change required to produce radio programmes acceptable to the Germans would not, perhaps, have been as great as might at first be supposed. Prewar BBC broadcasting, at least until Sir John Reith's departure in 1938, had been in spirit essentially 'conformist' to the attitudes of the then British government, it had largely avoided 'awkward' or controversial subjects, and its news and current affairs coverage had been, by later standards, both dull and inadequate. The outbreak of war had brought, after the disastrous first fortnight, immense improvements in every part of the output, and especially in the frequency and liveliness of news bulletins and news commentaries, while the old 'stuffiness' had gone for ever. If the Germans had taken over the BBC, however, they would not have found any insuperable difficulty in imposing upon the schedules that spirit of dull pomposity prevailing in their own broadcasting services. Many BBC programmes might well have continued. The news and 'postscripts' would still have been heard, though now based on German communiqués or delivered by German spokesmen, and there would certainly have been no lack of music, in whose virtues Hitler was a great believer. 'Broadcasts to Britain', he had advised at one time, 'must contain plenty of music of the kind that is popular among Britons. . . . In this way, when their own transmitting stations starve them of music, they will acquire the habit of listening in more and more to the concerts we broadcast for them.' The German-British Broadcasting Corporation, or whatever name the BBC would have been given under its new rulers, would not, one assumes, have been troubled by restrictions on 'needle-time' (the total number of hours of gramophone records which the musicians' organisations allow to be broadcast each week) and the British music-lover would probably have been better off under the Occupation than before, especially if he enjoyed the work of composers on whom the Führer had conferred the accolade of personal approval, such as Bruckner, Mozart, and, above all, Wagner. Brahms would probably have been heard less often as Hitler thought him overrated, while, on the basis of Channel Islands' experience, Jewish composers, notably Mendelssohn, might have vanished altogether from the schedules.

A more marked effect of the Occupation on BBC programmes would have appeared in the field of light entertainment. *ITMA* could hardly have continued to be broadcast now that 'That Man' had triumphed and there were men speaking like Fünf, and nearly as stupid, in every Town Hall, while anti-German jokes, which in 1940 played so large a part in many variety programmes, would have had to be hunted down and deleted from every script. But, provided the Germans did not object to gags about rationing and shortages, the other staple comic subject of the time, the comedians could no doubt have managed without too much difficulty.

The departments responsible for *Music while you Work*, which would have been more necessary than ever if Britain had lost the war, being perhaps privately renamed by some exploited citizen *Music while you Work for the Germans*, and for commissioning dance bands to play on the air, would also have had to adjust themselves to the new conditions. In the Channel Islands guests attending a dance which ended in the singing of 'We're Going to Hang out the Washing on the Siegfried Line' were arrested, but a local dance band managed to adopt as its signature tune, 'The World is Waiting for the Sunrise', without the Germans realising the double meaning, and a jazz version of 'There'll Always be an England' was very popular, though this had of course to be a non-vocal number. Most of the titles popular in the autumn of 1940 were, as it happened, non-political, and even the Germans could surely not have objected to 'If I had my way, dear', or 'A Nightingale sang in Berkeley Square', though they might have raised objections, on account of its title, to a top tune of October 1940, 'I'm Stepping out with a Memory Tonight'. Another hazard were songs that seemed to the Germans disrespectful to the military profession and in the Channel Islands 'Kiss me goodnight, sergeant major' was banned on this account. With patriotic titles forbidden, it seems possible that some non-political song might have been adopted as a substitute national anthem, though what it might have been one can only speculate. Perhaps some tribute to the English or Scottish countryside, such as 'Linden Lea' or 'Loch Lomond', might have been chosen, perhaps some totally frivolous song, like 'I've Got Sixpence', a veiled reference to the superiority of British coinage to German occupation marks, perhaps some traditional tune which had acquired unofficial words, like 'Colonel Bogey', which later in the war, if tradition is to be believed, was whistled by British prisoners of war as a gesture of contempt for their Japanese captors.[1]

The Nazis had been pioneers in the use of the film for propaganda purposes and some of their early works are still regarded, on technical grounds, as classics. In all the occupied countries cinemas were allowed to remain open, both for indoctrinating the population and to provide harmless amusement, though cinema-going was, of course, curtailed by the curfew which made it illegal to be on the streets after a fixed hour, usually in Jersey 9 or 10 pm, by rationing of electricity and, most of all, by the shortage of new films. In the Channel Islands the population had to make do with the few titles already there, until everyone was heartily sick of the sight of *The Barratts of Wimpole Street*, George Formby in *Keep Fit*, and Fred Astaire in *Top Hat*. The British Isles, with its own film industry, and a far wider range of releases already going round the circuits, would have been better off, though films about the British forces, or (like many productions of the period) pouring scorn on the Germans would obviously have been impounded at once.

The machinery for controlling the cinema and live theatrical performances was very similar to that affecting the press. Not merely the producers and distributors of offending items were liable to be punished, but the premises where they were shown could be closed down for three months, the manager or proprietor of the cinema being personally liable to imprisonment. There was one other pitfall for the cinema manager. In Article VII of the *Ordinance* governing public performances, with a hypocrisy surely unique in history, the Germans proclaimed themselves as guardians of the public morals. 'Whenever the authorities shall consider that a film shall be such as to be injurious to morals, they shall inform the delegate of the Military Commander', in other words, the propaganda chief for the district. 'The delegate may, if agreeing with the opinion, forbid immediately either the exhibition of the film wholly or in part or the admission of young persons under eighteen years of age. The Military

---

[1] 'Colonel Bogey' seems a strong candidate on two grounds. As anyone who had been in the Army, and many civilians, knew, a distinctly coarse expression ('B——! And the same to you') was commonly sung to its opening bars, like a more elaborate bawdy rhyme, composed during the war, which ingeniously insulted the four leading Nazis with, so far as is known, no justification in fact:

> 'Hitler has only got one ball,
> Göring's, it's said, are rather small,
> Himmler's are somewhat similar,
> and Goballs has no balls,
> At all.'

Commander may maintain or cancel the decision of the delegate or may order that the same measures be applied to such film throughout the occupied country.' This rule was never in fact applied on British soil, perhaps because a chaste lack of realism was still the order of the day in British pictures, while the Hays Office in the United States was busy rooting out even the mildest of bedroom scenes or bad language, but a few years later the German censors would surely have had their hands full.

If the British Isles had been occupied in September 1940 imports of films from the United States, which was still officially neutral, would presumably have continued, though with war films conspicuous by their absence. Westerns, musicals and gangster films—encouraged by the Germans as demonstrating the decadence of the United States—might still have flowed in, and there would have been no shortage of British films which the Germans were likely to find harmless—among them *The Gang's All Here, Jamaica Inn, The Lambeth Walk, Goodbye Mr Chips* and *Where's that Fire?* The proportion of war films being produced in the autumn of 1940 was relatively small, and the British film industry could, if required to do so, have stepped up its output of light-weight films to replace all productions of a more serious kind, so that one of the minor horrors of the Occupation might have been more cinemas offering films featuring 'Old Mother Riley' and the 'Crazy Gang'. True to the policy of impugning prewar British governments (not a very difficult task) the Germans would also surely have raised no objections to *The Stars Look Down*, showing exploitation of the miners, or *Love on the Dole*, about the Depression in Lancashire.

For the cinema-owner the main worry would have concerned not what was appearing on the screen but what was happening in the audience. During the first year of the war the British cinema-going public had become accustomed to responding to programmes with unaccustomed animation. Hitler was always good for a hiss, a British pilot for a round of applause, and a unit of goose-stepping German soldiers for a raucous laugh or loudly-voiced comments such as 'You forgot to take your coat-hanger out, mate!' Although a German victory would have removed from the screen feature-films and newsreels in which the British were the heroes, the Germans would certainly have included in programmes newsreels and propaganda 'shorts' of their own, sometimes, if experience in the Channel Islands is a guide, with English subtitles, written in what was meant to be a colloquial style, by a German who had learned his English in America. The results were often hilarious and a determined humorist could easily ruin, too, the dramatic climaxes of the most solemn film. A classic example occurred in Guernsey, where the bread was barely eatable, prompting one man to shout out as a German war film showed two soldiers standing sadly by the grave of their fallen comrade: 'The poor b—— probably died of indigestion!' Such pleasantries were well received by the audience, but not by the Germans who, in the Channel Islands, often had a block of seats reserved for them and who at any 'anti-German demonstration', such as untimely applause or laughter, ordered the lights to be turned up and the audience to leave. After a few such occasions, even if no further penalties followed, the entertainment-starved population would no doubt have preferred to keep their reactions to themselves, anyone who did try to interrupt being 'shushed' into silence by his neighbours.

But one type of programme if shown in Britain (it does not seem to have been seen in the Channel Islands) would surely have proved too much for even the most long-suffering audience. The Germans had produced a series of anti-Semitic 'shorts', the one most commonly shown in occupied Europe having only a one-line commentary and thus being easily dubbed for use in any country. It consisted of only two scenes. The first was a long shot of a bare, ugly corridor, down which came tumbling some forty rats, the ugliest, dirtiest, most vicious-looking specimens imaginable. The film then 'mixed' through to a precisely matching shot of a similar road, down which a band of ragged, half-starved, bedraggled Jews were shuffling under the orders of some unseen figure, glancing furtively towards the camera out of the corner of their eyes, the visual comparison being underlined by a guttural German voice remarking 'The Jews are the rats of Europe'. Whatever success this example of the German film-makers' art may have had in other countries, it is not hard to imagine its reception in Britain. The pictures of the maltreated Jews would undoubtedly have provoked sympathy, not disgust, while the sequence showing the rats would assuredly have been greeted with cries of 'Here come the Germans', 'Look out for Adolf' and the like until even the most obstinate local propaganda chief withdrew the film from circulation.

One excellent change which the Germans would certainly have imposed in British cinemas would have been to apply their own 'No smoking' rule in cinemas. It might briefly have become patriotic (though disagreeable to one's neighbours) to defy the new law, but, with tobacco scarce, it seems likely that it would have needed only two or three occasions when a German policeman hauled out the culprits and ground their precious cigarettes under his heel—as happened in Guernsey—to force even the most besotted addicts to toe the new line. The public would, too, surely have rapidly accepted, as they did in the Channel Islands, the mysterious transformation of the 'Exit' signs into notices reading 'Ausgang', and of the familiar 'Ladies' and 'Gents' into 'Damen' and 'Herren'.

Conforming to the regulations for the theatre, which were similar to those for the cinema, is unlikely to have presented the acting profession with much problem, for already the emphasis on the London stage was on undemanding comedy and revue, and these, with topical references deleted, could have continued. Of plays which had recently opened, only *Thunder Rock*, with its message of a better world after the war, seems likely to have incurred the Germans' displeasure. In the provinces most productions were revivals of old favourites, safely remote from contemporary events, and once the actors became accustomed to seeing Germans in uniform in the audience, and to dispensing with 'God Save the King', there was no reason why the theatre should not have continued to exist, Occupation being less discouraging to audiences than a blitz.

The Germans did, however, take very seriously the control of even the amateur theatre, which, as there was no resident professional company, flourished in the Channel Islands during the war. One keen local actor was astonished when the German propaganda chief in Jersey refused permission for his company to perform the three Noël Coward one-act plays known jointly as *Tonight at 8.30* because one of them, *Red Peppers*, included as a 'play within a play' two sailors singing a nautical song. This might, it was suggested, incite the audience to burst into 'Rule Britannia'. The same German's reaction when this actor appeared in *The Merchant of Venice* was even more unreasonable. 'He was very angry and literally foamed at the mouth', the former Shylock remembers, declaring that he was 'sympathetic to the Jews' and that the play was an attack on German policy. It was in vain that the actor explained that the play had been put on because a local school were studying it as a 'special subject' for a coming examination and that 'it never entered our heads that *The Merchant* was any different to any other Shakespeare play'. He was eventually ordered by the Germans to write an article for the Jersey *Evening Post* on 'Shylock as I see him', to which he agreed on condition it appeared unaltered, but it was never published.

One of the first warnings to the world of the barbarian nature of the Nazi regime had been the famous public 'burning of the books' which they had organised, a sizeable blaze since they objected to most of the world's great literature which was neither pro-German nor anti-Semitic. Although each local commander was free to indulge his own prejudices, the basic black list used on Guernsey covered fifty authors, among them such non-political names as Dennis Wheatley, E. Phillips Oppenheim and Peter Cheyney, as well as more predictable offenders such as Winston

Churchill, Duff Cooper (a particular target of German hostility) and H. G. Wells. No raids on private libraries seem to have occurred, but public lending libraries and bookshops were all ordered to surrender copies of the forbidden books, and of others referring critically to Hitler and the Nazis. One employee of Boots the Chemists in St Helier, which, as in many towns, also operated a branch of Boots Booklovers Library, still remembers the occasion:

The job was loaded on to me and with the help of the staff I sorted out something like 400 volumes – the number amazed me. In due course I packed these in wooden cases and got a horse and cart [the Germans had appropriated virtually all motor transport] and took them up to Sonder-Führer Hohl [the German propaganda-chief on Jersey] . . . deposited them on his doorstep and then knocked on the door and asked for a receipt. He seemed a bit bewildered . . . it's quite a lot, 400 volumes dumped on your doorstep, and he asked me what it was all about. I told him that they . . . all had references to Hitler in them. I placed one on top and I showed him. I said 'Look, it says here "Hitler is a cow".' He blew up at once and I said, 'I haven't said it, it's in the book. This is what it says in the book, not me. Please sign the receipt', which he did. I never knew what happened to the books. . . . I don't know whether they were sent out of the island or whether they were burnt or what.

Similar scenes would have been enacted all over the British Isles had the culture-loving Germans arrived, and the thought of some large, humourless German standing in a small Chain Library branch earnestly thumbing through piles of romances in search of some slighting reference to his countrymen is not unamusing, as well as providing for the subscribers an object-lesson in what Occupation really meant.

Chapter 12:
How long is a Crayfish?

All members of the armies of occupation and their families are forbidden to fish by
any means whatever unless in possession of an authorisation or a fishing permit.

Occupation Ordinances, *1940*

While in the summer of 1940 scores of his countrymen at Army headquarters were engaged in the congenial task of planning how to enslave
yet another country, one dedicated lawyer or bureaucrat somewhere in
the Reich was busy on a task hardly less agreeable to any true German,
devising pettifogging regulations. Of all the ninety pages of the draft
Occupation *Ordinances*, none reveals more vividly the obsession of the
Germans with the most trivial details affecting the lives of their conquered
subjects than the four devoted to *Fishery Rights*. A 'fishery officer' was,
the anonymous draftsman laid down, to be 'appointed by the commander' of each Corps area, 'to negotiate with the authorities of the
occupied country' and 'members of the armies of occupation shall have
the right to fish on condition that they shall have obtained from the
Military Commander the authorisation to apply for a fishing permit'.
This authorisation was to be presented to the 'owner or tenant of the
fishery rights', who was 'bound in all cases to issue a fishing permit,
either by amicable agreement, or failing such, by way of requisition,
except in the case of closed waters, that is to say, artificial breeding
grounds, fish-breeding establishments, portions of water-courses of
which the communication with other water-courses, lakes or ponds is
barred by grating, nets or weirs to keep the fish which have reached the
size demanded by law'. All very sensible, no doubt, to prevent over-
fishing, but perhaps a little over-elaborate considering that not a single
German angler had yet had the chance to cast greedy eyes over a single
British trout-stream.

The rest of the *Ordinances* on this subject bear out this impression.
Although they had never followed in international affairs the principle of
throwing back the smaller fry—Luxembourg could hardly be considered
a very big catch, for example—the Germans were sticklers for piscatorial
etiquette in this respect and solemnly laid down the 'minimum measure-
ments' under Occupation law which qualified a fish to be kept and eaten.
Salmon had to be fifty-three centimetres long, river trout eighteen, perch

fifteen, while it was even an offence against the dignity of the Reich for one not to return to the water a crayfish under eight centimetres in length.

Although carefully set out in English and German, with an appendix explaining the British system of local government, many of the *Ordinances* seem to have been drafted by someone who knew nothing of the British Isles or had some other place in his mind. The rules concerning *Hunting Rights*, for example, are spelt out in even more detail than those for fishing, and occupy four times as much room as the postal regulations. 'Forestry officials', it is laid down, 'may be allowed to shoot over state preserves', a significant statement in Westphalia, perhaps, but of doubtful value in England. The main purpose of the rules was, however, clear enough. The Germans were to have the run of every covert or grouse moor in the country, subject to forming themselves into officially approved shooting-clubs and coming to terms with the landowner concerned, though 'when all attempts at an amicable agreement shall have failed, the preserves shall be placed at the disposal of the German armies by way of requisition'. Here, too, the framers of the law had gone into fantastic detail, providing, for example, that the agreement could be terminated 'in case of transfer of the majority of the members of the club to another garrison or if, in consequence of negligence or complicity on the part of the gamekeepers, there shall have been a considerable decrease in game as the result of poaching'. The Germans, it is clear, had tried to think of everything, even the possibility of the local poachers getting to 'their' pheasants and partridges first—and of the gamekeeper for once turning a blind eye to their activities.

While the German Army was in this somewhat elephantine way imposing restrictions on freedom to kill game—though it recognised no close season for the shooting of human beings—the Gestapo was making far simpler plans to deal with other types of recreation. The Germans had had some success before the war in using international sporting events as a means of establishing contacts with other countries, a process which had reached its climax in 1936 with the holding of the Olympic Games in Berlin, but those dim-witted, athletic dupes of the Germans who had argued that 'sport was above politics' were in, when the invaders arrived, for a nasty shock. Armed with an academic thesis by some obscure German researcher on the subject of 'Sport in England', the 'commandos' expecting to leave shortly for London were instructed on 29 August that among the 'immediate measures' to be taken on their arrival were 'the suspension of the activities of all sports clubs, closure and seizure of the large sporting associations and of the branches of the Olympic Committee [and] confiscation of sports equipment'. What precisely the Germans had in mind was not stated, but it is probable that it was team games which were their real target, rather than private amusements like golf and tennis, since these not merely offered a ready-made framework for resistance, but also assembled crowds of spectators, who might engage in anti-German demonstrations. Even so the proposal seems strangely short-sighted, for the opportunity to take part in, or watch, sporting events would have provided a useful safety-valve. But this apparently did not trouble the Germans, and among their 'important targets' the Gestapo included not merely 'denominational and Jewish sports organisations', but also 'large sports associations, the Football Association, etc.'. No reference was made to local, amateur football league matches and similar activities, and these would probably have been permitted as they were in the Channel Islands.

The Gestapo were less concerned about the most traditional of indoor recreations, since this was an activity which only involved two people at a time, but the Army had not forgotten it. Its lawyers seem to have been under the strange impression that in Great Britain, as in some continental countries, there were 'licensed houses' registered for prostitution, instead of strictly illegal establishments whose existence, at least officially, was unknown even to the police. To the German mind, however, since one country possessed brothels all must possess them and the 'Civil Authority', to whom most of their orders were addressed, meaning the mayor of a town or the chairman of an urban or rural district council, would, had the Germans arrived, have found himself facing the embarrassing requirement to 'prepare without delay a list of:

1. All brothels in the district administered by him, with the names of the inmates.

2. The names and addresses of all known prostitutes, not living in brothels.

3. The names and addresses of all women known to be suffering from Venereal Disease.'

In view of the Germans' passion for carrying out the law to the letter, it seems unlikely that a mere 'nil return' would have sufficed, and the preparation of the required information might have given a certain amount of amusement to the local government officials deputed to assemble it if nothing else. It would, however, have been no laughing matter for the girls concerned, for the military commander was authorised to 'appoint officers especially to supervise the sanitary police regulations to be exercised by the Civil Authority', and, unaware of the furore caused half a century before when attempts had been made to enforce very similar laws in garrison towns in England, the Germans proposed, in their high-handed way, to brand as a prostitute 'any woman whose usual place of abode is outside the zone of occupation present therein without any visible means of support', and 'any woman who solicits or has illicit sexual intercourse with any person being a member of the army of occupation'. The German 'vice squad' were also to 'see that the measures taken by the Civil Authorities are not designed to prejudice, and do not in practice affect, the dignity or safety of the troops of Occupation'. There were, in other words, to be no conspicuous notices in English High Streets reading 'This brothel is for German troops only'.

The queues of officers and men outside their separate brothels was in fact one of the sights of Occupation in the Channel Islands, the establishments being staffed by local girls reinforced by others from France— 'very attractive', one local man remembers—the occupants, to the wry amusement of other Channel Islanders, being classed for rationing purposes as 'heavy workers'. The French girls were needed because too few local women volunteered for the job, but eventually some of them became redundant. One Jersey physiotherapist remembers being called on, as a qualified male nurse, to give injections at a local brothel, staffed by twenty girls under a French madame, until told that his services would not be needed in future as it was being closed down due to amateur competition from 'collaborators and local girls'. The scenes witnessed in London, Ipswich and elsewhere after the arrival of the Americans later in the war— though these were, of course, allies—suggest that in England, too, 'Jerrybags' would not have been unknown, especially if the Germans had, as they threatened, deported the whole younger male population to the Continent.

Experience in other countries also suggests that, once the immediate danger of revolt was over and their machinery for plundering the country had been set up, the Germans would have encouraged the resumption of a life as near to normal as possible, and this conclusion is borne out by a detailed study of both the military commanders' *Orders* and the Occupation *Ordinances*. Even the initial *Announcement regarding Occupied Territories* to be posted immediately the Germans arrived had ordered, as already mentioned, that 'all businesses, trade undertakings and banks are to remain open', and pegged prices at the prevailing level. Von Brauchitsch's *Directive for Military Government*, which contained dire threats as to what would happen to anyone resisting the Germans and made dark references to the taking of hostages, also promised that 'Laws of the country operative prior to the occupation will be upheld unless they are contradictory to the purpose of the occupation'. The Germans seem, in fact, to have envisaged several separate legal systems existing side by side. German troops, and the civilians who followed them, were to be subject solely to German military law, as was any British citizen aiding and abetting a German engaging in crime, and also outside the jurisdiction and protection of the British courts was any British citizen who committed any offence against the German troops, or Occupation authorities, and whom the Germans asked should be handed over to them. This would, no doubt, have happened to anyone charged with serious offences such as sabotage or spying and, if they behaved in England as in the Channel Islands, the German courts would also have dealt with people who failed to show proper respect to the occupying forces. In Guernsey this included that splendid woman subsequently nicknamed 'Mrs Churchill', who refused to say 'Heil Hitler' when offered her sweet at dinner-time in the German-occupied hotel where she worked, replying 'To hell with Hitler for a rice pudding—and made of skimmed milk at that!' a gesture which earned her six months in gaol.

With these exceptions, and the private undercover activities of the Gestapo, which are nowhere mentioned in the official literature, it was intended that the whole elaborate machinery of British justice should carry on as in peacetime though the Germans proposed to add an additional storey to the existing structure, with a new 'High Court', consisting of two German lawyers, one of whom would preside, and one British lawyer. To this court anyone who had been engaged in a civil action could 'if he considers he has suffered from a miscarriage of justice . . . appeal'. This innovation would obviously have been popular with unsuccessful litigants, who had nothing to lose by appealing and to whom the Germans, eager to impress the public with the excellence of German justice, would probably have been indulgent.

The very first article of the occupation *Ordinances* laid down that 'the ordinances of the military commander shall have the force of law and on publication shall be recognised as such by the German [authorities] and by the authorities of the occupied country', and it was infringements of minor regulations promulgated in this way which would have presented British courts with their greatest problem. Major offences the Germans would have dealt with themselves so that no British court would have been asked to condemn a fellow countryman to death for sabotage, but a British magistrate, or jury, might well have been called on to fine someone who had scribbled 'Down with the Nazis' on a poster, or guests who had rounded off a wedding reception by singing 'God save the King'. There were many such incidents in the Channel Islands, mainly concerning the illegal possession of radio sets, or the chalking up of the 'V' sign, and in July 1941 the Jersey authorities even offered a £25 reward for 'information leading to the conviction of anyone . . . for the offence of marking on any gate, wall or other place whatsoever visible to the public the letter 'V' or any other sign or any word or words calculated to offend the German authorities or soldiers'.

If the courts would have been at least as busy as in peacetime, so too would the Town Hall and municipal offices. The Germans laid upon the head of the local civil authority the task of operating the whole complicated machinery of the non-military aspects of the Occupation. He was, they declared, 'personally responsible for the performance of the duties assigned to him in any regulations issued by the German military authority and for the observance of civil laws and of military regulations on the part of the community administered by him'. If the Germans demanded billets or bicycles, it was the mayor and his staff who had to find them; if they wanted a list of Jews, or Freemasons, or Jehovah's Witnesses, a harmless sect which the Nazis had singled out for persecution, he had to provide it; if they demanded that the town's sports grounds be reserved for German use, or ploughed up to grow food, or be renamed 'The Adolf Hitler Memorial Park', he had to try to satisfy them. A good mayor and, perhaps even more, a good town clerk, since it was on him and his staff that the day-to-day burden of carrying out the German orders rested, was likely before long to be unpopular all round. The Germans would call him obstructive; his fellow-countrymen would accuse him of being 'too soft towards the Germans', if not actually collaborating.

The most senior public figure in the British Isles actually to face the problem of walking the tightrope between futile opposition to the Germans and active collaboration with them was Alexander, now Lord, Coutanche, formerly Bailiff (i.e. Prime Minister) of Jersey. Lord Coutanche had been born on the island but had trained as a barrister in England and served in the British Army in France during the first world war, later returning to the island and rising to the post of Attorney-General. When the Germans arrived he was forty-eight, not an age at which it is easy to adjust to totally new conditions, but he had no doubt where his duty lay. 'I considered my orders were contained in the letter from the Home Office which instructed me to assume the office of governor', recalls Lord Coutanche. 'My instructions were that I would do the best for the people of the island whether I could get instructions from London or not. That I regarded as the orders of my King . . . I hope I carried them out as intended.'

The situation on Jersey was very different from what it would have been on the mainland, for the Bailiff had been formally appointed governor, his predecessor having been ordered to leave with the departing British troops, and the German Commandant who moved in at Government House, the Buckingham Palace of Jersey, issued a proclamation that 'such legislation as, in the past, required the sanction of His Britannic Majesty in Council for its validity, shall henceforth be valid on being approved by the German Commandant and thereafter sanctioned by the Bailiff of Jersey'. Some similar device would have had to be adopted by the Reichs Kommissar in London, though strictly speaking everything that happened once the King and the government he appointed had gone would have been illegal. The Parliament of Jersey, 'the States', could legally have met but the Bailiff decided that to summon it to debate legislation would be too slow and cumbrous a process, so that Jersey was ruled during the Occupation by a Council of eleven men, who met weekly, the Bailiff himself, the two law officers and eight 'presidents' in charge of the main departments of the Council, though the states could still, Lord Coutanche has pointed out, 'abolish us at any time and resume the government'. Wisely, it may be felt, it did not do so and Lord Coutanche himself has no doubt, looking back a generation later, that 'the record of Jersey and the Channel Islands during the German occupation was an honourable one', a judgment with which most Channel Islanders, who still feel a deep respect and admiration for their wartime leader, would agree.

In the Channel Islands most people knew the leading citizens who were acting as a buffer between them and the Germans at least by sight, but in many British towns even the name of the mayor and councillors is often unknown to most of the population and here the unpopularity of carrying out the Germans' orders would have fallen upon the local authority's employees. The Germans recognised themselves that obstruction by these permanent officials would be at least as serious as opposition by the elected councillors, and the Occupation *Ordinances* threatened to 'remove from office any official . . . when such official fails or refuses to conform to the Orders of the Military Commander', although 'definite or specific charges in writing' were to be served upon him and he was to be given the chance to submit a defence. If his plea failed he would lose his job and, once out of work, the offending Town Clerk or Borough Treasurer or administrative officer in the Education Department would not have found it easy to find another appointment, for the Germans reserved the right to 'veto the appointment of any official designated to serve in the occupied territories if, in the opinion of the Military Commander, such action is necessary for securing the maintenance, safety and requirements of the Occupation Forces'. Nor was it only members of local authorities and local government officers who were at risk. The Germans also listed, as subject to removal or to a ban on their appointment, 'members of the police and customs, teaching personnel, personnel of mail and telephone services . . . prison personnel'. Thus the postman who grumbled on his rounds about the extra work caused by delivering German mail, the schoolmistress who taught her children to sing 'Hearts of Oak', or the elderly warder in the county gaol who expressed sympathy with the prisoner 'inside' for, say, working on his allotment after curfew, might suddenly have found themselves deprived of both job and pension.

As in Jersey, police stations and prisons might soon have been over-flowing with offenders against one of the Germans' innumerable regula-tions, and a particularly rich harvest of law-breakers would probably have been reaped by the pass laws. Passes and permits had always made a deep appeal to the German mind and Britain, which until the introduction of identity cards in 1939 had managed without any form of compulsory identity document, offered almost virgin soil. The Germans proposed for every British citizen over the age of twelve a more elaborate document than the National Registration Card already in use, containing not merely a photograph but a description of the person concerned, and the card was to be replaced every three months to prevent forgeries. Anyone travelling outside his own area also required a pass, giving particulars of the bearer and specifying the maximum amount of money he was allowed to carry, the quantity of goods he was transporting, and details of his route. Passes, the *Ordinances* laid down, were to be 'sparingly issued', and travel for non-business purposes would only be allowed for visits to 'sick rela-tions', defined as 'parents, sons and daughters and brothers and sisters', and the issuing officer had to 'satisfy himself of the seriousness of the illness', a system similar to that later imposed by the British government for people visiting restricted areas near the coast. Applied to the whole country, however, it would have proved extremely burdensome to ad-minister. Travel by night was even more strictly controlled, and the list of those likely to be eligible revealed a curiously nineteenth-century view of British society, covering merely 'doctors, midwives and . . . millhands working at night'.

The first year of the war in England had seen constant upheavals in many families, as children were evacuated, men joined the forces, and women moved to be near husbands working in a new district, but the Germans seem to have envisaged that under their rule life would settle down into a static tranquillity. Only under conditions of 'absolute neces-sity' were people to be allowed to 'cross the lines of examining posts', i.e. move from the area of one military command to another, and permission to do so 'should seldom be necessary except for doctors, midwives and persons travelling for revictualling purposes'. How the business life of the country was to be carried on under such conditions was not explained. Nor was any reason offered as to why, when the precious pass was granted 'to leave the district by motor-car not more than two spare covers and tubes will be carried'. How many drivers, it might have been asked, ever did have with them more than one spare tyre?

Although one of the Germans' first orders on occupying Britain would have been that 'all businesses, trade undertakings and banks' were to remain open, everyone who went out to work would soon have felt the effects of the presence of the occupying troops. Both large public companies and small private firms would have suffered from the wholesale requisitioning of a wide range of both raw materials and finished goods and many would have been turned over to producing articles solely for the Germans, at prices, of course, fixed by them. The railways, waterways and docks, while still also under British management, would have been supervised by special Commissions of German experts, ever on the alert for further pickings for the Reich, or for any sign of slackness on the part of managers or workpeople. Particularly elaborate instructions were drawn up for Britain's few inland waterways, the Germans apparently imagining that the British river and canal system was as vital a part of the transport network as in Europe, and judging by the volume of paperwork required the railways would have suffered even more. The Germans demanded from the harassed staff not only a daily return of coal stocks, but ten-daily or monthly statistics on the number of passengers, goods carried, locomotives, rolling stock and, not least, 'drivers, guards and breakmen', an all too appropriate slip in spelling, perhaps, considering how hard the Germans proposed to work their British subjects.

British factory-owners, like those in other occupied countries, would clearly have had to come to some understanding with the Germans and though their employees would have come into little direct contact with them, the Germans' presence would have been felt the first time the unions demanded an increase in pay or some other improvement in conditions of service. There was about the Germans' method of dealing with industrial relations an awe-inspiring simplicity. Since prices had been fixed at the prevailing level by one of the first *Announcements* to be issued by the Army commander, 'the raising of . . . wages . . . and remuneration of any kind above the level on the day of Occupation' was 'forbidden unless exceptions have been expressly authorised', and to offer more pay—and, presumably, to ask for it—was therefore a breach of the law. One of the next group of orders to be issued laid down that 'anyone stopping work with the intention of prejudicing the interests of the German forces of occupation, anyone who locks-out employees or who incites others to strike or to lock-out will be punished'. Since any interference with the country's economic life could be held to be contrary to German interests, this provision alone would have been sufficient to have landed any recalcitrant union official or shop steward in gaol.

The laws which the Germans intended to impose in the long term were somewhat less arbitrary, the ban on strikes applying only to public service industries, including the postal services, gas and electricity production, the railways and the mines, and everyone 'employed either directly by the armies or by contractors working under the supervision of the armies', though the Army Commander had the right to apply it also 'to any other undertaking which may appear necessary for the maintenance, safety or requirements of the armies of occupation'. As virtually everyone in the country would ultimately have been working for them, directly or indirectly, few businesses of any size would have been safe from intervention, and the principles which the Germans proposed to enforce bear many resemblances to those underlying the 1972 Industrial Relations Act. Any threatened dispute had first to be reported to the usual negotiating body, which had to announce its findings within eight days, and if they were not acceptable the aggrieved party could appeal to a three-man 'Board of Conciliation appointed by the Military Commander'. If its decision was unacceptable, there had to be an eight-day 'cooling-off period', and the occupation authorities had to be warned before any strike could legally be called. Even in the non-essential industries, once a strike had begun, the strikers could be ordered back to work and compelled to follow the same procedure as if they had been working for the Germans. Factory-gate demonstrations and trade union protest marches would have been dealt with even more high-handedly, since public meetings and processions of all kinds, irrespective of their purpose, were forbidden without special permission.

Away from his work, how would Occupation have affected the ordinary citizen? For anyone who lived through the years from 1941 to 1944 it is not hard to envisage the answer, for life in a German Britain would have had all the greyness and uncertainty of those years with none of the ameliorations. At the leading grammar school in Jersey, one teacher recalls, 'it was felt that the children's health would never stand up to sport, cross-country running, hockey, etc.' and 'a lot of these activities were severely curtailed' even before the buildings were commandeered by the Germans and the playing fields dug up to grow food. The pattern of events in Britain would have been similar. Gardening would have been a major activity, undertaken from necessity rather than pleasure; one could still have gone to the cinema, still have borrowed books from the library, still have gone to church, for the Germans kept their promise in every country to allow freedom of worship (meaning, of course, Christian worship) and faithfully carried out the injunction to their troops contained in *How to behave in England* that 'any disparagement of the religious practices of the country will be punished'.

Church would have become the only place where a British citizen could openly avow his patriotism, for prayers for the royal family (if the same rules applied as in the Channel Islands) would have been allowed and never surely would the familiar words of the Prayer Book, beseeching the Almighty 'with thy favour to behold our most gracious Sovereign Lord, King George; and so . . . strengthen him that he may vanquish and over-come all his enemies', have been answered with more fervent 'Amens'. The singing of the national anthem, whether in church or elsewhere, would have been forbidden, as would the displaying in public, but not in one's own home, of 'any national or other flag' unless forty-eight hours' notice had been given to the Germans, to allow them to discriminate between harmless displays of innocuous bunting at fêtes and the flying of the Union Jack. The only other visible reminders of the existence of 'the king over the water' would have been postage stamps, of which the Germans would probably have used up existing stocks, and the royal coat of arms on pillar boxes and public buildings. If practice in the Channel Islands was followed, there would, too, have been one other reminder of the imperial past, OHMS labels on official communications, so that envelopes bearing this inscription would have been received with unusual satisfaction.

Although the press and radio would have been strictly controlled, in an occupied Britain private communication would probably not have been greatly affected. The Germans warned that 'all postcards, letters and other postal packages will be subject to censorship', but no one in his senses would have expected otherwise, and the draft postal regulations imposed no restrictions except on the use of uncommon languages, on illegible handwriting (which might be a concealed code) and 'the use of ambiguous phrases, unintelligible marks or signs, code or cipher, shorthand or secret ink'. Handwriting, the Germans ruled, 'must be legible and in Latin characters when possible', and no doubt those whose illegibility had been inconveniencing their correspondents for years would suddenly have discovered that they could after all write intelligibly.

The rules for telephones were more drastic and would have had far greater repercussions on daily life for in 1940 under one and a quarter million private homes possessed telephones (thirty years later the figure was seven million), but the Germans proposed to close down 'all public call-offices', the official term for public telephone booths, and to restrict long-distance calls to 'urgent official, professional and business purposes' Public telephones in fact continued to be allowed in the Channel Islands. though many were put out of action by people stealing the receiver diaphragms for use in home-made radios, and in Britain, too, one suspects the ban would before long have been found unworkable. While it existed, people would no doubt have become accustomed to applying for the use of his telephone to the nearest neighbour or tradesman who possessed one.

Although in all their regulations the Germans used metric measures, they appear to have had no plans to decimalise the currency or to force metrication upon the British public, and in the Channel Islands the traditional British system continued to be followed by local residents. But one other long-cherished example of British individuality would have vanished overnight, the rule of driving on the left. Driving on the right was the rule of the road in Germany and everywhere else in occupied Europe, and the Germans announced its adoption within a month of their arrival in the Channel Islands, adding insult to injury with a warning from the Commandant on Jersey 'that the public must learn to use the roads properly', for, as missing gate-posts and wrecked traffic signs all over the island already testified, the Germans were easily the worst drivers in Europe. With their potentially lethal lorries and requisitioned cars charging madly about the narrow roads, which were virtually empty of civilian traffic except for bicycles, few of the population were disposed to argue, and driving (or more commonly, cycling) on the right became universal with remarkably little difficulty.

Even fewer problems would have been encountered in adopting European Time, which the Germans brought with them to the Channel Islands, where the clocks had to be put forward an hour, for in fact the British Isles adopted it, though under the name of British Double Summer Time, in May 1941 and retained it, on and off, for most of the war. This meant that in midsummer it was still light at 11 pm, but due to the curfew at 9 or 10 pm the inhabitants of occupied Britain would have had the frustrating experience of being forced to hurry home and stay indoors on even the finest evening.

The Englishman's traditional refuge from his troubles had always been the 'pub', and the Germans did not plan to interfere with this hallowed institution, though it might have been threatened by a shortage of supplies, as grain was requisitioned and sugar ceased to arrive from the West Indies. Whisky and gin, though produced in Great Britain, rum, which came from the Caribbean, and British-brewed beer would all have become scarce, but wine might actually have been more plentiful as the

Germans encouraged trade with their vine-growing Mediterranean allies and satellites. With other types of alcohol unobtainable, cider, too, might have come back into its own, since apples were often plentiful. One Jersey man remembers without pleasure the spirits he distilled from home-made cider and, even less successful, those made from Algerian wine, the result being 'pretty poisonous but warm', though only the bravest topers tackled it neat. Overall the drinking history of the country in the years after 1940 would probably not have been very different, though with public houses opening even later and, due to curfew, closing even earlier, and the sad notice 'No beer' being displayed even more frequently.

Curiously enough, the Germans' main anxiety over the sale of alcohol concerned their own forces. The details of control, the *Ordinances* laid down, were to be left to local commanders but anyone who sold a drink or even—a highly improbable event—gave one to any German soldier could be punished and, on a second offence, apart from any other penalty, the guilty establishment might be shut down for three months. But a far worse punishment was inflicted by the Germans on any of their own soldiers who made a nuisance of themselves in public. A Jersey policeman remembers complaining to the German field police after going to the rescue of a local girl being molested by a drunken soldier, who thereupon threatened him with a bayonet, though both escaped unhurt. Two days later, asking what had happened to the man, he was told simply, 'He's in Russia.' This was the fate held over any German who misbehaved in the Channel Islands and it helps to explain why the general standard of conduct towards civilians was as 'correct' as the official *Guide* demanded.

Although in the Channel Islands to see a member of the occupying forces drunk in public was a rare event, some Germans could after a few drinks display an aggressive amiability almost as trying as truculence. One wartime member of the Jersey police force remembers calling with a friend in the course of duty on a German officer, who pressed his visitors to have a drink. They asked for coffee, a far greater treat than alcohol to most people in occupied Europe, explaining that they were teetotallers, but the German reacted, the policeman recalls, by declaring ' "Now you're insulting the great German Reich and the German Führer. You will drink!" So he ordered three bottles of lager and three glasses, the lager was poured out and he said, "You will drink!" We didn't show any signs of drinking, so he drew his automatic, pointed it at me, and said,"Gentlemen, you will drink!" and we drank. I've never seen three glasses of lager vanish so quickly.'

Chapter 13: Requisitioned

The main task of military government is to make full use of the country's resources for the needs of the fighting troops and the requirements of German war economy.

Directive for Military Government in England, *1940*

The ability to milk a cow had long been common in the Channel Islands, and with the arrival of the Germans a number of residents developed a new skill: the 'milking' of cars. The occupying troops had seized so much of the islands' fuel supplies that the few people left with vehicles of their own were often forced to steal from the petrol tanks of enemy vehicles (frequently the former property of their neighbours) to keep their own on the road. A Jersey physiotherapist remembers how an acquaintance who worked at the Forum cinema 'used to let me know when the Germans were coming down with their big bus'. While they were safe inside enjoying the film he would be busy in the car park, siphoning off some of their precious petrol. A local hotel used by German officers every night served as another 'cowshed', where on many occasions he would fill a two-gallon can—the maximum amount unlikely to be missed—sometimes paying two or three visits in the same evening. Although often offered money, he never sold the stolen petrol, preferring to share it out among local doctors with scattered practices.

Petrol was so sparingly dispensed that even the local lifeboat had difficulty in obtaining enough. One member of the crew who indented for twenty gallons after an hour-and-a-half trip—more than had actually been used—to make up for a previous occasion when none had been claimed, remembers how 'next day I . . . found a German car in the drive of my house and my wife being bullied by a wretched German captain, revolver out, swinging it round'. After being questioned he managed to convince the visitor that the extra petrol had been properly used, 'but all the time he was fiddling around with this revolver . . . and he said, "If I catch you or your crew stealing one half a pint of petrol, I'll shoot you and all your family."' After that, this man admits, he ceased even 'hunting around for any odd drops of diesel oil' to eke out the household's fuel supplies.

Conditions in the rest of the British Isles would have been no different, for one of the Germans' first acts everywhere was to seize all the transport they needed, and the instructions to the Gestapo 'Commando Groups', as already mentioned, advised that in England a car should be acquired without delay. Although most vehicles seized were put to practical use, often in carrying away other goods commandeered by the Germans, a secondary motive was to acquire a status symbol, for the German Army still relied to an astonishing extent on horse-drawn transport. The comparable sign of prestige for an ordinary soldier was a private bicycle, for though the Germans had bicycle battalions—indeed one, as mentioned earlier, was earmarked for the defence of each Lines of Communication area in England—they were always keen to acquire extra machines. The present Town Clerk of St Helier, Jersey, Mr W. H. Marshall, then a junior official, remembers once 'they wanted fifty bicycles. We had therefore to work out some means of taking them away from the local people as fairly as possible. We tried to do this on the basis of whether a bicycle was necessary for one's job. A fellow living in York Street, for instance, whose work was in town had less need for a bicycle than a man who was working on the new North Road.' It was, Mr Marshall found, 'a heartbreaking experience' to have to persuade his fellow-citizens to give up this precious possession, 'but we never had a case where somebody resented it. . . . I think the local people understood that it was better to deal with us than to deal with the Germans.'

This was one of the basic principles of German Occupation; that every demand, however unreasonable, was to be made through the civil authorities, and it would certainly have been applied in Great Britain where the Occupation *Ordinances* called upon the civil authority to take a wide-ranging census of the potential loot which its area offered, pride of place, as in the Channel Islands, being given to 'carriages, motor-cars, motor-bicycles, horses, etc.'. The Germans also wanted details of 'all stores of the kind which can be used for military purposes, factories or public or private undertakings which can be applied to the manufacture and repair of military stores' and even 'the personnel necessary for working any of the means which should be liable to be requisitioned'. It would not have been long before few British citizens were left in possession of their own car, though this would have caused less widespread ill-will in October 1940, when there were fewer than one and a half million private cars on the roads, than it would have done a generation later, when the number was nearly eight times as many. The effect on firms which lost their lorries and delivery vans would have been more serious and an even more drastic pooling of resources would have been necessary than actually occurred in wartime Britain, while, due to the impact of petrol rationing, bus services, as on the Channel Islands, would have been savagely curtailed, with no buses running at all on some days of the week. What, however, seems likely to have caused most ill-feeling was the provision that anyone whose car was requisitioned had also to provide a driver and be responsible for its maintenance. 'The driver must remain with the car and may have to stay away from the place to which he belongs for an indefinite period', warned the relevant Regulation. 'The driver will get no pay from the German authorities. The owners of the car or, in the case of motor-cabs, the firm or municipality is responsible for paying him and must make their own arrangements for forwarding pay to him wherever he may be'—a typical example of the German passion for covering every detail. To discourage any conscripted driver who might reasonably object to driving Germans about the countryside in his car and at his own expense, the *Ordinances* stressed that 'for any neglect of his duty as driver he will be punished by a German summary court'. Nor did the Germans plan to stand any nonsense from dilatory garages, even though they would not be footing the bill. 'Requisitioned cars will be sent for repairs . . . to the most convenient workshop', they promised, 'and such repairs must be promptly carried out and at the expense of the government of the occupied country', which would later also pay for 'petrol, oil and tyres' supplied by the Germans, no doubt from stocks impounded from British garages.

In fact on the Channel Islands the Germans seem to have driven their own vehicles, or paid direct, like other locally hired labour, the civilian drivers they employed. What was totally indefensible was the ludicrous valuation they placed on the vehicles they impounded. Though bicycles and horse-drawn carriages and wagons had, with the petrol situation so uncertain, appreciated more in price than cars, transport of all kinds was at a premium and the prices paid by the Germans were hopelessly inadequate. The owner of one van costing £300, and now irreplaceable, received in the early days £165, but he was fortunate compared to later sufferers, where the Germans paid only scrap value for the stolen vehicles. A company owning a new £1000 bus received £1 for it, a private-car owner £5 for a car which had cost him £381 in 1939, and some people were given nothing more substantial than promissory notes, still unhonoured. A year after the Occupation had begun there were on Guernsey fewer than fifty private cars and commercial vehicles to serve a population of 23,000.

Up to the very end of the war the Germans were rounding up vehicles, though they no longer had any petrol for them. One Jersey woman remembers how, after she and her husband had been deported to France, the Germans not merely enticed away their much-loved terrier, left in the care of her brother, and ate him—this was the 'starvation Christmas' of 1944—but also seized their car, though they had to push it to their park, for her brother had removed the battery and stripped from it everything movable. The car was among the last consignment sent from Jersey, but they never succeeded in recovering it. For much of the war, though with little other work to do, the garages on Guernsey were kept busy spraying requisitioned vehicles 'battleship grey' for military use, and later, when this colour ran out, painting them in the African desert camouflage, of which the Germans had unlimited stocks.

Even families who did not own a car did not escape making some contribution to the Germans' war effort, or comfort. 'It sometimes seemed to me that we were always handing something over', one Guernseyman has written, recalling the calling in of all cameras and photographic apparatus to enable the Germans to speed up the issue of identity cards, and a house-to-house collection of mattresses 'for which chits were duly issued, supposedly for payment at some future date'. The Germans also raided the safe-deposit boxes in the local banks in search of bullion, but went away empty-handed, and even removed the swords which, according to local custom, were hung under memorial tablets in local churches, though most of these were returned after the war. The regimental plate of the Royal Irish Fusiliers, left on the island when they were recalled to England, was also taken, though later retrieved. By German standards these were all, of course, trivial achievements, but they indicate what the Germans might have accomplished on a far vaster scale if they had managed to hoist the Swastika over Buckingham Palace and Holyrood House.

The Germans had in fact prepared even more far-reaching plans for removing everything they wanted from the rest of the British Isles than they applied in the Channel Islands and here, too, they planned to use the local authorities as the collecting agents, the only exception being military equipment, which had to be handed over direct to the Germans, though 'the mayors, or senior local authorities', warned the relevant *Order*, 'will be made responsible'. The proclamation itself was, by German standards, very brief:

All fire-arms, including sporting guns, ammunition, hand-grenades, explosives and other war material are to be surrendered. The surrender must be effected within 24 hours at the nearest German administrative sub-area or local headquarters ... Anyone who, contrary to the above order, retains possession of fire-arms, including sporting guns, ammunition, hand-grenades, explosives or other war material will be condemned to death, in less serious cases to penal servitude or imprisonment.

The Occupation *Ordinances* went into a great deal more detail, attempting in the German way to cover every possible article, the list of Army stores running to thirty-two separate categories and that of Naval stores to sixteen. Every citizen in possession of any of these was enjoined to disclose them, though it seems in any case unlikely that anyone in possession of a 'battleship', 'armoured train' or 'field bakery', which were among the items mentioned, would be able to keep it hidden very long. The Germans also drew up regulations providing in detail for the destruction of any half-finished munitions or, where this task was beyond the factory concerned, it had 'to report amounts in triplicate to the nearest area commandant'. Later, some relaxation of the ban on sporting guns seems to have been contemplated, for it was laid down that members of bona fide shooting clubs could, under strict conditions, possess rifles and even pistols.

In the secret Orders for the Military Government of England which were drawn up by the General Staff between July and September 1940 the Commander-in-Chief, in whose name they were to be issued, made no bones about his true intentions. 'The main task of military government', stated his basic *Directive* bluntly, 'is to make full use of the country's resources for the needs of the fighting troops and the requirements of German war economy.' Later sections of the *Directive* made clear enough that the rights of the conquered people, to whom the country actually belonged, came nowhere:

An essential condition for securing the labour of the country is that law and order should prevail. Law and order will therefore be established. Administrative measures will not violate international law unless the enemy has given cause for reprisals . . . Laws of the country operative prior to the occupation will be upheld unless they are contradictory to the purpose of the occupation . . . The welfare of the inhabitants of the country and the interests of the country's national economy, the latter being the concern of the Defence Economic Staff and its headquarters, will be considered in so far as they contribute directly or indirectly towards the maintenance of law and order and the securing of the country's labour for the requirements of the troops and German war economy.

The task of the Defence Economic Staff mentioned in the *Directive* was spelt out in more detail in another document. They would, it was explained, 'be employed on the economic exploitation of the country' and would be directly responsible to the German War Office, their only contact with the Army Commanders being to divert some part of the food and other supplies seized for the immediate use of the occupying forces. The central Staff, presumably remaining in Germany, would operate through Defence Economic Commands which, said Orders issued on 9 September, 'will be stationed at first in the embarkation ports, then in the landing ports; later they will be permanently established in those particular types of industrial centres for which they have been specially recruited. . . . Their task is to seize, secure and remove raw materials, semi-finished production and machinery of military importance.' The Commands were to work through Economic Officers, who 'are the forward representatives of the Defence Economic Commands and will be stationed at the principal ports. Their task is to assist the troops in economic matters, to arrange and effect the removal of goods, and to secure transport space.'

The Germans seem, at least in the initial stages, to have thought solely of stripping British industry of its stores and plant and of removing them to the Continent, a logical corollary of their plans, to be mentioned in the next chapter, for deporting most of the male working population, which might presumably have found itself back at its old work-bench, now set up in Düsseldorf or Mannheim instead of Derby or Macclesfield. The only reference to leaving machinery where it was related to 'special instances', where the Economic Commands could 'examine and take over repair shops for unit purposes'. In fact it seems likely that wiser counsels, if the British Isles had been totally subjugated, would have prevailed. Why go to the immense trouble of moving a whole factory and its work-force to the Continent, with all the upheaval and interruption in output involved, when it might be left where it was, with an occasional visit from an Economic Officer—who would before long have become as familiar a figure as the Factory Inspector—to ensure that production was flowing smoothly? Certainly in France and other countries major industrial plants like the Renault factory were left alone, though now forced to work for the Germans, and this, on any common-sense assessment of the probabilities—though the Germans were sometimes impervious to common sense—seems what would have happened in Britain. No doubt some specially valuable items—machine-tools, automatic steel-handling equipment, patented processes on which some influential industrialist in Brunswick or Cologne had long cast envious eyes—would rapidly have been appropriated, but the general removal of Great Britain's economic capacity across the Channel seems not so much impossible as unnecessary.

Some more portable items would certainly have vanished at once, for one of the orders prepared beforehand contained a shopping list of essential items. The text is of a brutal directness which well illustrates the Germans' attitude, ninety per cent bullying, ten per cent reasonable, towards the now helpless British:

The following goods are hereby requisitioned:
Agricultural products, food and fodder of all kinds, ores, crude metals, semi-finished metal products of all kinds, including precious metals, asbestos and mica,

cut or uncut precious or semi-precious stones, mineral oils and fuels of all kinds, industrial oils and fats, waxes, resins, glues, rubber in any form, all raw materials for textiles, leather, furs and hides, round timber, sawed timber, timber sleepers, and timber masts.

Requisitioned goods may not be alienated, altered or moved to another place. They must be handled with the greatest care and must be protected against deterioration.

All goods are excluded from requisitioning which are part of a normal household stock.

Farmers and tradesmen, including innkeepers, may retain such stocks of agricultural products, food and fodder, as are essential for supplying their clients with absolute necessities. To the same limited extent petty craftsmen and shops may supply goods to consumers.

Anyone contravening these regulations will be punished.

How the 'normal household stock' was to be replenished, or the 'petty craftsmen and shops' were to obtain more supplies to replace those they sold over the counter was not explained. Presumably, as under the quota system adopted by the Board of Trade from 1940 onwards, manufacturers after the first frenzy of requisitioning had passed, would have been allowed to sell some part of their output to wholesalers and retailers who would have been rationed according to their prewar demands. Since, as part of the Civil Authority, government departments would have continued to function under the Germans, the actual regulations drawn up would probably have differed little from those actually imposed in the later years of the war, though with a far smaller volume of goods to be shared out, and with little guarantee, owing to the danger of sudden new demands from the Germans, of each shopkeeper's ration being honoured. If, of course, the Germans had carried out their threat of mass deportation, the civil population left behind would have been far smaller than in peacetime, while the demands of the armed forces, which took priority from 1940 to 1945, would have ceased altogether apart from the daily necessities of life. Appalling shortages there would no doubt have been but that anyone would actually have been reduced to rags, or frozen or starved to death, seems unlikely.

Despite their obviously high regard for Britain as an industrial nation, the Germans do not seem to have rated British agriculture very highly, for it is barely mentioned in their Occupation *Orders*, and occupies little space in the *Ordinances*. The invaders seem to have looked to the farms of England and Wales to feed the Occupation Armies rather than to provide wagon-loads of produce to be sent back to the Fatherland, and the exploitation of agriculture was left to a 'Chief Supply Officer for England', responsible to the main attacking formation, Army Group A, and not, like his countrymen how busily stripping British industry, to the Economic Defence Staff and the German War Office. His first job was to 'prepare on English territory a supply base', and later he was to 'be responsible for seizing such stocks of food, petrol, motor transport, horse-drawn vehicles, etc., in the country as all have already been taken over by the armies', but whether they were then to be exported to Germany or to be held against the future needs of the Occupation forces, was not made clear.

The Chief Supply Officer's terms of reference illustrate another facet of the German approach to their defeated enemies. They were not on the whole interested in piecemeal requisitioning and, though some items might well vanish during the initial burst of looting, German troops were better disciplined than most, and once it was over anyone indulging in further unauthorised 'removals' was liable to be severely punished. Readers of the *Guide on how troops are to behave in England*, which was ready for issue in September, were warned that 'acts of violence against orderly members of the population and looting will incur the severest penalties under military law; the death sentence may be imposed'. The acquisition of booty by individual units was also sternly discouraged. Rather ironically in the light of the plans of the Economic Defence Staff which were to be implemented once victory was won, the Commander-in-Chief ordered that 'unnecessary interference with the economic life of the country is to be avoided. Factories, workshops and offices are not to be disturbed; except where operationally necessary such places may only be entered by soldiers executing orders. The use of stocks of petrol, oil, machinery, tools, etc., found in factories and works is forbidden. . . . Goods of all kinds and military booty, especially food and fodder, and articles of clothing are to be preserved and secured.'

In the Channel Islands this policy was faithfully carried out. The Town Clerk already quoted remembers how, when the Germans wanted eggs in Jersey, they did not apply to the owners direct but, once again, to the local council. 'We had', he recalls, 'to collect two or three dozen eggs each week from the farmers. This again we did on a rota system, so that no one particular man was penalised more than any other.' But although German lorries rarely drove up to individual farms or factories to load up with goods, everyone in the Channel Islands knew that when they reached the market or depot the Germans took their share, and though the goods were usually paid for, it was at prices they fixed themselves and in their own currency. This was widely expected to be worth little more than 'inflation' marks or Confederate dollars when they had lost the war, so that an English pound note rapidly became worth nearly £3 or even more in German money. The Germans themselves, despite their supposed confidence in victory, showed a strong preference for sterling and on Guernsey were prepared to pay £15 to £22 for an English sovereign, and up to £2 15s (£2·75) for a pound note. Silver and even copper coins, too, rapidly disappeared, being sent to Germany, the British authorities replacing the missing coins by printing notes at values of 6d, 1s 3d, 2s 6d and 5s, which are now collectors' items.

But it was the seizure of stocks of goods already on the island, and of those being produced there, which had so serious an effect on its economic life, and a similar process would probably have occurred in Britain. Everyone from factory-owner to shopkeeper had less to sell and some occupations, like that of restaurant proprietor, ceased to provide an adequate living. One Guernsey farmer confided to his diary in April 1941, when the Occupation was not yet a year old and the worst shortages were still to come, that the Germans were already behaving 'like fat and vulgar locusts. . . . My car, lorry and row of trees are now gone and coal is to follow. I wonder if they'll want my wife?' Happily they did not, but many families did lose their pets, which in the last desperate winter of the war were often stolen by the Germans or fellow residents for food.

The Germans officially discouraged in their soldiers' *Guide* for troops going to England the wholesale purchasing of goods already in the shops. 'The soldier will be provided with all essentials by his unit', he was reminded. 'Unnecessary purchases are to be avoided.' It would have been unreasonable, however, to expect that any serviceman, loose for the first time in a foreign country with money in his pocket, would not have set out on a shopping expedition and one of the earliest signs of the arrival of the Germans in the Channel Islands was the appearance of the 'fieldgreys', as the Germans nicknamed their own troops, or the 'Jerries', as the inhabitants called them, staring into shop windows or going inside to explain by pantomime, as few spoke English, what they wanted to buy. The tradesmen of Jersey and Guernsey were well accustomed to dealing with a flood of summer visitors and the shelves of most establishments were well filled, but before long stocks were running low as the new arrivals discovered with surprise that Goebbels's stories of the starving, threadbare English were untrue. Ten days after the first troops had arrived on Jersey their commandant felt compelled to issue an order forbidding them to buy at a time more than '50 cigarettes or 25 cigars, 1 bottle of wine or two bottles of beer, three shirts, collars and ties, and one suit-length of cloth', while the sale of all foodstuffs to any soldier, except for 'fruit, biscuits and confectionery' was forbidden. One islander observed later that same July how 'new arrivals are to be seen standing in front of shop windows with their mouths open', and already the same transports which had brought them there were carrying away 'potatoes, spirits and other goods', while on this largely agricultural island the ration of cooking fats had already been halved, the first of many such reductions. Three days later an order was issued for two 'meatless days' a week, though it was soon forgotten and meat itself later became little more than a memory for most people.

The requisitioning of property, especially land or business premises on which one's livelihood depended—as in the evacuated cities of Great Britain there was no shortage of empty dwelling houses—pressed even harder on individuals than the wholesale commandeering of agricultural produce. Two years later, on Guernsey, one man charged with various thefts defended himself on the grounds that his 'premises had been taken over by the German troops and he had lost everything, including crops', for which he had received no compensation; the Germans' only reaction being to fine the acting editor of the local newspaper for including this evidence in its report of the trial.

There is no reason to suppose that the rest of the British Isles would have escaped any more lightly had the Germans landed, indeed the elaborate plans made by the Germans suggests that they would have been pillaged even more thoroughly. The only compensation would have been fixed by the Germans themselves, and disbursed through the local authority, who would in the first instance have had to find the money from rates, though perhaps able later to recover it from central government funds earmarked for Occupation purposes. The Germans seem to have assumed that, under the armistice treaty to be signed once their armies were victorious, the British government would have agreed, like the French government, to pay a large sum in reparations, as well as handing over war material of many kinds, including the British fleet. Later expenditure, for example on building roads and barracks for the German forces, or in compensating the owners of requisitioned premises or goods, would be charged against the 'Occupation account', in other words the British taxpayer would pay for the privilege of having German troops on his soil. This was the policy followed in the Channel Islands and the effects on the island's budgets were seen at once. On Jersey income tax shot up from 9d to 4s od in the pound, on Guernsey it rose from 1s 6d to 5s od, though this was still a long way below the British rate, which by the end of the war had reached 10s od. With the war apparently lost, of course, one huge item of government expenditure, on munitions and other military needs, would have vanished overnight, though Britain might still have been expected to meet the heavy cost of maintaining the two and a half million members of its former armies in captivity. As the Germans' demands seem likely to have grown rather than diminished the bill laid upon the British taxpayer as some new factory or industry began producing largely for enemy use, it seems certain that the British taxpayer would have faced a grim future, though if he had been left a reasonable share of his earnings there would have been little on which to spend it.

Happily the Germans never did cross the Channel, but in reflecting what their occupation of the British Isles would have meant one image remains in the mind, recorded in his diary by a Guernsey man in 1943: an old woman in her seventies trudging wearily for miles along a road carrying a heavy can of tar, the only fuel she could now obtain, while requisitioned cars and lorries driven by healthy young Germans roared past choking her with dust. Such scenes would have become a daily commonplace in the lanes of Devon and Yorkshire, of Angus and Inverness, of Carmarthen and Merioneth, had Britain fallen.

Chapter 14: Deported

By order of higher authorities, the following British subjects will be evacuated and transferred to Germany. . . .

Notice *signed by German Commandant on the Channel Islands, 15 September 1942*

The German plans for Great Britain were in one respect far harsher than those applied in any other occupied country. 'The able-bodied male population between the ages of 17 and 45 will, unless the local situation calls for an exceptional ruling', ran paragraph 5 of the Commander-in-Chief's *Directive for Military Government in England*, 'be interned and dispatched to the Continent with the minimum of delay.' The effects on the life of the country if this brutal instruction had been carried out would have been enormous. There were in 1940 around eleven million in these age groups in a male population of twenty-three million and a total population of forty-eight million, so almost overnight nearly half the men in the country and nearly one in four of all its citizens would have disappeared. The nation's working life would have been, for a time at least, almost paralysed, since in 1940 the mobilisation of women for employment in factories, and the replacement of men by women in a vast range of occupations, from dockyard crane-drivers to bus conductors and plumbers' mates, had hardly begun. Although there were already two and a half million men in the Forces, and the total, at its peak in June 1945, reached more than four million, even then nearly two out of three men of military age were still in civilian life, a few because they were medically unfit but the vast majority because their work was regarded as vital to the war effort. The Germans' deportation orders would have started lower down the age scale than the British government's call-up, which began at eighteen, and reached far higher, for though in theory by the end of the war any man under the age of fifty-two could be called up, very few over forty-one were in fact recruited. At the same time, a high proportion of the men in the forces were stationed in the United Kingdom, or later Europe, and were able to come on leave at regular intervals. There would from a German prison camp have been no 48-hour passes and no way out except to the gas-chamber.

If the internment policy had been applied in its full rigour, daily life for those remaining, apart altogether from the loss of their sons' and husbands' company and anxiety about their fate, would have become a travesty of civilised existence. Goods of every kind would have become desperately scarce as industries were swept bare of their labour force. Coal, gas and electricity supplies would have dwindled rapidly, as all the most active miners and the key technicians and engineers left unconscripted by the British government disappeared to fell trees or build fortifications in some German forced-labour camp. Business of every kind would have been almost at a standstill as the few younger men in key positions who had been deferred from call-up were crammed into the railway cattle-trucks which the Germans favoured for transporting their helpless captives—before the railways themselves virtually ceased operation as their essential workers, too, were dragged into slavery. Food production would have been even harder hit for farm workers of every type had been one of the largest single groups exempt from military service, while the import of food from abroad would have suffered as the younger dock-workers were themselves loaded on to transports (perhaps the very barges which had brought the invading troops across) for shipment to the Continent. Everywhere the surviving civilian turned the loss of men would have been apparent: the doctor, the chemist, the clergyman —the Germans had no plans to spare any of these. The phenomenon noticed after the first world war, that there seemed to be few younger men about, would have repeated itself on a far vaster scale.

The country, it was often remarked, had never recovered from the loss of almost a whole generation of its ablest, bravest and healthiest citizens. The results of a German round-up in 1940 of all those aged from seventeen to forty-five would have been infinitely more serious and would have led, before the end of the century, to the virtual disappearance of the whole population of the British Isles. The word 'genocide', for the murder of a whole race, had not then been coined—it needed German treatment of other communities to add it to the world's vocabulary—but this is what the policy proposed for the United Kingdom would have meant. The retention in captivity as prisoners-of-war of only two million Frenchmen for five years made an immediate mark upon the French birth-rate, which in the British Isles by contrast, after a dip in 1940 and 1941 when it was the lowest ever recorded, rose rapidly, so that the total number of children born during the war was about four and a half million, more than replacing the 1,800,000 civilians who died during those six years and the 300,000 servicemen and merchant seamen killed on active service. If all the young men in their late teens, twenties, thirties and early forties had been removed, few would have been left to father the next generation, for most men in their late forties and upwards were married to women past the age of child-bearing. The only children of British parentage to be born would have been those of the few men who had somehow escaped the great round-up, or who had married wives substantially younger than themselves.

The total lack of British men, not merely as husbands but as boyfriends, must have had a traumatic effect upon social life, especially if the Occupation had dragged on year after year, so that memories of former companions and consorts faded, and it began to seem inconceivable that they would ever return. The ordinary woman would therefore have faced the agonising choice of never fulfilling her deepest instinct, to bear a child, or of seeking solace in the arms of some older man (whose social horizons would have been transformed by the sudden disappearance of all younger competition) or one of her country's hated enemies, accepted first, perhaps, merely as a companion but ultimately as a lover and perhaps even as a husband. Even in the Channel Islands, where most of the men remained, several hundred illegitimate children were born to Channel Island women and German soldiers, although the details, and even the final total, were hushed up. Inevitably in England, too, some of those lonely, or worthless, women later known expressively as 'Yank-bashers' might have become 'Jerrybags' instead. One can predict even more confidently that, had the Germans issued in England the order they posted in Guernsey in October 1942, it would have had equally little effect: 'Sexual relations either with the German soldiers or with civilians are strictly forbidden during the next three months'—one instruction which was universally defied.

The consequence of the mass deportation of the male population would have been so far-reaching, and the mere physical effort of rounding up and transporting eleven million men would have been so enormous, that one wonders if it would have been attempted. Certainly it was not in any other occupied country, even those such as Poland and Czechoslovakia where the Germans behaved with exceptional brutality. Nor in the only British territory they occupied, the Channel Islands, was there deportation on this scale, or of this particular category. If, of course, the Germans had, as they also planned, robbed the British Isles of virtually its whole productive capacity, then it would have made sense to take the workers with their factories but, as suggested in the last chapter, wiser counsels would probably have prevailed, in which case the deportation policy, too, would surely have stayed unimplemented. Even if some plants could have been bodily removed, three industries at least, and possibly more, could not have been uprooted and replanted in Germany and these contained more men reserved from military service than any others. The Germans could not have carried away the British landscape, with its crop-bearing fields and pastures needed to support cattle and sheep. They could not have removed the coalmines, which alone meant leaving nearly 900,000 men where they were. Iron and steel smelting plants might perhaps have been dismantled and carried off, but their real value lay in being sited close to the source of their raw materials. Finally, the humblest German Economic Officer would have known that, though the generators of British power stations could be removed to Duisburg or Dortmund (although these places had sufficient power already), common sense and economic geography dictated leaving them where they were, on the coalfields which supplied them. For all these reasons the Germans would, it seems likely, have decided to 'forget' the internment order. Even as originally drafted it included a major escape clause, deportation being required *'unless the local situation calls for an exceptional ruling'*. This in many if not all parts of Great Britain is precisely what the local situation *would* have demanded.

A wholesale seizure of the younger male population might perhaps have occurred in districts where there had been resistance to the Germans, either by 'auxiliary units' or sabotage, or by workers who had gone on strike or 'worked to rule', thus enabling the Germans to get rid of the actual and potential troublemakers and provide a warning of what would happen elsewhere if the population were uncooperative. Deportation of all the men would, in other words, probably have been suspended over the British Isles as a permanent threat to would-be dissidents which, with the exceptions to be mentioned later, is what happened in the Channel Islands. One Guernsey man, well placed to judge and later himself sent to prison in France, recalls how 'throughout the German Occupation the biggest blackmail threat held over us by the enemy was that, in the event of the civilian population offending them, the Germans would "deport from the island all men between the ages of eighteen and forty-five years". The Nazis knew the effect this would have on everyone so they played it as their trump card.'

The knowledge that he might be carried off to work for the Germans abroad was also a strong inducement to every citizen to do as he was told, since anyone marked down as a 'troublemaker' was likely to find his name at the top of the list when 'volunteers' were required to join the Todt organisation, the vast mobile labour force the Germans moved about Europe to build factories, roads and fortifications. For the same reason it was dangerous to be unemployed, and one Jersey man, active in the resistance, remembers that after losing his job he 'refused to register with the local labour authority because I might have been sent to work for the Germans and I spent three years of the Occupation wandering round on a commission basis collecting overdue library books'. Although no British citizens seem to have been enrolled into the slave-labour force, the people of the Channel Islands had ample opportunity to see how its members were treated, for large numbers were employed on Jersey and Guernsey, building pillboxes and underground strongholds, and Alderney was taken over as a combined prison and camp for them. While many local people, as will be mentioned later, did their best to help these unfortunates, most were not unnaturally scared of these half-starved, ragged, wild-looking men, rendered desperate by the brutality with which they were treated, and having before them only the choice between being worked, or beaten, to death by the Germans, or being shot for stealing from the civil population. Fear dissolved in compassion, however, on occasions like that in 1942 when British deportees were being loaded on a boat at St Peter Port and a bucket of soup was knocked over on the ground, causing the slave-workers nearby to throw themselves on hands and knees to try to scoop up the precious puddles with their hands.

The life of a slave-worker was but one step removed from the hell of incarceration in a concentration camp. Many of those who experienced it died, but one who survived, though with his health ruined, is a Frenchman taken against his will from the Unoccupied Zone of France and sent to work in Jersey. This was his life—as it might have been the life of millions of British citizens, had the Germans carried out their deportation plans. The working day lasted from 6 am to 6 pm, or, in winter from 7 to 7 or 8 to 8, with one half-day off every fortnight, but this was as much to be dreaded as looked forward to for on that day there was no food after midday, the Germans explaining simply, 'Nichts Arbeit, nichts Essen'—'No work, no food'. The food consisted of 'cabbage soup without cabbage' and some coarse bread. The men tried to slake their appetite on potato peelings stolen from the dustbins, on bread thrown out by their German guards as uneatable, and on raw limpets, torn from the rocks, which the local people also collected, though to feed their pets.

Hunger becomes an attitude of mind. . . . You think about food, you hear about food, you wake up in the mornings thinking about food, you talk about food, all you can think about and talk about is food, food all the time. And when you cannot fill up that gap in your stomach you become a zombie.

They were not paid, received no luxuries or comforts of any kind and very few clothes and this man was conscious all the time of the deliberately brutalising effect of the regime imposed upon them. 'You become like an animal, you fight for everything, you fight for a place in the queue at night to get your soup . . . you fight to get a bunk . . . to sleep by the fire. Before you used to be compassionate. . . . Today you become hardened.' Many of his workmates died of malnutrition and ill-treatment—those who survived have since been crippled with rheumatism and other complaints—but worst-treated of all were the Russians, whom the Germans regarded as barely human. He personally saw one Russian murdered by a German guard who 'hit him with a shovel and practically cut him in half'.

No Channel Islanders were sent as slave labourers, but many were deported. The first warning came on Tuesday 15 September 1942, two years after the arrival of the Germans, and it was a clear breach of the promise then given that 'in the event of peaceful surrender the lives, property and liberty of peaceful inhabitants are guaranteed'. The German authorities on the islands were not, however, to blame. Lord Coutanche has since described how with the Attorney-General he called on the German Field Commandant, then installed in the boarding house of the chief island boys' school, Victoria College, and 'we protested as hard as we could protest' until the colonel concerned picked up a paper from his desk and said ' "That document, that order for the deportation of these people, is signed by the Führer himself and you've worked with us long enough here to realise that there is nobody on earth who can stop that order being carried out." '

The decision, which seems to have been due to Hitler's obsession that the allies planned to recapture the Channel Islands as a base for the invasion of Europe, was that anyone whose normal home was not on the Channel Islands, such as those caught there on the outbreak of war, and all men aged sixteen to seventy born outside the islands, with their families if they were married, would be 'evacuated and transferred to Germany'. The Germans planned, in their tidy way, to deport 2000 from Jersey and Guernsey together, but in the event they carried off about 1100 from the former and 890, later raised to 1000, from the latter, a total of 2100. It took them little time to decide who should go, for they had already compiled a nominal roll of all the islands' inhabitants, showing their place of birth, which became the vital test applied. Some absurd anomalies occurred as a result. Lord Coutanche personally drew attention to one, of a man marked down for deportation as English merely because his mother had gone home to her mother in England to have her baby before rejoining her Jersey-born husband in his native island. 'I went up and I explained what a fine chap he was, World War soldier and all that sort of thing. There was nothing to be done: "There he is on the list and there he stops", although that man was as much a Jerseyman as I am.' The present Town Clerk of St Helier also witnessed an example of German inflexibility, mingled with callousness, during the deportation of the second batch of local people: 'One man', he remembers, 'had a heart attack. There was some German officer just stood over him and photographed him while he was lying on the ground.' The unfortunate sufferer was eventually carried on to the boat, escorted by a nurse.

Behind the scenes this official, and other Jersey residents, were doing all they could to protect their fellow citizens. 'We had to go up to the commandatura at College House', he remembers, and 'go through the list with the Germans, and if there was any particular reason why a person or family should not be deported we had to give them those reasons. We did this reasonably successfully . . . so much so in one case they said, "Well, if we can't send all these fellows, we'll have to send you." ' In fact very few 'substitutions' by volunteers willing to take the place of those too weak to go were allowed. One elderly man killed himself rather than leave his home and a few girls born on the mainland escaped deportation by rapidly marrying native-born Jerseymen. One man then running a canning factory managed to save some of his employees by persuading the Germans that they were engaged on essential work and could not be spared, but 'the second time I went down there it wasn't quite so easy', though he managed eventually to get both the threatened men struck off the list. 'One I said was consumptive . . . and he was sent out straight away, he and his wife and a little baby, and the other fellow I said was our main agricultural engineer though he was just a labourer. I said that our work would stop if he was taken . . . and they let him off.'

On Guernsey, after a wretched weekend spent in packing, the unfortunates finally selected were assembled at the Gaumont cinema where, in happier times, they had queued for an evening's entertainment. Now, as the sad lines of elderly couples, young families, women with babies in their arms or with frightened children clustered round them, shuffled forward, they were checked in not by a commissionaire but, one watching journalist noted, by a 'superior-looking, fat-gutted Nazi overseer'. This unsympathetic individual acted as the final court of appeal, for some young people not on the list 'when a particularly aged or infirm couple came forward to be checked in . . . stepped quietly forward to say to the Germans "Can we go instead of this old couple?" '. 'It was a good job', admits one Jersey woman, looking back on her day-long wait with her two small children at the weighbridge near the former railway station at St Helier where they were assembled, 'that we didn't know before we left about those horror camps . . . otherwise I think we'd have just died of fright then.'

30 *German troops on Guern*

GUERNSEY'S OLDEST NEWSPAPER — ESTABLISHED 1813

The ✶ Star.

CXXVI.—No. 156   MONDAY, JULY 1, 1940.   GRATIS

ORDERS OF THE COMMANDANT OF THE GERMAN FORCES IN OCCUPATION OF THE ISLAND OF GUERNSEY

1)—ALL INHABITANTS MUST BE INDOORS BY 11 P.M. AND MUST NOT LEAVE THEIR HOMES BEFORE 6 A.M.

2)—WE WILL RESPECT THE POPULATION IN GUERNSEY; BUT, SHOULD ANYONE ATTEMPT TO CAUSE THE LEAST TROUBLE, SERIOUS MEASURES WILL BE TAKEN AND THE TOWN WILL BE BOMBED.

3)—ALL ORDERS GIVEN BY THE MILITARY AUTHORITY ARE TO BE STRICTLY OBEYED.

4)—ALL SPIRITS MUST BE LOCKED UP IMMEDIATELY, AND NO SPIRITS MAY BE SUPPLIED, OBTAINED OR CONSUMED HENCEFORTH. THIS PROHIBITION DOES NOT APPLY TO STOCKS IN PRIVATE HOUSES.

5)—NO PERSON SHALL ENTER THE AERODROME AT LA VILLIAZE.

6)—ALL RIFLES, AIRGUNS, PISTOLS, REVOLVERS, DAGGERS, SPORTING GUNS, AND ALL OTHER WEAPONS WHAT-SOEVER, EXCEPT SOUVENIRS, MUST, TOGETHER WITH ALL AMMUNITION, BE DELIVERED AT THE ROYAL HOTEL BY 12 NOON TODAY, JULY 1.

7)—ALL BRITISH SAILORS, AIRMEN AND SOLDIERS ON LEAVE IN THIS ISLAND MUST REPORT AT THE POLICE STATION AT 9 A.M. TODAY, AND MUST THEN REPORT AT THE ROYAL HOTEL.

8)—NO BOAT OR VESSEL OF ANY DESCRIPTION, INCLUDING ANY FISHING BOAT, SHALL LEAVE THE HARBOURS OR ANY OTHER PLACE WHERE THE SAME IS MOORED, WITHOUT AN ORDER FROM THE MILITARY AUTHORITY, TO BE OBTAINED AT THE ROYAL HOTEL. ALL BOATS ARRIVING FROM JERSEY, FROM SARK OR FROM HERM, OR ELSEWHERE, MUST REMAIN IN HARBOUR UNTIL PERMITTED BY THE MILITARY AUTHORITY TO LEAVE.

THE CREWS WILL REMAIN ON BOARD. THE MASTER WILL REPORT TO THE HARBOURMASTER, ST. PETER-PORT, AND WILL OBEY HIS INSTRUCTIONS.

9)—THE SALE OF MOTOR SPIRIT IS PROHIBITED, EXCEPT FOR USE ON ESSENTIAL SERVICES, SUCH AS DOCTORS' VEHICLES, THE DELIVERY OF FOODSTUFFS, AND SANITARY SERVICES WHERE SUCH VEHICLES ARE IN POSSESSION OF A PERMIT FROM THE MILITARY AUTHORITY TO OBTAIN SUPPLIES.

THESE VEHICLES MUST BE BROUGHT TO THE ROYAL HOTEL BY 12 NOON TODAY TO RECEIVE THE NECESSARY PERMISSION.

USE OF CARS FOR PRIVATE PURPOSES IS FORBIDDEN.

10)—THE BLACK-OUT REGULATIONS ALREADY IN FORCE MUST BE OBSERVED AS BEFORE.

11)—BANKS AND SHOPS WILL BE OPEN AS USUAL.

(Signed) THE GERMAN COMMANDANT OF THE ISLAND OF GUERNSEY
JULY 1 1940.

TO EVERY ISLANDER

The public are notified that no resistance whatever is to be offered to those in military occupation of this island.

The public are asked to be calm, to carry on their lives and work in the usual way, and to obey the orders of the German Commandant which are printed on this page.

CONTROLLING
COMMITTEE
OF STATES OF
GUERNSEY.

2 *German troops in St Peter Port, Guernsey*

33 *German tanks on occupied Guernsey*

31 *Occupation Orders, July 1940. (The first issue of the Guernsey* Star *ever supplied free)*

34 *A German military band in the Royal Parade, St Helier*

35 *A Guernsey cinema taken over by the Germans (the film on show is* Victory in the West*)*

36 *Anti-invasion defences under construction at Anne Port, Jersey. (In the background is a Martello tower, built during the Napoleonic wars)*

A captured French gun being towed into position on Guernsey for use against British shipping

38 and 39 *A gas-driven van and a horse-drawn van on Jersey*

40 *Residents of Jersey collecting Red Cross food parcels*

1 *The Germans burying the washed-up bodies of British servicemen with full military honours*

42 *The New Jetty, Guernsey, awaiting demolition in case of an allied invasion. (The bombs were never in fact detonated)*

Most people reacted remarkably calmly to the news of impending deportation, partly because rumours about it had been circulating for some time. One Jerseyman, then aged twenty, who had fallen foul of the occupying forces a few weeks earlier, was not surprised, he remembers, when 'I went home one particular day for my lunch and my mother handed me an envelope and it was my sealed orders as to what to do to prepare myself for the Fatherland'. As a single man he was philosophical about the coming ordeal. 'I thought, "Well, if I do go to Germany I couldn't be any worse off than under German rule on the island. They could do what they liked with me" in either place.' Another man and his wife endured a week of waiting after reading the notice of the impending deportations in the local newspaper, and were then ordered one afternoon to report the following morning. She still vividly remembers the moment when the blow actually fell:

My husband was out, and a parish official came with a German, and he handed me a bit of blue paper. He said 'This is your instructions, will you please read it? And sign it?' And then my husband came in and . . . he was very cross and he read this notice and said, 'I'm not going to sign this. I don't wish to take my wife and family to Germany. So our official, poor old man, he was rather old, he said, 'Come, come, Mr Stevens, do be reasonable, don't upset things.' So my husband got even crosser, he said, 'No, I will not sign this. I'm not going to Germany. I don't intend to go to Germany', and looked at the German and said, 'I'm not going to sign your paper. You can shoot me, if you like.' There was a tense moment, then this German said, 'I'm sorry, I'm not allowed to shoot you.' So I thought 'To hell with all this', and I signed the form to get rid of them.

The instructions the Stevens had been given were to take all the clothes and bedding they could carry for themselves and their two children, then aged two and six, with food and drink sufficient for forty-eight hours. Of their actual departure Mrs Stevens remembers, 'It was quite an incredible feeling. You've got a whole house, you've got your belongings and you're walking out of your house, on a hot September day, with literally all the clothes you can get on your back and round your neck, and that's all—as far as you know, that you've got in the world.' Her fears for her children, she remembers, were tempered with 'regret they weren't older because, not only did we have to carry ourselves and our clothes and our blankets, but we had to carry the children and the children's belongings, which made it a really terrific load'. Light relief, of a kind, came a few minutes later when they reached the bus provided to carry them to the assembly point and found on it a family from 'down the road, with a small boy, and he was really being extremely fractious and his mother turned round to him and said, "Gerald, if you don't be quiet, I won't take you to Germany with me." '

Parliament Square, July 1940

One Jersey man, then a boy of seven, remembers that his first reaction 'was a sense of excitement'. A woman of the same age also does not 'remember feeling scared or worried or anything', though a friend later reminded her how she had 'stood outside the sweet shop', stamped her feet and said 'I'm not going'. Her chief memories of a day that must have been one of appalling anxiety for her parents were not disagreeable, but of sleeping on the deck of a boat with a life-jacket on, and carrying her doll wrapped up in a blanket.

All told, about four per cent of the wartime population of the Channel Islands were deported, representing a cross-section of both sexes and all ages, compared with the twenty-five per cent of the population, drawn exclusively from the younger adult males, whom the Germans talked of removing from the British Isles. How did the vast majority, who were not personally affected, react to this blow to their neighbours? Most, despite the obvious temptation to look the other way for fear of offending the Germans, behaved, at least before the boats left, with a humanity that did them credit. In the weekend before the first ships left Guernsey—they were supposed to go on Monday 21 September, but did not in fact sail until Thursday 24—the other residents, despite their own shortages and the prevailing rationing, provided gifts of clothes, shoes—who knew how far the deportees might have to walk?—and food while a young local caterer, on the list himself, organised the collection of food and provided a supply of soup, sandwiches and hot drinks. On Jersey the departure of the deportees, some of them wearing small Union Jacks in their hatbands, was made the occasion of a mass demonstration of sympathy from the other islanders, who lined the streets leading to the harbour, setting up shouts of 'Churchill!' and 'England!', and eventually fourteen youths, who were playing football with a German helmet, were arrested.

Curiously enough, however, no sooner had the boats left or, in some cases, even before they had left, than the looters moved in. The couple who had climbed on the bus with the fractious small boy, for example, were sent home late that night to await another boat, and, the husband remembers, 'We came back and found the house fairly well emptied of anything valuable like spare food, spare clothing, quite a lot of wine I had and the obvious valuables. It wasn't wanton looting but people who had perhaps no luxuries heard or saw that we were going and came in and said to the girl we'd left in charge to clear up the house, "Mr Stevens has some wines, Mr Stevens has some tea, he said if he ever went away we could have it." And it went.' Others who returned home in similar circumstances had equal shocks. One family was forced to borrow coal to keep warm for the few days of liberty left to them. Another, arriving home in the dark, found that even the electric light bulbs had vanished since that morning. One child, whose father had, from humble beginnings, built up his own garage business, was moved to tears at his father's distress at finding 'everything missing, windows broken and stuff [gone] that my father treasured for years'. 'If it had been the Germans who had taken it', one woman feels, 'well, you could have accepted it, but to know that it was your own friends that had stripped the place, it was terrible.' Often bombed-out families in England, finding possessions which had survived the blitz looted, suffered a similar sense of outrage, though they were spared the experience many families deported to Germany suffered three years later when they came back to discover their furniture gone and sometimes even the roofs stripped from their houses and the floor-boards taken up, a silent monument to the shortage of fuel.

Though boatloads of young Englishmen of military age might, of course, have had a very different reception, the actual conditions of the removal, and subsequent detention of the Channel Islanders were probably as good as the authorities could provide in the circumstances, though far inferior to those which Germans and Italians detained by the British were currently enjoying (not without many a complaint) in the hotels and boarding houses of the Isle of Man. Conditions at the first camp to which they were sent were primitive but after six weeks the whole party were moved again to a modern German barracks at Biberach in southern Germany not far from the Swiss frontier, which proved to be a model of its kind, efficiently and humanely run. The atmosphere was not unlike a prisoner-of-war camp, with daily counts of the inmates, presided over by a German nicknamed 'Donald Duck', and, with the help of Red Cross food parcels, the occupants were much better off for food than the fellow countrymen they had left behind, the worst feature of life being, as one woman recalls, that 'you were stuck in the blooming compound'. But those who volunteered to go out to work were allowed outside the camp and found many of the local people friendly, and everyone was struck by the beauty of the countryside. As the wife of a British army sergeant who had retired to Guernsey, and now found herself unexpectedly in Bavaria instead, remarked, 'If the Germans have got such a lovely country as this to live in, why do they want to come bothering other people?': a fair question, still unanswered.

Chapter 15:
See Germany and die

They told me I was going to a special camp which was much better than any other.

A Jewish woman, 1942

The first Gestapo Commandos to arrive in Britain would have had the benefit of the 'Special Search List', a 350-page document listing the offices of nearly 400 suspect organisations, including political parties and trade unions, such as the Amalgamated Society of Journeyman Felt Hatters which hardly seem likely to have provided the nucleus of a resistance movement. The same report also included the names of 2300 individuals, indicating which section of the Security Service was interested in them. Although many of those named later boasted of being on the Germans' 'Black List', the document seems to have been basically a directory of everyone whose name had at some time or another, not necessarily as a potential opponent, come to the notice of the Gestapo. By far the largest single category consisted of foreign refugees, many of them Jews, and this was followed by politicians, drawn impartially from all three parties, journalists and academics, to whom the Germans were always inclined to ascribe more influence than they actually possessed, the best-known being Professor C. E. M. Joad, the future star of the BBC *Brains Trust* programme. By no means all those on the list had been noticeably anti-German. Lord Halifax, for example, had been a notorious appeaser, while one woman author mentioned was an active pacifist, whom it would have paid the Germans to leave at liberty. There were some unexpected omissions. The first world war Prime Minister, for example, David Lloyd George, who might conceivably have become Prime Minister in 1940 in place of Churchill, was not included, though his daughter Lady Megan Lloyd George, a future Labour MP, was. But the 'Black List' is in any case a document of interest rather than importance, for no evidence exists that those on it were marked down for permanent detention, much less liquidation. The Jews and anti-Nazi refugees might indeed have been lucky to emerge again from the wine-cellars of the Reform Club, or wherever it was the Gestapo kept its prisoners, but most of those mentioned would either have gone underground before the Occupation began or have been released once the Gestapo had satisfied itself they were not a potential threat. In the Channel Islands, although the population tended to describe every particularly obnoxious German as belonging to the Gestapo, it never really operated; no one was arrested without some reason being given, and the only person executed on the Islands was a young foreigner who landed there after escaping from France.

One organisation suppressed in the Channel Islands which would assuredly have suffered the same fate in Great Britain was the freemasons, who numbered about 450,000. Many British people have expressed distrust of this supposedly powerful secret society, but Hitler's hatred of it reached the dimensions of a phobia and he believed it formed a conspiracy second only to his old adversary 'international Jewry'. Freemasonry, despite the links between the Grand Lodges in different countries, made no known contribution to rescuing the victims of Nazi oppression or to any resistance movement, but Hitler described it to his cronies in 1942 as 'an immense enterprise of corruption' and (without irony) as 'a handful of men who are responsible for the war'. A month later he returned to the subject, boasting that he had known 'little towns that were entirely under the dominion of masonry', and had himself once refused an invitation to a 'full-dress gathering' of a local lodge with the courteous response 'Save your saliva. For me, freemasonry's poison.' Its rituals, he considered, 'transformed men who were quite sane and sober in their ordinary lives into informed apes'. The movement had been suppressed in Germany shortly after Hitler came to power, and former freemasons could only become Nazis if he gave his personal approval, but, he told his listeners, 'I grant absolution only to men whose entire lives bear witness to their indisputably nationalist feelings'.

Shortly after their arrival on Jersey the Germans closed the Masonic Temple and forbade the Provincial Grand Master, the local head of the order, from holding any further meetings, and in 1941 a task-force of no fewer than thirty Germans—another of those 'column-dodging' groups with a soft job which flourished within the Security Service—arrived to make a detailed photographic record of the temple and strip it of all its elaborate decorations, which, with the ceremonial regalia, were shipped off for exhibition in Berlin, apparently to prove that British freemasonry was under the control of the Jews. Thereafter one or two small masonic meetings were held in private offices but officially 'the craft', as its members called it, had ceased to exist on the islands. 'Most of us felt a great loss', recalls one Jersey freemason. 'It was like losing something that you had owned from boyhood. But I think there were other things that worried us more at the time.' The sequence of events would have been the same in England, for Section III at Gestapo headquarters had already laid down, on 26 August 1940, that 'a separate Commando Group' was needed 'to deal with English freemasonry, with special attention paid to the relations between England and France and the Balkan countries, which to a large extent involve freemasons'—further evidence of Hitler's belief in an international conspiracy of which Germany was the victim.

Although Hitler seems to have had no personal vendetta against them, the Germans distrusted on principle any international organisation and often assumed, as with the Boy Scouts, that its activities were a cover for the British Secret Service. Lord Baden-Powell, the founder of the movement, appeared on the Gestapo 'Black List' and both Scouts and Guides would no doubt have been shut down, as they were in the Channel Islands, though owing to evacuation there were few children left. More suffering, at least among the worst off, would have been caused by the closing down of the Salvation Army, also objected to on internationalist rather than ideological grounds. The Germans also suppressed on Jersey and Guernsey, and planned to close down in Britain, such totally harmless friendly societies as the Royal Antedeluvian Order of Buffaloes and the Ancient Order of Rechabites, which combined sickness and similar benefits with a little harmless ritual. The objection here, too, seems to have been to any allegedly 'secret society' which might help people to unite against the occupying forces, particularly if it had links with other countries, and this was no doubt the reason why Rotary International was also to be closed down, although its major activity was nothing more sinister than holding regular meetings of the younger businessmen in any community. Even more revealing of the limitations of the Germans' knowledge of British institutions was their decision to exempt from closure the Ancient Order of Foresters, a friendly society like the others, but assumed by the Security Service to be dedicated to raising timber for the long-term benefit of the Fatherland. The same misunderstanding, one supposes, might also have led the Woodland Folk, a left-wing youth organisation, to be spared.

But the first target in England as everywhere else would have been the Jews. In every country the Germans occupied there was the same sequence of events, beginning with the arrest of leading Jews and the closure of synagogues and Jewish organisations, continuing with the public labelling of Jewish businesses and individual Jews and their segregation into ghettoes, and ending with their removal to a destination unknown then but only too well known now. Even the 'model protectorate' of Denmark, with its freely-elected Parliament, was forced to pass anti-Jewish laws, though the Danes helped almost all the Jewish population to escape to Sweden. There was, to use one of Hitler's own phrases, no 'Jewish problem' on the Channel Islands, for the tiny handful of Jews—about ten each on Guernsey and Jersey—had no synagogues, owned no banks or large businesses and played an inconspicuous part in public life. The authorities on both islands took the view that it was not worth risking a major confrontation with the Germans to protect a group consisting of only about one resident in every 500, and they accepted, with only one protesting vote, the publication of anti-Jewish edicts and the compilation of a register of the names of Jews, not knowing, of course, that this might one day form part of a file in the camp office at Belsen or Dachau. On both islands the order that the words 'Jüdisches Geschäft'—'Jewish Business'— should be painted across the windows of Jewish-owned shops was obeyed, thought it affected only three establishments in Jersey, and when, later, the Germans ordered that they must be sold to Gentiles, one, a drapers was taken over by the manager in trust for the real owner, who had escaped to England, and to whom he returned it after the war. Lord Coutanche and his colleagues did, however, draw the line at publishing a German order that all Jews should wear a bright yellow star on their backs, and the Germans did not make an issue of the point. 'The Jews were, I think', recalls Lord Coutanche, 'called upon to declare themselves. Some did, some didn't. . . . Those that didn't weren't discovered. I've never heard that they suffered in any way.' Looking back he believes that there is no more he and his Council could have done to help them. The orders about the Jews were 'one of many, many hundreds of things that happened', and no one then realised their terrible significance.

What in fact did become of the tiny number of Jews on Jersey and Guernsey? Rather ominously, no one has so far succeeded in finding out; some seem to have been murdered in German camps, and at least one returned to the islands after the war. One, the wife of a British officer and thus doubly in danger, was hidden by the St Helier physiotherapist previously mentioned. The scene he describes could equally well have occurred, if the invasion had succeeded, in St Austell or St Helens.

The bell rang on the door of my clinic one day and I thought it was a patient. I went to the door and . . . it was Mrs R, and she was agitated and shaking. I said, 'What's wrong with you?'

'Well, can I come in?'

I said, 'Yes, come in', and she said, 'The Germans are after me.'

I said, 'Where are they?' and she said,

'I don't know. I left them in my flat. They made me pack up all my jewellery and good stuff and told me as I was married to an English officer . . . I was going to a special camp which was much better than any other camp in Germany, so I was to bring all my best things . . . trunks, never mind how much, and I'd be well treated. Well,' she said, 'during this time my father, who was an invalid downstairs, he called out to ask if we'd like some tea and I said, "Yes". A German soldier came to me . . .

I was at the passage by then. I said, "You go down and tell my husband to make the tea and we'll come down and fetch it. He did, but I went into the next room, which gave on to the fire escape, and escaped down it and ran here.'

The family with whom this Jewish woman had taken refuge hid her for three years, for part of which she slept in the cellars of an adjoining house, then, when the troops who knew her by sight had been posted away, in a folding bed in a room in the front of the house, until later on in her stay she was even able to sit out in the garden wearing dark glasses. Her host managed to feed her from food which he received from farmer-patients in payment for his professional services.

If the Germans had landed in Britain, few Jews are likely to have escaped detection. The mere size of the Jewish community, estimated at 450,000, of whom 340,000 were, nominally at least, of Jewish religion and thus on the books of at least one Jewish organisation, would have made it impossible to hide more than a few of its members. The Germans, of course, branded as Jewish anyone with Jewish blood—even a Jewish grandmother made one a 'non-Aryan—'and the first victims, because the most easily identified, would probably have been those strictly 'orthodox' families which kept every Jewish festival, ate Jewish food, spoke Yiddish among themselves, and conducted most of their business and all of their social life with members of their own race. Later it would have been the turn of all those with Jewish forbears, Jewish names and Jewish appearance, and finally of those who had anglicised their names, become Christians, lived and worked among Gentiles, and perhaps thought of themselves, and were accepted by their acquaintances, as being one hundred per cent British.

How would the non-Jewish population have reacted to these events? A striking feature of German occupation in every country (with the sole exception of the bitter battle in the Warsaw ghetto in 1943) was the virtual lack of opposition to the persecution, followed by the internment and removal, of the Jewish population, and the larger it was the more easily it seems to have succumbed. In Germany and Poland especially, which had contained a large number of Jews, little seems to have been done to help them, far greater efforts being made in Holland and Denmark, especially the latter, where the Jews numbered only about 2000 in a population of four million, relatively fewer than in the Channel Islands.

Anti-Semitism, like colour prejudice, flourished most where its victims were most numerous. A small Jewish population who had 'merged with the landscape' rarely suffered persecution. It was where, as in Eastern and Central Europe, they formed a community within a community with its own language, religion, diet, schools and customs, inter-marrying with each other, favouring each other in business and having little contact with the life of the country which sheltered them, that they were most unpopular. Around 1899, in the Dreyfus case, anti-Semitism had split France into opposing parties, and between the wars the whispered warning 'Don't let the Jews drag you into another war!' had been the most effective of all Goebbels's arguments. In the freedom-loving United States, with its large Jewish population, 'anti-Semitism', noted Sir Oswald Mosley after a visit in 1926, 'appeared in various sections of American life from top to bottom'. He was, he says, shocked to find that even the bathing beaches in some areas were divided into 'Jewish' and 'non-Jewish'.

Mosley himself insists he was not anti-Semitic; his quarrel was only with those Jews, or indeed anyone else, who wished to see Britain involved in another war with Germany. Not all his supporters, however, were equally guiltless and there had been ugly scenes in the East End in the 1930s when Jewish shops were attacked during Fascist marches and individual Jews chased and assaulted. The British public reacted promptly. At a time when ordinary Germans stood watching elderly Jews being forced to scrub the streets and Jewish shops were being openly looted, the British people compelled its government to pass an Act making the wearing of military-type uniforms illegal, there were widespread public protests at the violence used at Fascist meetings, and crowds of Gentiles, as well as Jews, gathered to break up Blackshirt processions in Jewish areas. All this suggests that Hitler would have had nothing like as easy a passage in enforcing anti-Jewish measures in Great Britain as in other European countries. It would be dishonest to deny, however, that beneath the surface the Jews were unpopular with many British people who were violently anti-Nazi, and the war by no means destroyed this feeling. It was widely stated in 1940, in print as well as by word of mouth, that Jewish faces predominated in many air-raid shelters (as indeed they did in the East End, where they formed a large part of the population) and a little later at least one author (although, oddly enough, he was on the Nazis' 'banned' list) drew attention to the large proportion of Jewish names among those charged with black-market offences. During the flying-bomb raids in 1944 the old stories about 'cowardly Jews' never leaving the shelters or, alternatively, fleeing in hordes to safer areas were widely heard again. Those who passed them on, or who told anti-Jewish jokes, of which many circulated during the war, were as horrified as anyone else at later revelations of German atrocities, but whether there would have been a general strike to protest, or even violent riots, when the signs reading 'Beware Jew' began to appear on little tailors' shops in

Whitechapel or on kosher restaurants in Finchley, seems more doubtful.

The Gestapo 'Commando Group' for Judaism should, it was suggested in Berlin, take over the house of Sir Herbert Samuel, a leading British Jew, as its 'operational base', to which in due course such other key victims as 'Rothschild' (though which member of this famous financial family was not specified), 'Hore-Belisha' (the former War Minister) and 'Mond (Chemical Trust)' (presumably the second Lord Melchett, a director of Barclays Bank and deputy chairman of Imperial Chemical Industries) were to be brought. A document listing 'Opponents of Germany', produced a week later, listed a curious rag-bag of other candidates for early attention, among them 'The Chairman of the Committee for Jewish Refugee Children (name not known) in Blackpool', 'The manager of the Kailan Mining Association . . . his country house is said to be in Somerset', 'Sir Benjamin Drage, Jewish director of Drages Ltd, London [who] expressed himself in *The Times* as in favour of accepting Jewish emigrants', *The Cabinet Maker and Complete Home Furnisher* [which] is a Jewish paper', and most oddly of all, a bookmaker 'regarded as the king of East London' and a Woolwich Jew 'known as a cigarette adulterator'.

For the ordinary citizen without close Jewish friends the first reminder that anti-Semitism was now official policy would probably have been the signs reading 'Jewish business' over every Marks and Spencer store and over all the branches of many food shops, cinemas and restaurant chains about whose ownership the public had hitherto shown little interest, German propaganda no doubt making the most of the extent to which the nation's economic life now depended upon Jewish businessmen. Later such businesses would probably have changed their names, as the owners disappeared, or as Gentile friends took over the business to protect it from confiscation. The greatest effect would have been on the men's tailoring trade, the women's fashion trade, especially among smaller 'rag trade' manufacturers, and bookmaking. Kosher restaurants and delicatessen shops would have disappeared, and synagogues have been offered for sale as storerooms or warehouses. More defensibly, Jewish slaughter-houses would also have been shut down, though not before the maximum publicity had been given to the methods of killing in use in them, against which many British people, in no way anti-Jewish, undoubtedly felt—as they still do—intense revulsion.

The Jews in Great Britain had always been concentrated in a few areas, especially London, and their removal would have thrown on the market a great deal of property at knock-down prices, tempting some eager purchasers not to enquire too closely what had become of the previous owners, though property in London in 1940 was in any case very cheap. In Bethnal Green and Stepney, in Hampstead Garden Suburb and Marylebone, the 'For Sale' and 'To Let' boards would have been everywhere, though many Jewish estate agents' businesses would themselves have been up for sale. Other signs of the times would have been slower to appear, like the disappearance of 'Jewish New Year' cards from the stationers' counters, of Jewish recipe books from the bookshops, and, by the time the 1942 editions of diaries and almanacks appeared, references in them to Passover and other Jewish religious festivals would have vanished. Within two or three years, if not before, all evidence that the British Isles had ever had a large Jewish population would have disappeared, apart perhaps from a thinly patronised anti-Semitic exhibition set up by the Nazis in some corner of the National Gallery or the British Museum left vacant by looted art treasures.

After being warned that they were listed as Jewish, the next step on the road to the concentration camp for British Jews would probably have been the order to assemble, with no more luggage than they could carry, at a local assembly centre, two obvious choices being the Golder's Green Hippodrome and the People's Palace in the Mile End Road in Stepney, and here, as in other capitals, Red Cross workers would no doubt have done their best to help the assembled crowds who might otherwise have been left, as happened in Paris, without food, medical care or even water for several days. At this stage, much of the organisation would probably have been in the hands of leading Jews themselves, who might well, with German help, have set up ghettoes where they could at least practise in peace their own religion and the rigid dietary rules and other taboos associated with it. When the day came that they were ordered to prepare for a move to the Continent, like their coreligionists in Europe they would surely have gone, if not willingly, at least non-violently. What else, after all, could they do? Both they and their countrymen would have believed they were merely going to internment; but even had they known their real destination, the prospects of successful resistance would have been small.

The present Chief Rabbi, the Very Rev. Emmanuel Jakobovits, was in 1940 a young minister who had himself arrived in England as a refugee from Germany only a few years before. He believes today that in 1940 'much the same pattern would have been witnessed here as in all the other countries of Nazi occupation', and the loyalty of many Jews to their religion would, he believes, have made their detection easy. As he explains:

There are quite a number of communal records . . . which preserve with very minute detail entries on Jewish marriages and Jewish burials and Jewish registration of membership of synagogues and Jewish organisations and schools and so on, so that the documentary evidence itself may well have given away the bulk of the Jewish community, which was highly organised here. Most Jews were in fact members of some Jewish organisation or community or other. Those not on those lists may well have been found through the indiscretion or malice of some neighbour or someone else who happened to know or had old scores to settle or some personal grievance . . . as happened on such a massive scale in other European countries. The possibility of Jews actually getting away with it simply by not being detected as Jews . . . would have been very remote indeed. I know of hardly any cases on the Continent where this was the cause of the survival of Jews. They survived in hiding or by flight, but not by non-detection.

Flight from the British Isles, with the nearest friendly land nearly 3000 miles away across the Atlantic, would have been almost impossible but when it came to hiding the Chief Rabbi believes that 'compared to the situation in other European countries, the Jewish community here was extremely well placed. Anti-Semitism . . . had in no way struck anything like as wide and deep a root in society as it had done in Germany or in Austria, let alone in Poland or in some of the other Central and East European countries. . . . My guess would be that at least as many Gentiles here would have been found to risk their lives, if necessary, by protecting Jews and keeping them in hiding as were found in a country like Holland or . . . Denmark.'

Some British Jews, Dr Jakobovits believes, would have put up a fight before surrendering. 'I would think that resistance would have been altogether highly organised here and that Jews would have been among some of the main resistance fighters in much the same way as Jews played a principal role in the Maquis in France.' But the fate of British Jews would not, he thinks, have been particularly influential in encouraging the United States to come to the rescue of the British Isles.

Anglo Jewry has had a peculiarly insular past, by regarding itself as somewhat distinct from the Jewish communities on the European continent on the one side, and the American Jewish community on the other. There were very few Jews . . . in America who were of British origin. I would think that American Jewry would be likely to be touched more deeply by the fate of Central and Eastern European Jews, from which after all the bulk of American Jewry was drawn, and where everyone had relatives and a family or possibly a place of birth with which to identify in a personal way.

With resistance probably futile, and no outside help forthcoming, what does the Chief Rabbi consider would have been the fate of British Jews if their country had been occupied?

At first, I think, Jews would have been herded together in closely packed ghettoes reserved exclusively for a Jewish population and almost hermetically sealed off from the rest. There would then have set in a process of deportation of large numbers of people beginning with the leaders and then eventually entire family units would have been shipped across the Channel and then right through Europe to Eastern Europe and . . . the various concentration camps. There may have been quite a number of Jews who would have found refuge in hiding with Christian neighbours who, themselves, at the risk of their lives would have protected a number of families, as indeed did a great many families in Holland, where quite a few thousand survived the occupation by living in hiding. [But] while that occupation eventually came to an end because of the final victory of the Allied Forces, had Britain been occupied I doubt if redemption could have come in time to secure those people from detection. And therefore if there had been a prolonged occupation exceeding two or three years it would probably have been physically quite impossible to hide them away for ever.

All over Europe Jews turned in the hour of desperate need to their ministers, for guidance and spiritual comfort. The advice they gave is unknown, since pastors and their flocks are alike dead. The Chief Rabbi in Great Britain has considered what comfort he too might have been able to give his people if in 1940 the Germans had landed:

I would hope that under the burden of such a challenge I might emulate the example of countless rabbis who were in fact placed in this position and first of all give those in my spiritual charge not only a message of faith in ultimate triumph and the ability in fortitude to withstand the kind of suffering and martyrdom which . . . is the hallmark of our history, but I might also by personal example and by reference to . . . our . . . literature, evoke the kind of popular response that would enable spirit to prevail over matter. And that would enable our people under such excruciating conditions to see itself as really a speck in a long line of history, and not merely view the present as being a disconnected self-contained unit unrelated to a past and a future . . . One would have stressed under such conditions the supreme importance of strengthening ourselves from within, by shoring up our family life, by trying . . . to spiritualise our day-to-day existence and thus take the mind off some of the pressures from without . . . Very often we don't realise our own potential in the face of adversity until we meet it. It is only under stress of those burdens that sometimes the fineness comes out in man. I would never despair of the ability of a human being to withstand ordeals which rationally speaking one would imagine he is bound to succumb to.

About what would have happened to British Jews who were caught, there need be no speculation. One Jersey woman, then a child, has not forgotten the strange sight which caught her young eyes on the boat on her way back to the island from internment, for travelling with them was one of the few Jews who had also survived. 'She had her hair all shaved off, her arm was in a sling and there was a number printed on her arm.' A little earlier, when they were still detained, she remembers her mother, having quarrelled with some Germans, being threatened with being sent to Belsen, a name that meant nothing to them until, just before the war finished they realised its significance when a lorry-load of survivors from that terrible place were brought into the camp.

They were all Jews and . . . we were at the gate to see them come in . . . You just couldn't believe they were human beings any longer. [There was one of them] well, we didn't know if he was a man or a boy or what he was, he was so thin. He had Army boots on and as he dragged his feet he just came out of them. His legs . . . just wouldn't stay in . . . The people were very lousy, they had to be taken into the baths and their clothes were put into the corner and I'm not telling a word of a lie when I tell you that those clothes were literally moving . . . Tears were rolling down the commandant's face, he just didn't believe it. He shook his head and he said . . . to us, 'How can we win a war when we treat people like that?'

Chapter 16: Resistance

Armed insurgents of either sex will be dealt with with the utmost severity.

> Directive for Military Government in England,
> *September 1940*

While in June 1940 the French government was planning to surrender, the British government was planning to resist even if its country were overrun. No one at this stage was thinking of a permanent underground resistance movement such as later sprang up in all the occupied countries, but merely of a small military force behind the enemy lines, which would harass the Germans in the rear as they advanced and give the forces defending the 'stop-lines' inland more time to prepare. During the Norwegian campaign, even before Hitler's offensive in the West, dumps of explosives for this purpose had been hidden at various points around the country, and after Dunkirk a full-scale, if small, organisation was set up to form 'stay behind' parties in a coastal strip thirty miles deep, from John o' Groats in the far north of Scotland right down to Lands End, in the far west of Cornwall, and then round the Atlantic coast as far as Pembrokeshire in South Wales. The stretch of coastline from there back to Scotland was left unguarded, the colonel in charge deciding, rightly we now know, that no danger of an attack from that direction existed.

At the start the whole of the area to be protected was divided into twelve sectors, each manned by a 'striking force' of twelve soldiers, led by a subaltern, signallers, clerks and a storeman being added later. They were recruited by one of a small team of officers looking for initiative, resourcefulness, and an enthusiasm for 'irregular' operations, rather than the more orthodox military virtues, and the men who did the selecting were themselves of this type. In the area of highest risk, for example, in the south-east, where XII corps was protecting a front from Greenwich, well up the Thames estuary towards London, to Hayling Island, nearly at Portsmouth—thus covering almost precisely the territory chosen by the Germans for the initial lodgement of Army Group A, and the Army Command objective after the subsequent break-out—the man responsible was the author and explorer Peter Fleming, a hostilities-only Guards officer with the unconventional outlook to be expected of a successful journalist, author and explorer. Eventually some twenty Auxiliary Units, as they became known, manned by soldiers, were set up, but they were reinforced by a far larger number of 'cells' or 'patrols' recruited solely from civilians, who carried on with their ordinary jobs, but were expected, if the Germans arrived, to retire to their secret hideouts and become full-time guerillas, emerging after dark to blow up an enemy petrol dump or sabotage a troop of tanks.

Many of those invited to take on this lonely, dangerous and, of course, unpaid job, offering in full measure Churchill's 'blood, toil, tears and sweat' with the chance of getting shot thrown in, were already members of the Home Guard, from whose rolls they were quietly dropped—so quietly that some were threatened with court-martial for not turning out on parade with their old units. But the Auxiliary Units also recruited civilians, especially men like gamekeepers and farmers, and even a Master of Foxhounds, who knew the country intimately, as well as clergy, doctors and local officials, who could travel round after an occupation without attracting attention. Other recruits were selected because they, too, showed the right spirit and aptitude, among them tin miners in Cornwall, coal miners in the industrial North, fishermen, blacksmiths, hotel-keepers and publicans. Some were aged no more than seventeen, some were in their seventies. But all, though they would never have put it in such terms, were ready, for their country's sake, to live a cramped, dangerous, secret existence, while their homes were destroyed and their families killed, knowing that the best they could hope for if caught was a speedy execution. Paragraph 3 of the Commander-in-Chief's *Directive for Military Government in England* warned that 'armed insurgents of either sex will be dealt with with the utmost severity. If the population initiates active operations after the completed conquest of a locality, or in places behind the fighting front, the inhabitants involved in the fighting will be regarded as armed insurgents.' The poster prepared for public issue went even further. 'I warn all civilians', read von Brauchitsch's proclamation, 'that if they undertake active operations against the German forces they will be condemned to death inexorably.'

In fact, technically speaking—and when it was one's life at stake technicalities mattered—it was doubtful if many members of the Auxiliary Units, even though they wore Home Guard uniform, were really Home Guards at all, for their former units had disowned them, or they had never belonged to the organisation, while no central records were kept of the three special battalions on whose strength they were supposed to be, which existed on the ground rather than on paper, a reversal of the usual situation in 1940.

The first approach to a man to join an Auxiliary Unit often came from someone already connected with it over a quiet drink after a Home Guard parade, and the potential recruit would then be exhaustively 'vetted' by local enquiries. Once accepted, his evenings and weekends would be spent in training, either locally or at a country house at Highworth, near Swindon in Wiltshire, acquired for the purpose in 1940. One farmer recruited to a patrol at Romney Marsh, Kent, remembers the training as 'really good', and this impression is confirmed by the 'saboteur's handbook' issued to members, an innocuous-looking buff-coloured booklet, labelled 'The Countryman's Diary 1939', with, printed below it:

HIGHWORTH'S FERTILISERS
DO THEIR STUFF UNSEEN
UNTIL YOU SEE
RESULTS!

This, quite literal, 'cover' story may have been designed to discourage prying eyes, though it seems more likely to have been a private joke, but the contents in any case fully lived up to the promise on the front, consisting of fifty-two pages of admirably forthright and lucid information, sufficient to convert any man not incorrigibly clumsy into a dangerous saboteur. The section headed 'Some Improvised Mines', which is illustrated by cut-away drawings, gives an idea of what the Germans would have been up against.

These are all things you can easily make yourselves, as the materials are easy to find.
The first step is to make a 'burster'. This can be made by filling a small cocoa tin with Gelignite—1 lb is enough—and moulding in a small knot of Cordtex . . . Bring the spare end out through the lid.
The next step is to make the 'shrapnel' part of the mine. The shrapnel itself is usually small pieces of scrap metal such as nuts and bolts, nails, etc. If you can't get these use small, sharp stones . . . The more shrapnel the better—but remember you will have to carry the thing about.
A very good method is to use an old motor cycle cylinder filled with gelignite. The fins fly very well . . . With a little imagination dozens of other ideas will present themselves . . . The essential point is that for outdoor booby traps you must aim at killing by splinters—not by blast.

Later sections of the booklet were equally informative about attacking 'shell and bomb dumps', 'petrol dumps' ('in large dumps concentrate on the up-wind end of the dump. The wind will help to spread the fire'), 'Aeroplanes: the Tail is the best part to attack', 'Armoured cars' ('fix a charge of 2 lb primed gelignite on . . . the side of the engine'), 'Trucks' and 'Tanks', the advice here showing a vast advance in realism on the days of Molotov cocktails and blankets hung across streets: 'Best of all attack the repair lorries which always go into 'harbour' with the tanks and let the field army do the "tank bursting".'

The Auxiliary Units would have concocted their lethal devices, and lived their solitary lives, in tiny hideouts officially known as 'Observation Bases' or OBs. By the end of 1940 about 300 had been constructed, some of them being in the cellars of ruined castles or abandoned farmhouses, in caves unknown to tourists, in abandoned coalmines and, in Scotland, in the 2000-year-old dome-shaped stone dwellings last used by the Picts. The secret of their location was well kept. The Kent farmer already quoted remarks that 'I had two brothers-in-law in another patrol and had not the slightest idea where their OB was'.

This was the more remarkable because many had to be specially built by Army engineers in hillsides and in woodland, the finished result resembling a small, concrete-lined, underground kitchen, the domestic atmosphere being heightened by paraffin lamps, cooking stoves and piles of tinned food sufficient to enable the five or six occupants to stay literally underground for at least ten days. After 1940 other refinements were added to the organisation, including an elaborate signals network, manned by Auxiliary Territorial Service girls, who were asked to volunteer for 'an interesting and possibly dangerous assignment', and were interviewed, as if to underline the basic respectability of the whole organisation, in the public lounge of the most aristocratic of London department stores, Harrods, by the niece of the then Archbishop of Canterbury. By that time the total strength had reached 5000 men, well equipped with the latest weapons and explosives, such as the invaluable 'stickybomb', which attached itself to a tank and directed a concentrated explosion at the armour. In 1940 numbers were smaller and it would all have been a far more desperate affair, with bands, one suspects, of rather dirty and unshaven desperadoes slipping out of their hideouts in the darkness to stab a sentry in the back or lob a grenade into the German headquarters established in some local country house, many of which had already been reconnoitred with this very prospect in mind. The basic aim, however, was not so much to kill people, who could easily be replaced, as to throw enemy plans into disorder by destroying equipment. 'The whole object of our existence', another Kent Auxiliary Unit member recalls, 'was to go behind the enemy lines to do as much damage as we could, blast petrol dumps, ammunition dumps, lorries or anything. . . . In the course of this one might come up against sentries. . . . We were taught to kill these. . . . One went behind the sentry, put the knife behind his ear, gave a sharp push, and you had a very, very quick death, and a very quiet death'—to be followed, of course, by a very noisy explosion.

The Germans would not have tolerated such action for long. Reprisals would have been immediate and savage, and would certainly have included the taking of hostages, for the German *Directive* already quoted advised that 'when taking hostages those persons should if possible be selected in whom the *active* enemy elements have an interest'—meaning presumably the families and neighbours of men suspected of being involved. Would this have caused the Auxiliary Units to stop their operations? A group of former members to whom this question was put in 1972 were unanimous that it would not. 'We'd taken the job on', one pointed out, 'and if people that we knew had been shot we couldn't have brought them back to life by stopping. I think we would have owed it to them to go on despite what might have happened and, if we'd seen things destroyed that we'd known for a great many years, I think it would have made us go on and on . . . as long as we stayed alive'. Even if his own loved ones had been put at risk by his activities he believes that they, too, would not have wished him to stop: 'I'm sure their feeling would have been to go on. Mine would have been anyway.' Another of the unit agrees. 'If they killed hostages', he would, he believes, have decided it was 'up to me to get my own back and kill some of them'.

The Germans also hoped by reprisals to force local people themselves to discourage military resistance. This policy had some success on the Continent, where even the most loyal patriots sometimes urged the resistance men to go away and cause trouble elsewhere, but it was generally ineffective. 'The reaction', comments one Auxiliary Unit member, was never against the resistance movement, it was always against those who caused what had happened, in other words, the invaders.' The attitudes of peacetime, he points out, offer little guide to one's feelings in such a situation. 'If the Germans had been here . . . our minds would have been very different from what they are today. What future would there have been other than try and get rid of the invaders— and do your damnedest while you were alive to do it?'

How long would the Auxiliary Units men in fact have stayed alive? Although their stores were originally only intended to last ten days, some members believe that, if given a sufficiently remote hideout from which to forage for further supplies, they might have stayed hidden for months. Peter Fleming felt that most might have escaped detection for six or seven weeks, if the invasion had come around 20 September, until the leaves began to fall from the trees and the frosty ground betrayed their give-away tracks to low-flying aircraft. In distant areas, like the north of Scotland (with few German targets to attack but equally few enemy to observe them) they might have gone on living their curious lives for years. But this was not the real aim for the Units really existed to cause behind-the-lines disruption before the battle had been lost and they had been given no instructions what to do if the Germans were finally victorious, each Unit having to search its own collective conscience as to whether there was any point in fighting on.

If, of course, the Germans had carried out their policy of rounding up for deportation all the men from seventeen to forty-five, this would have settled the matter, at least for those in this age-group, for they would have had nothing to gain by surrender and would have been too conspicuous to settle back again into civilian life. It seems likely, too, that as others immediately threatened by the Germans—Jews, Communists, leading politicians, left-wing journalists—went underground the Auxiliary Units men would have found themselves, whether they wished it or not, as the spearhead of a larger resistance army, forced to cope, against their will, with an influx of untrained, unskilled and probably unsuitable recruits, who might well have been more a hindrance than a help. What would have happened after that one can only speculate, but certainly the experience of every country in the world has been that an internal resistance movement cannot by itself defeat an occupying army though it can give valuable assistance to a liberating one.

Independently of the Auxiliary Units, a few selected Home Guard officers and others were involved in preparing caches of weapons, which would not have been surrendered when the Germans arrived but kept hidden against some future need. In one Kent churchyard dummy graves were dug, containing not bodies but rifles and shotguns, The construction was undertaken personally by the foreman of a local firm of monumental masons, while the paving and curb stones were supplied, with no questions asked, by a local councillor from the council's road-mending stores. Here, too, near the Thames estuary, ammunition and grenades were buried in sealed watertight containers, the design being based on standard Admiralty lockers, easily assembled in the dockyard. These were sunk in the mud, the sites being marked by small buoys which floated at high tide —the subject of some future 'fishing expedition' for which even the exhaustive German regulations had not provided.

An even more dangerous and lonely job than that of the Auxiliary Units would have been undertaken by a few men who would have stayed 'above ground' and pretended to collaborate with the Germans while in fact spying on them. The official name of the organisation to which they belonged, and even the fact of its existence, have never been disclosed, but to the few members of the Auxiliary Units who were in the secret it was known as 'the other side'. Even to them the identity of the individuals concerned was never revealed and the Auxiliary Units knew only that messages about possible targets might be left for them at certain selected spots, though they had no means of contacting their unknown informants.

One area where 'the other side' would have been active was around Sheerness, near the mouth of the Thames, on the Kent bank, facing across the river towards Southend and Canvey Island on the Essex shore. Around Sheerness lies the Isle of Sheppey, a mainly flat, rather run-down area, flanked on one side by the Thames, on another by the narrow tidal inlet known as the Swale, and on a third by the River Medway, running inland to Chatham. The island was linked with the mainland only by a single road and rail bridge across the Swale, while the other broad and shallow channels surrounding it on the landward side were impassable except at very low water, and then only by those familiar with the area.

Sheerness had been one of the assembly points from which the 'little ships' had sailed to Dunkirk and it was a key base during invasion summer for the 'V' and 'W' class destroyers patrolling the Channel and guarding the river approaches to London, while its fall, by blocking the exit from the Medway into the Thames, would have rendered the docks at Chatham useless. The defending commanders had, therefore, recognised that the area was likely to be one of the Germans' first targets and might well be overrun, but its early recapture was regarded as vital, both to secure the dockyard and to regain the use of the airfield on the island, and one local Home Guard officer found himself approached, in a way which seemed fanciful then, but has become familiar in espionage trials since, to organise a signals network which could continue to function under the very noses of the victorious Germans, to warn the British forces on the mainland of the enemy strength and dispositions. This potential agent had the type of background which made him both a particularly valuable recruit, and one whose bona fides, as a disgruntled British citizen, the Germans might readily accept. After joining the Army as a boy soldier and serving for many years as a regular in the Royal Signals, he had left the service after a disagreement with his superiors and had joined the Post Office Telegraph Department. Here he had fallen foul of the law over a fraud involving faked postmarks on football pool coupons and had served a short period in prison, but by 1939 had rehabilitated himself so success-fully that he was employed on responsible contract supervision work by the Admiralty at Sheerness. After the formation of the LDV, later the Home Guard, in 1940, he had been one of the first to be commissioned (although military ranks were not formally introduced until later in the war) and seemed to have put the past behind him—until, with invasion threatening, it suddenly caught up with him. One night that summer he was visited by a mysterious stranger, apparently a civilian, who identified himself by reference to various mutual acquaintances in the Army and then asked his surprised host if he were willing to do something dangerous for his country. When this officer agreed he was told he would be contacted again, and was assigned the codeword 'Wormwood', to which the counter-sign was 'Woodworm', these being chosen, it was explained, because the Germans found great difficulty in pronouncing their 'W's.

Sure enough, while attending a Home Guard parade at the Drill Hall in Sittingbourne, he received instructions to go to a local public house, The Bull, and, on leaving this in the darkness, he was stopped by a girl who whispered the codeword, and then drove him to a large country house, strictly guarded, where he was shown into a dimly lighted room and found himself facing three men he had never seen before. They explained to him that if and when the Germans arrived word would be leaked to them that he had no reason to love the British authorities, and it was hoped he could ingratiate himself with the invaders and pick up useful information. Seeing that it reached the proper quarter, however, would be far more difficult than collecting it and he was asked to devise some system that could still be used to convey information from the Isle of Sheppey, even if normal communications with the mainland were severed. He would, he was told, later receive another visitor to whom he should pass on details of the scheme he had worked out.

By then he was ready with his plan. Conventional communications equipment of all kinds was desperately scarce at that time, and a radio transmitter operating on the island would, he believed, rapidly be located by enemy direction-finders, but there was a method of signalling which cost nothing, could be operated by totally untrained staff and had at least a good prospect of going undetected—the homely domestic clothes line. In those pre-washing-machine days, he remembers, much of the district seemed to be almost permanently covered by clothes hanging out to dry, so that the few vital lines which carried a secret message concealed amid the surrounding shirts and petticoats would have been in little danger of detection. On a clear day—and most days that summer *were* clear—a signal could be read through a telescope from as much as twelve miles away, though the system was, of course, useless in bad weather or after dark.

Although all those in charge of the operation would have been men, it was felt that any male seen hanging out a basket of damp clothes would look distinctly conspicuous, so a number of women—mainly the wives of serving officers—were let into the secret, and the Germans, who firmly believed women's place was in the home, might well have smiled on them approvingly as they trudged about the garden pegging out the washing, refusing to allow a mere invasion to upset their regular domestic routine.

These 'operators' needed no training or special equipment, the duty of the first in the chain being merely to hang out the garments she was told, in the order specified, while all the later 'stations' merely had to hoist the same pattern of articles on their line, until it had been copied in turn by the next. They did not need to know what message they were passing on, and it was probably better, considering the risk of capture and torture, that they should not, this being known only to the Home Guard major who originated it and some far-off recipient miles away inland.

The basis of the code was the Morse alphabet, with a large article like a sheet or tablecloth signifying a dash, and a smaller item, such as a towel or a tea-cloth, a dot. Nappies would clearly have been excellent, as a whole row flying in the breeze would have attracted no attention (provided there was a baby in the house), but anything smaller, such as a handkerchief or pair of underpants, was not large enough to be 'read' at a distance, though acceptable if the receiving station was not far away. The articles forming each letter were hung close together, with a larger space between letters or words, and, by prior arrangement, other refinements could be incorporated, such as a prop part way along the line to indicate the start of a new message.

The major who devised the system also made use of the conventional abbreviations familiar to every Army signaller or civilian telegraphist, who knew, for example, that 'X' meant 'This message is not for you but is to be passed on', and that 'A' stood for 1 o'clock, 'B' for 2 o'clock and so on, with further letters signifying the minutes. Such experts could readily interpet a line of, say, a sheet hung between two pillow-slips (dot, dash, dot), two tea towels and a tablecloth (dot, dot, dash), and two groups close together, each of two bath-towels and a hand-towel (dash, dash, dot, repeated twice), which spelt out 'R U GG', as 'Are you going . . .'. As in naval flag signals, single letters could stand in the codebook for short standard messages or single words, and by flying a coloured garment at the start of the message a whole additional range of variations was possible, blue, for example, signifying a single ship, one company of troops or a flight of aircraft, and red indicating a naval flotilla, Army battalion or Air Force squadron. The alphabet was similarly divided up to indicate the type of enemy forces, 'A' to 'F' meaning various kinds of ship, from destroyer to pocket-battleship, 'G' to 'L' being used to signal the approach or presence of fighters, fighter-bombers, gliders and other aircraft, and 'M' to 'R' being reserved for land forces, with 'N' warning of armoured cars, 'O' of heavy tanks and 'Q' of transport vehicles.

Like so much else that summer, signalling by clothes-line was an echo of the Napoleonic wars, when, from a semaphore station on the roof of the Admiralty in London, messages had rapidly been flashed all the way to the coast via a network of similar stations, on hills and high buildings, each consisting solely of long wooden arms mounted on a post, though in this case there had been no need for secrecy. It would be pleasant to think that one day that summer the long-distance clothes-line mounted at the water-pumping works on Southdown Hill on the Isle of Sheppey and designed to be read on the mainland, might have flown Nelson's classic message before Trafalgar, 'England expects . . .', but the brutal truth is that in 1940 there would probably have been no time for romantic gestures of this kind.

Psychologically there were resemblances between the atmosphere of the Channel Islands and that which would have existed in an occupied Britain, but in most ways conditions were not comparable, for the Islands had been formally disarmed and legally surrendered, the normal civil authority was still in being, and there had been no bloodshed to embitter feelings on either side. On Guernsey and Jersey, due to Hitler's belief that they were to be the allied stepping stones back into Europe, there was, however, nearly one German to every two inhabitants and sometimes even more, by far the highest proportion in any occupied country. Even in London, where there would have been most German troops, the numbers would have been relatively much smaller, and outside it many places might have gone for weeks or months together without seeing a single enemy soldier. A garrison of at most 500,000 and more probably of half that number, would have had to be spread over a population of forty-eight million, or at least thirty-five million even if all those in the Forces and in the threatened age groups had in fact been carried off to the Continent.

Lord Coutanche still firmly believes that 'we couldn't have done any more to help the major cause' through more violent opposition to the Germans. He and his colleagues, he recalls, 'neither encouraged nor discouraged "pin pricks" against the Germans', though these, he points out, can be prompted almost as much by boredom as by patriotism. 'Bear in mind here's a population with no coal, no gas, no electricity, no heat, the only thing to do is to go home and go to bed, when its dark. They must have something to think about and there were small bands of people who decided to paint V signs or decided to cut telephone wires. We neither discouraged it nor encouraged it. I respect their patriotism but frankly I didn't think then and I don't think now that it did any good to anybody.'

The cutting of telephone wires was the most serious sabotage which occurred on either Guernsey or Jersey, and the Germans dealt with it by ordering the residents of the affected districts to provide nightly guards for local telephone lines. 'I think', says Lord Coutanche mildly, 'the people who were compelled to leave their houses . . . to stay up all night guarding a telephone wire which went from nowhere to nowhere in particular . . . thought it was rather a waste of time.' Others on the islands were also critical of this particular gesture. One Jersey policeman remembers going to see a suspect in his office, who 'lifted up a carpet and showed me a piece of the wire. I said, "You're a damned fool, because it only means the public are going to suffer for that; you're not hurting the Germans. If and when the British land you can cut any telephone wires, that's up to you, but not at this time." That's the kind of thing that I didn't approve of at all. It was purposeless.'

To avoid embarrassing conflicts between their official duty, to carry out the orders of the German commandant, and their natural patriotism, this policeman and his colleagues relied on that most valuable part of any good policeman's equipment, the blind eye. Often, he admits, they knew when people had secret radios, the commonest of Occupation offences in Jersey, but kept quiet about it, unless an informant compelled them to take action. They did their best, too, not to run into offenders engaged in another wartime crime, curfew-breaking. 'Half the time we stayed in the police station', he remembers, and if there were still fellow islanders illegally about 'the Germans collared them, we didn't'. People caught stealing presented a more difficult problem, though the police's private rule was simple. 'If people stole theirs'—i.e., property confiscated by the Germans—'we didn't worry, if people stole ours, we jumped on them.' It was not long before some local villains began to take advantage of this policy, as the same police officer discovered:

I met a chap coming along one morning with a sack on his back at daybreak, asked him what he had in the sack, he said he'd just broken into a German store and stolen some coke for his wife and children. I was about to let him go when I asked him to open the sack—and he'd got the sugar ration from a local shop. Of course he was off and I was after him but I picked him up eventually. But had he had coke from a German store . . . I'd have let him go.

Fortunately, perhaps, for the inhabitants there were no hidden stores of arms on the Channel Islands and no attempts to provide them, so the local resistance movement was, by the standards of neighbouring France, where both collaboration and opposition reached far greater extremes, a very mild affair. As in France, however, its inspiration was largely left-wing, its real founder in Jersey being a local man who had emigrated to Australia and returned to Europe to fight in the Spanish Civil War, though it had ended by the time he arrived. The movement began with groups of half a dozen or so like-minded people meeting in each other's homes and eventually had a network of contacts all over the island, providing information, food for people on the run, and vital supplies like paper for illicit publications. Its membership rose by the middle of the war to fifty or sixty and to around a hundred after D Day, being in the words of one of its earliest members, a seventeen-year-old who had just left the local grammar school, an instinctive response to the 'tremendous almost physical shock' at 'the outrage of foreign occupation'. Like the governor and the police, they saw cutting telephone wires or destroying German signposts as 'meaningless', and apart from constantly urging a firmer stand against the Germans by the authorities and producing illegal leaflets, their main work lay in helping slave-labourers, especially the Russians, collecting food and clothing for them, and even providing places where they could hide. The results were striking. 'You could go to 50% of people in this island and get an immediate response', this man discovered, 'even if they didn't agree politically with you at all.'

Among those applied to for assistance on behalf of the Russians was the present Town Clerk of St Helier. 'Two Russians escaped . . . from the prisoner-of-war camp,' he remembers, 'and a friend of mine got in touch with me and asked if I could take their photographs to put on identity cards to help them in their escape. I arranged to meet the two Russians and the man concerned in town; we took the photographs at my mother-in-law's house, and I then took the photographs home, developed them, printed them and . . . stuck them on the identity card and matched up the German stamp . . . across the photograph with the new photograph that I put on.' The cards themselves came from new ones issued by the Germans in replacement of those declared lost, or from those dropped in the street and found by sympathisers with the resistance. Some, 'regrettably', says Mr Marshall, were stolen for the purpose, for to be without one's 'papers' in an occupied country was a serious matter, though the really dedicated resistance worker in any country was always willing to sacrifice his countrymen for an end which he believed to be right.

This same local government officer, then far more junior, also regularly engaged in another hazardous enterprise, listening to and circulating the news, or Churchill's speeches, which he heard on an illicit radio. This involved taking the broadcast down in shorthand, typing it out, duplicating the copies on the Town Hall duplicator, and passing them to various trusted members of the staff, and the police, to distribute in their turn to 'safe' people known to them. On one occasion he bumped into a German officer while on his way to hand them over to the police sergeant, who was one of the main 'newsagents' involved, and dropped all fifty copies on the Guard Room floor. The German, however, 'bent down, picked them up, collected them, handed them back to me and apologised profusely for being so clumsy'. There were other narrow escapes. 'I can remember cycling home in great worry at times and digging a hole in the garden and putting everything in it, including the radio set, which of course I dug up as quickly as I could in case the damp got to it.'

One of the most depressing, and alarming, features of the occupation of the Channel Islands was the number of people who, whether from envy or sheer malice, anonymously denounced those of their compatriots who had managed to retain a radio. One Englishman, later deported to Germany, remembers a notorious informer who selected his victims by listening in food queues for anyone passing on up-to-date British news. When, later, he arrived in the deportation camp himself, he had to be kept shut up for his own protection. But if there were traitors in the Channel Islands (and it seems surprising that some blatant ones should have escaped unpunished at the end of the war) there were also many people in key positions quietly working to frustrate their efforts. One man still remembers with gratitude the postal employee who spotted a letter addressed to the Commandant in the heavy capitals favoured by one informer, and quietly appropriated it. It was, as he had suspected, denouncing another local resident for possessing a radio, but never reached its destination.

Although, for reasons already explained, it seems unlikely that the Germans would have confiscated all radio sets had they occupied Britain, if they had done so the population would no doubt have reacted with the same ingenuity as in Jersey. The physiotherapist mentioned in earlier chapters concealed his in electrical equipment used in his work, a screw turned one way energising the appliance, and the other turning on the radio. He recalls an occasion when he was treating a small boy and turned the screw the wrong way, causing the patient to remark suddenly, 'You know I can hear my daddy's voice', his father in fact being in the garden at the time. Another family managed to satisfy the Germans by surrendering a small 'car-type' set, taken from their boat, but kept a small portable hidden under the floor connected to what appeared to be a power point in the room above, and a loudspeaker, normally kept hidden in a cupboard, could be plugged into this when it was safe. Possession of a loudspeaker was legal and less suspicious than earphones, which were widely used on the island linked to home-made crystal sets.

Many illegal news bulletins circulated on both Jersey and Guernsey and several of those concerned in preparing them, or found in possession of them, were sent to gaol, but far more serious from the Germans' point of view were leaflets urging resistance to any of their orders, such as one which was circulated advising people to hide their radio sets. This was one of the occasions when the Germans took hostages, selecting for the purpose local residents with a reputation for being 'uncooperative'. The sensations of one man, a hitherto law-abiding factory-owner, who found himself in this position were typical of those which many thousands of people in Europe must have experienced, though in their case the ending was usually less happy:

On Friday evening I'd had a tip that something was wrong and on the Saturday morning I arrived at my office and a German handed me a slip of paper and it said that I was under temporary arrest. I said, 'What's all this about?' He said, 'It's because some pamphlets have been issued and we've taken some hostages.' I said, 'Is this going to be a long job?', and he said, 'I don't know, it can be short.' I said, 'When will there be a trial?' He said, 'There's no trial.' . . . I was numbed, I didn't know quite what had happened to me. . . . One minute to be out in the bright sunshine and the next minute to be in a cell. . . . One chap [a locally-born warder] used to pop in and see that we were all right and try and cheer us up and then he'd go off and throw pebbles at the window in our cell and say 'That's all right, chums, you're going to be all right'. It was very nice, very cheering—but in actual fact I think we both felt a bit worse after.

Up to that time the Germans had not executed any hostages in Jersey and in fact they never did, but to this man, in June 1942, it seemed 'well on the cards' that he would be the first. Recently he had, with other islanders, laughed at the Germans for talking of their opponents being 'fuselated', instead of 'shot'. Now, he admits, he was 'no longer very amused'. Happily, after a week in prison, he was released, the offending pamphlet's authors having given themselves up.

This man, who had done much in a quiet way to obstruct the Germans, does not believe that on the Channel Islands more active resistance would have been possible. 'It had to be of a passive nature and I think that Jersey did that' is his verdict. 'The things that hurt the Germans most was being ignored and they had a fair dose of that.' He contributed his own share of the 'dose' so effectively that, as he still remembers with amusement, he was formally, if not very convincingly, admonished for his attitude by the Governor in person:

He was called to College House [i.e. German headquarters] and I met him on the road coming back. He stopped and said, 'Tony, I've been called to College House and they've been complaining about you not being co-operative. You'll try and be a better chap, will you?' And I said, 'Yes', and I winked back and that was it. It didn't make much difference to my attitude and I'm sure it didn't make any difference to his.

Many Channel Islanders, like this man, automatically made life difficult for the Germans whenever they got the chance. The physiotherapist previously quoted told a German soldier who came to him for treatment that he was 'full up' with civilian patients, and was as a result called before the Commandant, who had the effrontery 'to read me the Geneva Convention and told me that I had to work for them or be deported'. Knowing that his other patients needed his services, he eventually agreed 'to do so many patients a day' from the German garrison, but drove the toughest bargain he could. In many shops the assistants ignored German customers, but after one barber had pointedly not cut the hair of a waiting German, an order was issued that Germans must be attended to first—the sort of unwelcome reaction that resistance was always liable to produce. Many firms made the most of all the difficulties involved when ordered to supply the Germans, and on Guernsey two which were ordered to supply German flags managed to misunderstand the simple instructions they were given so that the first Swastikas they produced had to be scrapped. Such gestures made, of course, not the slightest difference to the course of the war, but they did help to sustain morale among everyone who heard about them.

In the Channel Islands no one was shot for resisting the Germans, though a sizeable number were imprisoned, mostly for two or three months, their gaolers sometimes managing to make 'mistakes' over the release date and letting them out early, another useful method of passive resistance. There could have been a blood-bath at the very end, for after D Day the left-wing extremists in the resistance movement, one remembers, 'contacted a committee of German Socialists and Communists, who were organising a mutiny of the garrison, to hand the island over to the allied forces', though this came to nothing. This was fortunate, perhaps, for the German Commandant in the closing stages of the Occupation was a fanatical Nazi admiral, very different from his comparatively easy-going military predecessor, and only too eager to call out the firing squads as a prelude to fighting to the last man. Life in the resistance did, however, have its effects upon those involved in it, providing, as in other countries, a unique political education. When the Occupation began one member of it was, in his own words, 'a very starry-eyed Communist of seventeen'. When it ended he was a man of almost twenty-three. It turned him, he believes, 'from a very green sort of youngster with lots of high ideals and illusions into a rather cold, calculating politician'.

And most British people on the Channel Islands came out of their five years' ordeal with their self-respect unscathed, if not a little raised. Besides the thousands who chalked up V signs or wore hidden badges, often made from British coins, with V inscribed on them, there were many who made more public protests, which helped to keep hope alive even if they did the Germans no harm. A young girl employee in Boots the Chemists 'just didn't seem to care', one of her colleagues remembers. 'She always made sure that the German customer knew no English at all and then with a smile on her face proceeded to call him all sorts of names. She never got caught.' Nor did a kindred spirit of an older generation, an elderly retired colonel who, punctually at nine o'clock every morning, would march with soldierly stride down the main street of St Helier to a shop which contained a huge portrait of Hitler in the window. He would then halt smartly, 'stand rigidly to attention in the middle of the road and spit'.

Chapter 17: Collaboration

The following have been named as persons and firms of a friendly disposition towards Germany.

Memorandum of the German Security Service,
11 November 1940

'No one knows how he will behave during an Occupation until it happens.' This is the verdict of many of those British people who endured five years under German rule in the Channel Islands and it commands respect. 'There were', one man who himself spent a period in gaol as a hostage believes, 'people who were a bit over-friendly, but in the circumstances it's difficult to judge. There are people with stronger wills than others. The stronger wills were able to resist, the weaker wills gave way a little.'

Apart from the 'Jerrybags', whose crime was probably a desire for comfort and company rather than treason, and the anonymous letter-writers, who seem to have been prompted by malice and envy rather than disloyalty, there were in this solitary part of the British Isles which actually experienced occupation exceedingly few who, to quote an eighteenth-century politician, 'drank of the wine that makes men forget their country'. A few, a very few, tried to trade on working for the Germans to try to obtain preferential treatment, but they were mostly very young. The manager of Boots, having dismissed one young girl friendly with a German security man, 'was forced to take her back under threats', and a Jersey policeman remembers how on 'one occasion . . . a young boy about fifteen was riding a cycle the wrong way up a one-way street. I asked him what he was up to. He said, "Can't you damn well read? Look at the back of my mudguard, I'm working for the Germans." So I told him, "It doesn't excuse you from obeying the law." He said, "If you go on at me like that I'll report you to the Commandant." I said, "The war won't last for ever. One of these days I'll kick you up the backside from here to the Commandant's office." I didn't get any more from him. He was gone.'

In Denmark, Hitler's 'model protectorate', which in many ways was far better treated than the Channel Islands, it was commonly estimated at the end of the war that ten per cent of the population had collaborated to some degree, ten per cent had actively resisted, and the rest had done neither. On the Channel Islands one active resister who was himself sent to prison estimated the percentage of collaborators on Guernsey at only two per cent. In the whole of the Channel Islands only twelve people were considered for prosecution at the end of the war but in not a single case was the evidence strong enough for a charge to be brought.

Although for the rest of Great Britain the hope of liberation after a successful invasion would have seemed far more remote, all the evidence suggests that in trying to find British people to work with them, let alone for them, the Germans would have faced an equally uphill struggle, for the surviving German documents suggest a truly desperate desire to discover some 'persons and firms of a friendly disposition towards Germany' to offset those voluminous lists the Gestapo had compiled of its avowed enemies. To balance the 2500 names on the 'Special Search List' there are only some fifty who were even believed to be well disposed towards Germany, and, apart from a German restaurant which many would recognise, apparently included merely because it was German, the documents include not a single well-known person or establishment. Even those on the list are there only because they had been tolerant of Germany before the war; there is no guarantee that they would not have been wholly patriotic once the Germans had landed, as Sir Oswald Mosley, whose name, incidentally, does not appear on the German 'White List', says he would have been.

Whenever any potential supporter came to their notice, local Gestapo branches seem to have sent details to Berlin, and typical of those reported in this way, in October 1940 by the Graz section, was an Englishman believed to be living with his sister in the Midlands who had 'given proof of his objective attitude towards National Socialism' when lecturing at an Austrian university, while the country was still independent, to such an effect that he had spent a month in gaol as a Nazi courier before being released on the intervention of the British Consul and expelled from the country. He had popped up again later that year, in Germany itself, holding a university post there until forced to return to England on the outbreak of war. Whether or not his attitude had changed since then was not recorded—German intelligence in England was always abysmal.

Another list was compiled in Brunswick a month later by those same devoted officials who had suggested to headquarters that they should remove the Elgin Marbles and the Gutenberg Bible from the British Museum. Ten people or companies were suggested, and someone in Brunswick had obviously lived in Lancashire for six of those named came from the Manchester area, among them a schoolmistress, a judge (married to a German), a firm of calico printers, a member of a company of wholesale druggists, and two private citizens, one a man of unnamed occupation, the other his married daughter. Elsewhere in the country the Germans looked hopefully in the direction of a City firm of shipping agents (apparently because of their connection with a German firm), an engineer with offices in Victoria in Central London, and most surprisingly, a spinster living in the High Street of a small town in North Wales, though her qualifications were not disclosed.

Since avowed friends of Germany seemed, even to the Nazis, to be distinctly thin on the ground, the Security Service section in Luneberg (which had also discovered such dangerous opponents of Germany as the 'cigarette adulterator' and the 'King of East London' mentioned earlier) were reduced to drawing up a list of *Critics of Conditions in England*, apparently assuming that these too might be turned into active collaborators. It included the Scottish MP, Captain Ramsay, who was already detained under Regulation 18B and who would surely have been surprised to find himself in the company of a 'cabaret dancer [who was a] supporter of Mosley', a 'Catholic priest, Father —— [who] in a review of the anti-Hitler book by Professor Freud described Hitler's anti-Semitism as a good thing', a fairly well-known author expelled from the Labour Party for a book contrary to its policy, a former MP, described only as an 'opponent of Churchill', the author of a book on the problems of the clergy in rural areas and, most unexpected of all, a member of the staff of the 'Aberystwyth Agricultural Station', with an impeccably Welsh name, who 'is fighting in support of farmers against capitalism'. Far more promising sounds a member of the 'Ladies Army and Navy Club', the wife of a colonial Civil Servant, who had been 'a member of the Fascist League, for years active in propaganda for National Socialism', and was 'one of the best propagandists, who has extensive connections'. Alas, however, even this fish had slipped through the net for, the author of this memorandum complained, after recommending her to the 'Overseas Office' of the Party in 1936, 'unfortunately no notice was taken of my request to remain in touch with the lady'.

The main German 'White List' containing 'Addresses and Short Character Sketches of English people friendly towards Germany', prepared in the Munich office of the Security Service and sent to headquarters on 9 September 1940, contains thirty-nine names, of which seventeen are of women. The criterion for inclusion seems to have been at least one visit to Germany, usually to attend or lecture at a German university, and almost all of those listed appear to have been middle class. No titled person is included, nor anyone who appears to have been a manual worker, although, apart from one clergyman, none of the entries specifies the occupation of the person mentioned. The Germans were, however, interested, at least to the extent of recording it when they could, in the appearance of these potential contacts and, following the classic pattern of intelligence agents, they scrupulously recorded any emotional attachments their subjects had formed in Germany. The favoured thirty-nine seem, however, to have been a highly conformist, not to say respectable, body and no hint of scandal, much less of deviation, appears against any name. These were not government servants to be blackmailed into spying, but independent, if misguided, private citizens who, if they had collaborated, would have done so out of admiration for Germany and National Socialism.

Heading the list, though it does not seem to have been in any particular order, and receiving the longest entry, was the daughter of the headmaster of a well-known boys' school in the Home Counties. Of her the unknown informant had written:

Known to me from daily teaching and personal acquaintanceship as a true friend of the new Germany. She showed genuine enthusiasm and real agreement with all its institutions. She evinced genuine admiration for the characteristics of the Germans. Her own character is incorruptible and extremely reliable. She managed, in spite of strong resistance from English circles, to persuade her parents to visit Germany. . . . Her parents, too, whom I got to know very well, expressed themselves in every way as appreciative and in praise of the Germany of today. They were opposed to the Versailles 'Diktat' and in favour of the return to Germany of her colonies. They [had] spent a considerable time . . . in the former German colonies and told me that none of the natives there had ever forgotten Germany and hoped for their return to German sovereignty. They had repeatedly found this to be so.

Miss —— wrote to me in the early Summer of 1939, after her return to England, as follows: 'I know that, now that I have been in Germany and have got to know this country and its people, I can never again be happy in England.'

Miss —— did not have any love affairs which might have given rise to such an attitude.

More susceptible, however, seems to have been the next name on the list, the daughter of a Surrey businessman, a woman 'small of stature and a very nimble personality', who had also read for a doctorate at a German university until forced to go home in 1939. 'She was', wrote the German who had watched her, 'a true Englishwoman, but genuinely and obviously devoted to the new Germany and worked hard in her own circles in England for more understanding and sympathy. She became acquainted in Heidelberg with a German who was [a member of a non-Christian religious sect]. She herself belonged to the High Church, but this did not wreck the beautiful friendship which existed between the two people.' Tributes hardly less lavish were paid to a Cheltenham woman who had taught English in a girls' school in Heidelberg and was 'devoted to

Germany with her whole being' and 'accepted the world of National Socialism', another woman, from Berkshire, who had taught English in Munich, a bachelor girl from Knightsbridge, 'who showed lively interest in German culture', and a Devon woman who felt 'it should never come to war between Germany and England'. Some fortunate Nazi had also had the job of escorting around Munich Miss Jean —— of Blackheath, a middle-class suburb in South East London, 'a very winning girl of great beauty', who 'returned home a friend of German culture . . . in the form in which she had experienced it here'.

Besides an admiration for all things German, and the desire to avoid another war, the other most common reason why so many people professed sympathy for Germany was horror at the poverty and despair which mass unemployment and inadequate social insurance and welfare arrangements had bred in Britain between the wars, for the Nazis' achievements in both fields were impressive. A woman whose home was in Derby, which had not escaped the sufferings of the Depression, was quoted as desiring to see German experience repeated 'in the social scheme of her own country', while a Harpenden woman, 'an upright and straightforward character in every respect . . . always spoke with great bitterness of conditions in the English working-class districts' and was 'an ardent admirer of the social innovations in National-Socialist Germany'. So was another German sympathiser, from Woldingham in Surrey, who had, it was said, been 'particularly impressed by the whole system of education' in Germany and who 'wanted to see . . . changes in the social abuses in her own country'.

As their 'black radio' activities had shown, the Germans hoped to exploit for their advantage the nationalist dislike which they believed many Scots and Irish to have for the English, and four of the women mentioned lived in Scotland, one of these, who was 'of Irish extraction' reaffirming 'in her letters some years after her return home' to Edinburgh that she was an 'opponent of English despotism and of social abuses in England'. In Scotland, too, the Germans hoped to contact 'a patriotic Scotswoman', living in Ayr, who 'always bore in mind the evil things which England had once perpetrated on her native country'. In Aberdeen could be found Helen, 'a true Scot' who 'took in everything she saw as there were no such social and educational achievements in her home country', and in Dumfries, Dorothy, another 'true Scot' who 'often complained about the poor social conditions in England and in her own country and regarded Germany as a model for their modification'. Similar indignation inspired Diana, 'a very attractive girl of Irish descent' whose background 'was the reason for her dislike of the abuses of English power politics and of the poor social conditions, especially in London', though she cannot have seen much of these in her everyday life, as she lived in a comfortable part of prosperous Kensington. The only other Irish-born girl on the list lived at a much less impressive-sounding address in Belfast and passionately 'desired the liberation of Northern Ireland from English domination'.

All the women on whom the compilers of the White List had, politically speaking, set their sights, seem to have had certain characteristics in common. Although their ages are not given, the fact that they were all unmarried and had visited Germany shortly before 1939 either as post-graduate students or to teach English suggests that they were still young, probably in their late twenties. The addresses of most suggest a comfort-able background, and certainly there were none from either very poor homes or from particularly wealthy or aristocratic ones. While they might, from the Nazi point of view, have done useful propaganda work in their own circles, it is impossible to see any of them as a potential Fräulein Quisling, especially as the Germans, and the Nazi Party in particular, were basically anti-feminist and never considered women for high office.

Far more potentially important, therefore, were the twenty-two men on the White List, but these, too, were an undistinguished collection, useful perhaps as advisers on local conditions or as Nazi nominees on some recalcitrant council, but not the stuff of which major traitors were made. One of those listed, whose 'friendship for us was open and honest', was not a British citizen, since he came from Dublin and was 'a convinced Irishman and an opponent of English despotism in his country'; one, with a Scandinavian name, living in Surrey, was 'an Englishman of Danish extraction', and there was one Welshman, from Glamorgan, who—under-standably since he came from one of the areas worst hit by the Depression —'frequently expressed his admiration of [the] social achievements of National Socialism which, he said, were in stark contrast to English conditions'. Six of the twenty-two males mentioned were Scots, all of whom had apparently read theology at Heidelberg, the source of most of the information in the document. It was a Scot who headed the list of men's names, and also received the longest entry for a male:

Address: Edinburgh. . . . An open, honest and straightforward character, as was his whole presence. Although he was aware of the political disputes in which the Church in Germany was involved, he was very devoted to the new Germany. He demon-strated this in his discussions with his fellow-students and especially to me during German lessons, whenever a debate started between the foreigners. He was in every way averse to solitary tendencies. On Sundays, he often helped the farmers in the neighbourhood of Heidelberg, because it gave him pleasure to get to know the

German farmer in and out; he often said that there was nothing like that in Scotland or England. In addition he helped voluntarily with the harvest in Pomerania . . . and returned home shortly before the war. An opponent of war between England and Germany.

'Scottishness' seems to have made a great appeal to the Germans for most of the entries relating to the other Scots, from Perthshire, Aberdeen, Dundee and Edinburgh, contain such phrases as 'self-evident Scotsman', 'a true Scot' or, even more approvingly, 'a convinced Scot, who often inveighed sharply against the English character'. What is more alarming is that, like so many Christians in Germany, these Scottish theologians seem to have brushed aside all the evidence of the basic incompatibility between their religion and the Nazi philosophy, and of the persecution of the Protestant Church in Germany. (The Roman Catholic Church, which enjoyed Hitler's grudging admiration, had never incurred the regime's wrath by actively opposing it.) Thus one son of the manse (as his address reveals) 'did not allow himself to be influenced by arguments between the Church and politics but formed his own sensible opinion on these phenomena, coming down in support of the new Germany'. Another academic from Edinburgh, who, it was said rather cryptically, 'had a positive attitude to life and was worldly . . . rejected the prejudices of German theologians against National Socialist institutions', while another theology student from the same city, 'taking a world view . . . accepted all innovations of National Socialist Germany and . . . the church disputes in Germany did not affect his friendship' towards it.

This curious willingness to be seduced by Nazi arguments about religion and to turn a blind eye to the Party's excesses afflicted others besides the Scots, as the references to the eleven native-born Englishmen on the White List confirm. One of the most enthusiastic tributes is paid to a clergyman, from south-west London, who 'came to Germany to study the social and educational institutions of National Socialism and to learn about the position regarding German theology. He expressed high praise for the former and regretted that large numbers of theologians had not formed a proper relationship thereto, as their outlook was too limited and too narrow.' Another convert, described as 'open-minded', came from an unspecified theological college in Cambridge. Apart from this, however, and their similar social background, there was little in common between the other Englishmen pinpointed by the Security Service's informant. They came from places as scattered as Southport, Cheltenham, Esher, St Ives in Cornwall, Birmingham, Odiham in Hampshire, Twickenham in Middlesex, Derbyshire, Brighouse in Yorkshire, Stockport and Kidderminster, and all seem to have had in common an admiration for

German achievements at home and a desire for peace, even at the price of returning the German colonies. One gains the impression that many were somewhat vain people, easily duped, genuinely anxious for peace, ready to let their heads too easily rule their hearts, but nowhere is there any real hint that they were ripe for treason.

Chapter 18:
Which way to the Black Market?

An Order will follow for the complete stopping of rations to the civilian population.

Directive from Commander-in-Chief of the Armed Forces
to the Commandant of the Channel Islands, 18 September 1944

If the Germans had plundered the British Isles as thoroughly as they planned, the surviving inhabitants would rapidly have found that problems of day-to-day living loomed larger in their minds than either the memories of absent loved ones or the dreams of liberation. It was difficult under such conditions to avoid becoming a human animal, concerned only with securing food, warmth and shelter. To survive from day to day was much; to endure until the nightmare had passed was the utmost limit of any man's ambition. 'We became very, very hungry indeed', recalls one Jersey schoolteacher, and 'there was in many cases no heating, no fires, no light and this also reduced people's mental resistance in many ways. . . . I've met many people of the intellectual type whose intellectual interests dropped to a surprisingly low priority, where the main interest was virtually one of a kind of natural survival. One was more interested in discovering whether one could obtain something for the next meal rather than any deep philosophical thoughts.'

This man had seen in his own life as a wartime schoolboy the far-reaching effects of occupation. 'Materials, writing books, pencils, paper . . . became worn out, textbooks became rather battered but generally teachers made every effort to continue things as normally as possible', even though the time came when they were leading their classes down to the communal kitchen to queue up to cook for their dinner a solitary potato apiece. He had hoped to specialise in science but the school soon began 'to run out of apparatus for physics and chemistry and . . . chemicals. Doubtless it was thought some of the chemicals might be put to far more illicit purposes than ever entered the ideas of a schoolboy.' So science lessons soon became confined to theory and as it was no longer possible to take 'Higher Certificate' (the equivalent of the postwar 'Advanced' level GCE) he left school at nineteen to work in a local government office, using the German he had learned to read scientific textbooks, to translate instead German documents and interpret in 'cases against local nationals who had been convicted of the tremendous crime of owning a crystal set or distributing leaflets dropped by the RAF'.

The schoolboys of Victoria College, St Helier, had one lesson in practical chemistry unnecessary in normal times, sometimes being given permission to 'go on to the beach, where it wasn't mined . . . to get a bucket of the ocean and boil it up for a bit of salt'. The lack of this vital flavouring was one of the greatest afflictions of the whole Occupation, and in St Peter Port the Model Yacht Pond became an open-air evaporation tank. Horse-drawn wagons toured inland areas offering sea water for cooking at twopence a quart, attracting much wry comment about the inhabitants having to buy back their own ocean. Larger establishments obtained their supplies wholesale, and two nuns from one nursing home could regularly be seen driving to and from the shore a horse-drawn carriage laden with a bath.

The Islands' basic problem was its total lack of home-produced coal. Every lump was soon being cherished and a Guernsey farmer described in his diary in October 1944 the 'very special ceremony of our Sunday treat', when 'after dinner all the family gathers in the sitting room to watch mother strike the match which lights the weekly ruddy glow'. Gas was by now on for only three hours a day and was expected to be permanently cut off by the end of the year, as it had already been on Jersey, and electricity was also available at that time only for a few hours a day, and was supposed to be used mainly for lighting. By midwinter the population were keeping warm and cooking by wood fires, and people visiting friends dragged a log along with them, but the shortage of kindling was so acute that even the small trees in ornamental gardens were being hacked down and a man might find his own front door missing. Much cooking was done in bakers' large ovens or in communal kitchens set up by the authorities, to which one took one's simple provisions, most commonly turnip stew, the various articles being identified by numbered discs.

Artificial light was equally scarce. As early as late 1940 the candle ration on Guernsey was only two a week. 'Candles are like sovereigns and can't be procured at all', the Guernsey farmer already quoted noted in his diary four years later, and on the Black Market they changed hands at £1 apiece. In the hospital at St Peter Port the nurses on night duty sat in darkness, each becoming literally a 'lady with a lamp'—though of a kind more primitive than any Florence Nightingale had carried nearly a century earlier. Churches ceased to take a pride in their stained glass, since it restricted what daylight was available, and it became the rule to sit in darkness while the clergyman conducted the service with the aid of a single candle, lights for the congregation being provided only for the psalms or hymns.

For much of the Occupation, lighting on Guernsey and Jersey slipped back to the standards not merely of the nineteenth but of the eighteenth century, before cheap wax candles became available, so that the commonest source of illumination was a home-made lamp. The Guernsey farmer mentioned earlier relied for his early-morning milking on the glimmer from a bootlace wick burning a mixture of paraffin and vinegar. In the hospital on the same island a piece of tape threaded through the lid of a jam-jar filled with diesel oil served the same purpose. One member of the Jersey lifeboat crew remembers using white spirit, used for dry cleaning, mixed with diesel or even lubricating oil, which produced a light that was 'a bit smoky but better than darkness'.

Unless the Germans had deported all the younger miners, or dismantled and removed the generating and gas-production plant, it seems unlikely that the rest of the British Isles would have suffered a fuel shortage on such a scale, though even with mines and power plants working flat out there was from 1941 onwards a continuing fuel shortage, frequently reflected in empty coal scuttles and chilly offices. The picture which one writer has drawn of Jersey's leading citizen, Governor Coutanche, sitting in his 'fireless office, clothed in sweaters and overcoat, with his feet in a foot-muff containing a hot water bottle', while 'outside sat his interpreter swathed in blankets', is little different from that which many people in Britain witnessed during the later years of the war, though the overall shortage was never as bad. The difference is well illustrated by the attitude towards the water supply. In Britain itself there were appeals to people not to waste water, for example by having only five inches of water in the bath, and by limiting the number of times a day they washed up. On Guernsey, where little washing up was needed and there was rarely enough hot water for baths, the Germans called for a ban on the use of flushing lavatories, to save power used in pumping, suggesting the use of outdoor earth closets or buckets, and when the local Medical Officer of Health protested he was dismissed. He was later reinstated and the original order was withdrawn, but even so the taps on the island ran for only three hours a day.

It seems unlikely, too, again assuming that the Germans did not, as they might well have done, remove vast quantities of British chemicals and chemical-manufacturing plant, that the British Isles would have suffered as badly as their kinsmen in the Channel Islands from a shortage of soap. Soap was rationed in England in February 1942 but the amount was adequate, if one were careful, unlike the situation on the Channel Islands, where the Germans regarded it as a luxury for which there was no shipping space to spare, so that by January 1944 a single tablet of English toilet soap was fetching 10s 8d. Soap from France was available, on ration and at controlled prices, for much of the Occupation, but one resident remembers it as 'terrible stuff. When you finished washing your hands there was always a little pile of sand left in the bottom of the basin.'

As suggested in an earlier chapter, one immediate effect of a German occupation would probably have been, as in the Channel Islands, an immediate reduction in both public and private transport due to the requisitioning of vehicles and the Germans' constant demands for petrol. Britain had large stocks of fuel oils and gasoline in 1940 but these would soon have been run down and, as in the Channel Islands, bus services and taxis might have vanished altogether for a time. The horse and the bicycle would again have been lords of the road, with wedding guests, and even the happy groom, removing their bicycle clips as they entered the church, and mourners at funerals following, like their forbears, a horse-drawn hearse or farm-wagon. Bicycles, which became hard to buy in Britain and lost all their prewar refinements, would no doubt have commanded, as on Jersey, prices of up to £50, ten times the 1940 price, and one might perhaps have seen, as one did there, German soldiers carrying their saddle with them when they entered a shop to protect their machines from theft. In the *North Norfolk News* or *Glamorgan County Times* one would have seen the same 'small ads' as in fact appeared in the *Jersey Evening Post* or *Guernsey Star*, offering 'cycle rear wheel, as new, for what permissible' (i.e., whatever it was not illegal to sell in this way) or 'exchange bicycle tyre for circular saw'. The Germans' hunger for rubber was as insatiable as their thirst for petrol, and bicycle tyres and other spares would soon have been at a premium, the shortage being temporarily overcome by ingenuity, as on Guernsey, where one dealer made valve rubber from electric cable insulation and brake blocks from wood. The final substitute for the tyres themselves was garden hose or lengths of rope tied round the metal rim.

Clothes and footwear had gone on ration in England in June 1941 but, though there was much patching and making-do, no one ever went either ragged or barefoot, largely because Britain had large textile- and garment-producing industries, and manufactured its own boots and shoes. Here occupation would assuredly have made an enormous difference, for the Germans had long been jealous of the supremacy in world markets which Lancashire and Yorkshire cotton and woollen goods enjoyed, and might well have taken over many of their mills, while the supply of imported wool from Australia and of raw cotton from India, though not the United States, would have been cut off overnight. Garment manufacturing, especially for women, would also have suffered with the removal of the Jewish population, and however hard the Civil Service had tried to apply a rationing system it could not have succeeded if the essential pre-requirement were absent, namely an adequate supply of goods to share out. The devices and expedients to which British families became accus-tomed between 1941 and 1945 would therefore have been more necessary than ever—the painted legs, the parachute-silk underclothes, the children's dresses made of flour-bags, the overcoats made of Army blankets. One would have seen, as on Jersey, people working in the fields in shirts made of brightly patterned curtain material, and clothes being offered for sale at fantastic prices like £3 for a pair of imported underpants (the average weekly wage was then around £2), £17 10s for a raincoat and 16s for a pair of socks.

The most serious clothing shortage on the Channel Islands was undoubtedly of boots and shoes and this would also have affected England very severely, for, despite all the Board of Trade's efforts, it was by 1944 difficult to find women's and children's shoes of the right size. What would probably have occurred is what happened in Jersey, a return to clogs, which even in Lancashire came back into use during the war, fulfilling many a dire prophecy about 'clogs to clogs in three generations', and the universal re-making of boots and shoes that would normally have been discarded as worn out. On Jersey the owner of a boot-and-shoe factory which had closed down was asked by the civilian Council to re-open it. 'We started by making clogs', he remembers, 'and very fortu-nately there was an old clogger on the island, who'd been doing this in Lancashire in the old days and he had some tools with him', the soles being made of beech, and the uppers from 'canvas or bits of leather or bits of anything we could find to trim the shoe and make it as comfortable as possible'. The factory-owner admits himself that they were 'not really comfortable but they got you about and kept your feet dry and that was the main thing'. The same invaluable citizen came to the rescue of those with worn-out shoes and boots of a conventional kind, 'cannibalising' old pairs to fit new soles to still-weatherproof uppers, but by the end of the Occupation even secondhand shoes, one Jersey businessman remem-bers, were fetching £10 to £15. 'I managed to sell a pair of old boots for £14', he recalls, pointing out that such transactions were essential to finance one's purchases of necessities on the Black Market.

The British Isles would undoubtedly have suffered, too, as the Channel Islands did, from one shortage which would not have affected at all a large part of the population but which would have seemed to the rest almost worse than the lack of food, namely tobacco. Even in England, although the government decided against rationing tobacco, addicted smokers came to understand what a cigarette-famine meant, with long queues for popular brands, frequent 'No cigarettes' notices, and bitter accusations that favoured customers were being supplied from under the counter. If in the Channel Islands these symptoms of tobacco-starvation were less in evidence, it was because cigarettes became too scarce even to quarrel over. On the Islands, unlike the mainland, there was at one time an official ration of forty, and later twenty, cigarettes a week for adult males (sweets and chocolates, when available, being reserved for women and children), but before long most smokers were largely having to rely on home-grown tobacco, which in the warm climate of Jersey did not do badly, but which was so strong it would 'knock out' even a hardened smoker if smoked while still green. Those without the gardens, or patience, for such ventures smoked various substitutes, most of them highly unsatisfactory, though better in a pipe than in cigarettes home-rolled in tomato-packing paper, which, even if they contained tobacco, were hard to keep alight. Dried cherry leaves, dock leaves and rose petals were all used and a cartoon in a Jersey newspaper in 1942 showed a man puffing contentedly at his pipe while sitting on a horse with a shortened tail, the caption being 'Dammy, I had to smoke something!'

Every British soldier who was in liberated Europe at the end of the war will remember the high price, or barter value, which cigarettes commanded, £1 a packet being common, equal to a private's pay for a week. On Jersey and Guernsey the same situation had long existed but with the German troops as a source of potential supply, 22s 4d being offered for a packet of German, French or Belgian cigarettes. At one time tobacco ration cards were changing hands at £1 15s and as much as 2s 1d was being asked and paid for a single cigarette. Similar prices would no doubt have prevailed in England if the supply of tobacco from Rhodesia and other Commonwealth countries (though not, presumably, from the United States) had been cut off.

Women faced, to a relatively mild degree in wartime England, and to a far worse one in the Channel Islands, many shortages which left men unaffected. Occasional, if inadequate, consignments of cosmetics arrived in the shops of both countries, though far more on the mainland, but British women never suffered, like those on Jersey, from an embarrassing shortage of something far more essential than lipstick or face-powder, sanitary towels. The gap here, when imported supplies ran out, was filled by the resourceful manufacturer mentioned earlier who collected clean woollen and cotton waste and meat cloth from the Island's now largely unemployed butchers, selling the results in unwanted wrapping paper from the same source at sixpence a packet. Other feminine, or medical, needs were met by using packing paper for cotton wool, wax, olive oil and colouring for lipsticks, dried Irish Moss in cough medicine, and wreath wire for hair-pins. British people on the mainland, who showed similar resourcefulness in meeting numerous wartime shortages, would no doubt have risen to such additional challenges in an equally enterprising way.

Children, although to a much lesser extent in England, inevitably missed many of the toys and treats of childhood; Christmas dinner for one Jersey family in 1944 consisted of two slices of bread each. British house-wives, too, would during an Occupation have seen even fewer eggs than they did, with no tins of dried egg from the United States to replace them, and even less milk, the Channel Islands' ration shrinking at one time to only half a pint a week. During much of the Occupation, how-ever, the Channel Islands were almost the only occupied country receiving full cream rather than separated milk, and many people developed the art of butter-making on a small scale by shaking up the skimmed-off cream. By 1944 this supply had almost dried up and in January a pound of butter on the largely agricultural island of Guernsey fetched 42s and an egg 7s 6d.

By this time one person's official rations could be bought for about 3s, consisting as they did of two ounces of butter or margarine, two ounces of cooking fat, three ounces of sugar, half a pound of barley or two ounces of vermicelli (a form of macaroni), and a pennyworth of salt. All of these shortages, except the last-named, also affected the housewife in England, though the rations were usually rather larger and—more important still—they were always honoured. The English housewife, too, thanks to the excellent 'points' rationing scheme introduced by Lord Woolton's Ministry of Food in December 1941, could also regularly, if infrequently, buy a tin of corned beef, fish, 'spam', and tinned fruit, to relieve the monotony of the basic rations, each ration book containing a number of 'points' which could be spent as she wished on a wide range of inessentials from biscuits to baked beans, 'points' also covering duller articles like rice and porridge oats, the bulk-providing items which the Channel Islands most conspicuously lacked. The supply of tinned food, under a German occupation, would largely have dried up, as it did almost totally in Jersey and Guernsey, as shipping space was taken over by the Germans for their purposes and canned pears from Australia and tinned meat from New Zealand no longer reached the British market.

Most British families would not have greatly missed unrationed coffee from East Africa and Brazil, though all over Europe this, along with tobacco, is still remembered as the first, worst, and longest-lasting shortage, the universal substitute, made from roasted and powdered acorns, being recollected with equally universal revulsion. But what would have struck a major blow to morale throughout the British Isles would have been the disappearance of tea, of which supplies from British possessions in the Far East would have been cut off by a German victory. Many people on the Channel Islands consider the lack of tea as the worst of all the deprivations they endured. One Guernsey man was moved to pay £2 for a quarter of a pound (the official price for a whole pound was 2s 8d), 'and what a treat that was. We saved the tea leaves, dried them in the oven and brewed them time and again until there was no life or taste left in them.' At an auction on Guernsey in January 1943 another tea-lover paid £7 7s 6d for a half-pound packet, to enable his wife and himself to enjoy their first cup for two years. A year later, on both Jersey and Guernsey, a single pound of tea was fetching £25 to £28. The various substitutes that were tried, bramble leaves and strips of dried carrots, are remembered by the Guernsey man already quoted as 'vile', while one Jersey tea-drinker, who brewed 'tea' from chopped-up parsnips, describes the resulting liquid as 'foul'. To sweeten one's 'ersatz' tea, after the official ration of three ounces of sugar (about twenty-seven lumps) was used up, or ceased to be honoured, one used 'ersatz' sugar, made while fuel supplies lasted by stewing sugar beet for hours and then thinning out the resulting liquid, a process difficult to complete without it boiling over or burning. It was also very wasteful of sugar beet, ten pounds being needed to produce two pounds of treacly, black syrup, which was also used in puddings or in place of jam, though many people found it uneatable. To such straits would the British housewife have been reduced if the supply of sugar from the West Indies had been cut off, although a far smaller ration, based on home-grown sugar beet, might still have been met.

One major change which the British people would have noticed during an Occupation would have been the growth of a Black Market, which hardly existed during the second world war on any major scale. This was less, perhaps, because of the essential law-abidingness of the population, though this was certainly a factor, than because real essentials were still available and rations were always honoured, however small. In the Channel Islands there was not enough of many items to go round however carefully they were shared out, so what was available tended to go to the highest bidder. The bartering of rationed goods was officially forbidden, but advertisements in the press offering such items as a wheelbarrow or a clock often implied that food would not be unwelcome in exchange, and public auctions of scarce items were common. There was also a regular, if strictly speaking illegal, trade in food, and it was rarely difficult, one Jersey man remembers, to find what you were looking for. Such businesses often operated under cover of 'secondhand shops' offering 'some odd bits of furniture or something like that for sale' with 'the real business done in the parlour at the back'. Sugar, poultry and meat were the main items offered, especially pork, as pigs were easier to raise in concealment than sheep or cows. One Jersey farmer claimed to keep pigs in the attic of a deserted house, where they lived undetected by the official inspectors, and they were perhaps the source of the two pork chops for which one man remembers paying £7. So well-established did undercover transactions become that the wife of one leading resident went up to a policeman in the street and asked him, 'Can you tell me the way to the Black Market?'

Two articles in which there was never any hint of a Black Market in Great Britain were potatoes and bread, which were never rationed, for these were the basic items Lord Woolton called his 'fillers'. On the Channel Islands both these essentials had to be rationed and later they became appallingly scarce, as the Germans removed shiploads of potatoes and the flow of imported wheat dwindled, for the Islands had always gone in for dairy-farming and horticulture rather than growing cereals. The British public became heartily sick of potatoes but their compatriots tuning in to *The Kitchen Front* on illicit radios on Jersey and Guernsey listened in amazement to talks and recipes designed to encourage people to use more of them, for after the official ration of five pounds a head a week fell to one pound and then to none at all, potatoes became a luxury, especially compared with the swedes and turnips on which by late 1944 many people were living. The Jersey physiotherapist quoted earlier remembers suggesting to his farmer patients '£5 and a bag of potatoes' as payment for a £10 bill, and a Guernsey dentist who extracted four teeth from one agricultural official in 1943 ('quite an ordeal', the victim remembers, as supplies of cocaine had almost run out) was 'emotionally grateful' to be paid, at his own suggestion, 'a few pounds of potatoes of sorts' instead of a fee.

Bread and flour became even more precious, and as the amount dwindled the quality deteriorated. One Jersey man remembers that the flour, of which the official ration was seven ounces a head a week, was 'terrible stuff. It occasionally had nails in it and pieces of sack, and always corn husks. The bread was also a terrible colour and a terrible taste, containing all sorts of objects.' By November 1941 one Guernsey farmer's family were eagerly debating after each meal who was entitled to the last crust, and on Good Friday 1942, he noted in his diary, they dined off 'blackberry leaf tea with half a saccharine, a home-made bun of barley flour and sticky, sludgy brown bread'. A Jersey farmer remembers going downstairs one night after his wife and child had gone to bed and looking hungrily at the two slices left in the larder. 'I was really tempted to eat the bread', he admits, 'but I held myself back', and it remained for the family breakfast.

By September 1940 the British Isles were already beginning to feel the benefits of the government's policy of ploughing up waste-land and grassland to grow crops, and if the Germans had occupied the country and Canadian wheat had ceased to arrive this policy would presumably have been pressed on even more energetically. Some bread, therefore, there would still have been, though it would have had to be strictly rationed and flour might, as on the Channel Islands, have been so badly adulterated that even the dark brown or black 'Army issue' bread supplied to German soldiers would, as there, have been in demand in preference to it. Undoubtedly in Britain, too, those living in the country would have rediscovered the ancient art of gleaning, for which whole villages had once turned out at harvest-time. One Guernsey man, a journalist in everyday life, remembers this as 'one of the most back-aching jobs I ever tackled in my life. . . . Even today my back aches at the thought of it. We would go into a wheat or corn field after the crop had been harvested, kneel down and scan the surface for the precious little seeds which had fallen as the sheaves were gathered' and 'pick up the seeds one by one. . . . But all your pains were forgotten when you went to the mill with your gleanings for grinding into flour and carried home with you the small bag of flour. . . . My first grinding to me was more precious than gold – and the cake my mother made, even though without sugar, tasted heavenly compared with the minute husk-filled flour ration.' It was also preferable, no doubt, to the cakes made of millet, normally fed to cagebirds, which some people on the same island produced at this time. Eventually the supply of bread and flour almost ran out, and the population were only saved by supplies sent in by the Red Cross, which reached the Channel Islands at the very end of 1944 and early in 1945. People were seen laughing hysterically as they went to fetch their loaves from the bakers, and ordinary families smiled inanely at each other as they sat down to a meal of almost forgotten white bread, eaten by itself or spread with Red Cross cheese or marmalade. 'In the houses which still retained some remnants of their prewar prosperity', one Jersey man remembers, 'these loaves would be put out on silver salvers or cake dishes and sliced as if they were some fantastic cake at a banquet.'

The arrival of the food parcels was the last act in the Channel Islands' struggle to survive. There had been no sudden plunge from sufficiency to near-starvation, but rather what one man remembers as a process of 'the screw being put on little by little' with rationing 'gradually getting worse and worse and worse until you've got practically nothing'. The same process, to a far more limited extent, happened as food and goods of every kind became scarce in wartime Britain, but conditions would clearly have been far worse had the Germans arrived, and only a few items— tomatoes from Guernsey, which had a glut of them throughout the Occupation, onions from Brittany, sadly missed in Britain after 1940— would have been more plentiful. And what would the end have been? In the Channel Islands, as the Germans prepared to fight to a finish, and ships from the French mainland ceased to arrive, stocks of almost every item reached danger level and starvation became an imminent possibility, until in November 1944 the Bailiff of Guernsey sent a despairing message to the International Red Cross in Geneva:

Conditions rapidly deteriorating here. Will soon become impossible. All rations drastically reduced. . . . Bread finishes 15 December, Sugar finishes 6 January, Ration of separated milk will be reduced to one-third pint per head by end of year. Soap and other cleansers . . . completely exhausted. Vegetables generally inadequate to supply civilian population through Winter. . . . Clothing and footwear stocks almost exhausted. Gas and electricity finish at the end of year. Coal stocks exhausted. Many essential medical supplies already finished.

To his colleagues on Jersey, who a few days later sent off a similar message of his own, he wrote, 'Starvation begins to stare us in the face and I can see no way out of it.'

The Germans had already done their best to wash their hands of the Channel Islands' problems. Supreme Headquarters in Berlin, in the shape of Hitler's immediate subordinate, Field-Marshal Keitel, had in September issued an order that civilian rations were to be cut to 'the barest survival level', and had warned that 'An Order will follow for the complete stopping of rations to the civilian population and for measures to inform the British government that this has been done', the intention apparently being to herd the population into one corner of the islands and leave Britain to remove, or feed, them. Hitler himself suggested deporting all the residents, except able-bodied men who would remain to work for the Germans, though where they were to go was not explained, and eventually wiser counsels prevailed and the Germans agreed to a Red Cross ship being sent to the islands, stocked with parcels from the Canadian and New Zealand Red Cross societies, of the kind sent to prisoners of war, and these arrived regularly thereafter.

What would have happened in Britain if there, too, the supply of imported food had ceased? With greater natural resources conditions would probably not have become quite as desperate, unless the Germans had deliberately starved her people to try and force the United States to support them, which it seems inconceivable that she would have refused to do. Alternatively America might herself have demanded the right to send food ships to the British Isles and to escort them with warships, even at the risk of war. If, however, Europe had been liberated before Great Britain, the Germans on the British Isles might, like those on the Channel Islands, have found themselves cut off from their bases and rapidly becoming worse off even than their captives, until forced to forage for food in the fields and even in the civilians' dustbins. 'You haven't got an Army,' the Dame of Sark told the German Commandant on the island at this time, 'you've only got a pack of thieves and beggars. They're either coming round to one door begging for potato peelings to eat, or else breaking in another door trying to steal something.' In fact the Germans' discipline remained extraordinarily good, even though by now German officers were eating raw cabbage stalks pulled from the fields, and one soldier was seen to scrape clean and eat ravenously a tiny turnip thrown on a dung heap. One German declined some cigarettes offered by a civilian he had helped with a household job because, having arrived on the Red Cross ship, they were for civilians only, but the shared experience of empty stomachs broke down old resentments to such an extent that at least one kindhearted woman, shocked at the half-starved look of some of the young soldiers, furtively pressed crusts upon them. The final tribute to the Germans' self-restraint came in an anonymous letter to the authorities on Jersey. The distribution of Red Cross parcels should, the writer suggested, be entrusted exclusively to the Germans, since they were the most trustworthy of all the hungry people on the island.

Chapter 19: The New Order

1941 will be the crucial year of a great New Order in Europe.

Adolf Hitler, 30 January 1941

For the people of Great Britain one visible symbol of defeat would have been the disappearance of Nelson's Column from London. For the citizens of Germany the tangible proof and reminder of victory would have been the new Berlin which Hitler planned to build as heart and centre of his New Europe. Hitler had always been interested in architecture. To the very end of his life he amused himself studying the models and drawings of grandiose projects of which not a brick would ever be laid, and he had drawn up imposing plans to reconstruct such Nazi shrines as Munich and Nuremberg, as well as Linz in Austria where he had been brought up. Here he proposed to set up an enormous observatory, to which 'thousands of excursionists will make a pilgrimage every Sunday' to 'have access to the greatness of our universe'—and to reflect, perhaps, on the glory of their town's association with the Führer. But his most dramatic plans were for the capital of the Reich, and he entrusted the preparation of them to a young architect he had discovered, Albert Speer, who later, in 1942, became a spectacularly successful Minister of Armaments and Munitions.

Hitler's taste was for the massive and the monumental, faithfully reflected in the new Chancellery, the combined 10 Downing Street and Buckingham Palace, or White House, of Berlin, which Speer actually built for him in 1938, and in his plans for the new government quarter of Berlin which were based on sketches Hitler had made as far back as 1925, eight years before he came to power. Speer recalls Hitler's eagerness to see his plans implemented when the two men discussed them in 1936 and he himself was, he admits, immensely enthusiastic 'to have such a huge task. . . . For an architect just thirty years old it was an unheard of order, one couldn't dream of.' The centrepiece of the whole scheme was to be 'a huge avenue . . . similar to the Champs Elysées' but far wider and longer, stretching four miles through the heart of the capital. 'On both sides were the ministries of the greater Germany, as Hitler said. and also cinemas and theatres, operas and shops, everything mixed, so that life would continue also at night in this new centre of Berlin.'

Hitler planned to retain the existing Reichstag, only recently rebuilt after it had been burned down in 1933—an event exploited by the Nazis to assist their seizure of power—but to create alongside it a new and far larger one, with seats for the representatives of the 140 million people in the new German Empire. At that stage no provision was made for any 'members for Great Britain', but the chamber would no doubt have been large enough to accommodate them, too, when this last province was finally incorporated into the Reich. The new Chancellery was also to be kept, but demoted to being the home of Hitler's deputy, Rudolf Hess, since Hitler proposed to erect for himself a huge new palace, of long, low, colonnaded buildings surrounding a central square, rivalling in size and magnificence the home of the French kings at Versailles, where Germany had suffered the humiliation which had set Hitler on the road to power. Parisian influence was also reflected in the vast Triumphal Arch, 300 feet high and 400 feet wide, dwarfing the original Arc de Triomphe, which was only half its height, and designed to stand in the middle of the main Avenue. It had been designed by Hitler personally, prompting Speer to tell him, 'You are the architect, not me', and the approaches to it were to be lined by 'guns which Hitler already said should be trophies from wars of the future'.

There were echoes of the Invalides in Paris, too, though again the copy was far vaster than the original, in the Hall of Military Fame—the creation of which was entrusted to another architect. This was to contain other spoils of successful wars, including the railways carriage at Compiègne, where the German surrender of 1918 and the French surrender of 1940 had been signed, and which was destined later in the war to be blown to pieces by a British bomb. Below the Hall was 'The Memorial Crypt of the Field-Marshals', Germany's greatest heroes, which was to contain the bodies of President Hindenburg, 'stabbed in the back' in 1918 according to Nazi mythology, Field-Marshal Ludendorff, who had been actively involved in the unsuccessful Munich 'putsch' of 1923, and, another Nazi idol, the soldier-king Frederick the Great, who had died in 1786. Another future resident might have been Reichs-Marschal Göring, for the new and imposing building from which he was to control his varied interests, from the Luftwaffe to the economic exploitation of conquered territories, would have overlooked the mausoleum. Whether Göring would have been allowed any say in the design of his headquarters—such as including in it a picture gallery for his splendid collection of old masters—seems doubtful. The Führer, Speer points out, also planned to include in the new government quarter the 'administration buildings of I. G. Farben, Siemens and other big firms', but 'Hitler decided what he wanted to do' and the companies concerned were 'not much' consulted.

Hitler's plans for his new capital were rounded off by a brand-new central railway station at one end of the Avenue, and, its crowning glory, a huge assembly hall at the other, consisting of a cupola, mounted on free-standing supports, rather like a bridge, 750 feet across, beneath which, Hitler had calculated, 180,000 people could assemble to listen to speeches from himself and his successors. This fantastic construction would have dominated the whole city, for it was to have a height of 800 feet, compared to the eighty-five feet of that other prominent architectural feature of central Berlin, the Brandenburg Gate, and, Albert Speer remembers, 'the cupola would have been covered with copper and would have been green in a short time, so the whole thing would have looked like a huge mountain, surpassing every building in Berlin'. (It would in fact have risen almost to the height of the television transmission masts which now tower above the city.) Speer's reaction as the whole fantastic and unbelievably costly scheme was unfolded before him was, he remembers, that 'everything was out of human scale', and he was reminded of 'Cecil B. de Mille's buildings for his famous *Ben Hur* film, which I saw when I was a young student'. To Speer it seemed that the new Berlin was designed to 'express in some way the whole authoritarian system, the whole of Hitler's aims', and the enormous German eagle which he planned to mount on top of the Assembly Hall dome was to be a concrete symbol of Germany's supremacy in the world. The scheme was very much a practical blueprint, not a mere layman's dream. Under Speer's direction a staff of architects prepared models and detailed construction drawings and preliminary orders were even issued for the huge quantities of granite needed, the whole project being designed to be finished by 1950.

Just as the Berlin which Hitler meant to build seemed at the time no empty vision, so Hitler's talk of a thousand-year Reich, of which the city would be the centre, was no mere rhetorical flourish but a sober statement of policy. What role Britain would have played in it is uncertain, for Hitler always insisted that he was content to leave her alone to develop her own Empire, but about his plans for the East, to which from July 1940 onwards his thoughts increasingly turned, there was no uncertainty at all. In Russia there could never, he believed, be a reconciliation between rulers and ruled, for Hitler regarded the Slav races as an intrinsically inferior people, destined to remain the vassals of the Germans for all eternity. Russia itself was to lose its identity and become a mere province of Germany. 'What India is for England', he declared in August 1941, six weeks after the start of the campaign in the East, 'the territories of Russia will be for us. . . . We must no longer allow Germans to emigrate to America. On the contrary, we must attract the Norwegians, the Swedes, the Danes and the Dutch into our Eastern territories. They'll become members of the German Reich. . . . The German colonists ought to live on handsome, spacious farms. The German services will be lodged in marvellous buildings, the governors in palaces. . . . Around the city, to a depth of thirty to forty kilometres, we shall have a belt of handsome villages connected by the best roads. What exists beyond that will be another world in which we mean to let the Russians live as they like.' 'We shall soon supply the wheat for all Europe, the coal, the steel, the wood', he predicted two months later. 'To exploit the Ukraine properly —that new Indian Empire—we need only peace in the West. . . . When we are masters of Europe, we shall have a dominant position in the world. 130 million people in the Reich, ninety in the Ukraine. Add to these the other states of the New Europe and we'll be 400 millions as compared with the 130 million Americans.'

The role of the occupied countries in the West in Hitler's Europe was to remain quiescent, while his dreams of glory were to be fulfilled in the East, and they might well have been accompanied by a relaxation of German rule, and a lessening of German depradations, in the other occupied countries. Here perhaps lay the greatest long-term threat to national survival. The best of all prophylactics against contemplating, much less accepting, the idea of a future as part of the new German Empire, was hatred of individual Germans, as many a Pole of Czech could testify. The truth was, however, that most Germans, at least for most of the time, were not hateful. So far was every German governor of an occupied country from being a brutal, unfeeling tyrant, that one at least, Dr Best in Denmark, was constantly in trouble with Hitler for not being stern enough. So far was every German soldier from being a drunken, thieving, bullying brute that, as was seen in the last months of the Occupation in the Channel Islands, the German Army behaved, with rare exceptions, with exemplary restraint. The ordinary civilian, provided he did as he was told and kept well clear of resistance movements, was far less likely to see soldiers brawling drunkenly in the streets and causing wanton damage if he had a German unit billeted in his town, than some Scottish regiments, who gained such an evil reputation in Germany after the war. The German army was the best disciplined in the world and crimes like robbery and rape involving its members were extremely rare and were punished at least as severely as by the American Forces later in the war. In a German-occupied country, unless one belonged to one of a number of suspect groups, including Jews, anti-Nazis and prominent left-wingers, the danger to one's life was small. Outside these categories, the ordinary civilian living in a target city like Birmingham or Bristol went in far greater danger of being killed in an air raid before the Occupation than of being shot after it had started. In the Channel Islands not a single British citizen died in front of a firing squad, though a few perished by their own hand or had their lives cut short by privation. It was unpleasant, humiliating, frustrating and sometimes frightening living under German rule but, with the exceptions mentioned and unless one was unlucky enough to be seized as a hostage, it was not dangerous. Nor was daily life necessarily intolerable. The civilian population of Europe, the inmates of the ghettoes and concentration camps apart, were not, for most of the war, kept unreasonably short of food. Rations were not much lower than in Germany itself and at least one occupied country, the 'model protectorate' of Denmark, fed a great deal better throughout the war that the people of rationed Britain.

An even greater barrier to keeping fresh one's sense of outrage at one's country being occupied was the existence of good-natured individuals in the occupying forces who were a living contradiction of that popular wartime saying 'The only good German is a dead German'. Two people on the Channel Islands, with every reason to dislike the Germans, can recall instances of not wholly untypical kindness. One policeman who asked a Czech friend, who worked at a German officers' hotel, to try to obtain some oranges for his sick daughter was given a dozen by the German commandant, who refused to accept payment, and a few days later asked after the child and pressed a large slab of chocolate upon him. 'He wasn't a very genial man, but I think at heart he must have been a kind man', this police officer considers. The Guernsey woman sent to gaol for refusing to say 'Heil Hitler' for a rice pudding, was later, when she was visibly pregnant, sometimes given a loaf of bread or a bag of flour as she passed a German barracks on her way home. With the war over, such instances might have multiplied, making it harder to resist the insidious but dangerous temptation to distinguish between 'ordinary decent Germans' and 'those horrible Nazis'.

Such a distinction had in fact been made by successive British governments, which had always been reluctant to admit that the country was fighting the German people at all. Even in 1914 there had been some suggestion that it was the Prussian military clique surrounding the Kaiser who were the real enemy, while Chamberlain in declaring war in 1939 had referred to the need to destroy 'Hitlerism' not Germany. Even Churchill tended to denounce 'the Narzees' rather than the Germans, and the Germans would no doubt have done their best to exploit this distinction. A typical instance occurred on Guernsey where the officer in charge of a fatigue party sent to cut down the trees in one particularly beautiful garden apologetically told the owners that he had an equally fine garden at home and that after the war they must unite to keep every Nazi out of power.

It seems highly unlikely that Nazism, as distinct from passive acceptance of German rule, could ever have taken root in the British Isles; certainly it did not in the Channel Islands. The mere word 'Nazi' conjures up a vision of a beefy and brainless thug, or a short and sinister sadist, but in fact what made Nazism so formidable was that is exponents were not merely drawn from these groups. During the 1920s and 1930s its claims to be considered as a respectable political theory, leading to an efficient method of government, were taken seriously by many educated people, not only in Germany but elsewhere, and though its book-burning tactics and anti-Semitism were contrary to the whole spirit of academic life, some of its earliest successes were in the universities. In Austria, even before the *Anschluss* in 1938, many students proudly wore a Swastika badge in their lapels, and, even during the Occupation, there was a Nazi group in the university of Copenhagen, while, as has been seen, the Gestapo was largely staffed by men of high academic attainments.

The foundation of Nazi teaching lay in the so-called 'ideal theory of the state', stated in its simplest form by the philosopher Hegel and echoed by many subsequent German thinkers: 'The individual does not exist; only the state exists.' Applied within the Nazi Party itself this doctrine was interpreted to mean that no individual, whether German or alien, had any rights of his own, and it had hence justified such crimes as the murder of Hitler's old friend and ally, Ernst Röhm, the sterilisation of the unfit, the carrying out of medical experiments on helpless prisoners, and the attempt to breed perfect Germans from selected youths and girls to ensure the future of the Fatherland. Many, perhaps most, of those who staffed the concentration camps and Gestapo interrogation centres were no doubt depraved monsters, enjoying cruelty for its own sake or utterly indifferent to it, but the experiences of occupied Europe suggest that a few such people are to be found in every country, though Germany itself seems to have had a good deal more than its share. Anyone who has witnessed examples of senseless bullying at boarding school or in the Forces, or who has ever read in the press of cases of cruelty to children or helpless lunatics, will hesitate to assert too confidently that none at all would have emerged in the British Isles. The mass murderer Adolf Eichmann, and many humbler concentration-camp staff, always insisted that they were merely 'obeying orders' like loyal and conscientious officials, and the results of recent experiments in the United States, to see at what point a normal man will rebel against inflicting pain upon his fellows when ordered to do so are, to say the least, disturbing. Some authorities believe that inside almost every innocent-seeming ordinary citizen there is, however deeply buried, a potential gas-chamber attendant, though happily British history has provided no opportunity to put this hideous possibility to the test.[1]

But apart from its appeal to the perverted sadist, who would have welcomed it not for political but psychological reasons, how could Nazism, or at least cooperation with Germany to the point of ceasing active opposition to the new regime, as the price of a less disagreeable daily life, have been 'sold' to the British public? The partners in a London advertising agency, to whom the problem was put in 1972, made first the classic observation that 'one cannot sell a bad product' and 'National Socialism as it was projected under the Hitler regime is a product which one couldn't really market in this country'. But, accepting that the British people would have had no alternative to it, since other parties, if allowed at all, would not have been free to attack the Occupation, these experts believe that 'one possible route that the Germans might have taken' would have been to play on the public's desire 'for a better way of life', offering 'more dignity, more hope for the future, a bit more self-respect'. This was, of course, the basis of the Nazis' original appeal to their fellow-countrymen, but the British people being basically different from the Germans, the method of achieving this aim would have had to be different. 'What you wouldn't do, for instance', one advertising man points out, 'is have jack boots and black uniforms and SS regalia about the place', effective though these had been in Germany. It would have been essential to drop the very name 'Nazi', with its unfortunate 'brand image', and to replace it by a more neutral one such as 'The European Commonwealth Party', thereby giving 'the British people an opportunity to identify with National Socialism', the operation of Western Europe as a single economic unit being one of Hitler's basic intentions.

Goebbels's Propaganda Ministry were past masters at the use of film and short films aimed at indoctrinating the British public into accepting this and similar ideas would undoubtedly have been shown regularly in

[1] This refers to the famous 'Newhaven experiment', conducted by an American psychiatrist, in which a large number of American citizens, picked at random from the voters' list, were asked in turn 'in the interests of science' to administer an apparently painful electric shock to an unseen partner in another room whenever he failed to answer a question correctly. When sternly ordered to do so by an authoritarian figure in a white coat the vast majority ignored the protests and even screams from the next room continuing, though grim-faced and reluctantly, to do as they were told. The suffering 'victim' was in fact a tape recording, the electrodes having, unknown to the 'teacher', been removed from the 'pupil' before his interrogation began.

the cinemas and, once it became a significant medium, on television. Before being shut down in 1939 television had reached no more than 20,000 homes but, with the war over, development would presumably have been resumed in 1940, instead of, as happened in reality, 1946, and it might then have overtaken radio as the chief source of information and entertainment by the late 1940s, instead of, as actually occurred, around 1953.[1] The commercials making up the campaign designed to promote acceptance of German rule would, the advertising agency believes, have stressed the positive benefits of Occupation, such as the absence of unemployment. One, they suggest, might have involved 'two fellows sitting on a bus, both middle-class, clerical grey suits . . . one cheerful, the other pretty miserable'. As the bus passes a Ministry of Labour Employment Exchange, which has no customers, the two men would be heard talking. One, explaining why he looks downcast, would remark 'I liked it better before.' The other replies, 'You must be joking! All that unemployment and those queues, can't you remember? My missus said she didn't like to go out because of all the comments she got from the blokes hanging around on the street corners.' To this the first man, beginning to weaken, replies, 'I know all that, I often prayed it would get better . . .' leaving the viewer to make the obvious deduction that under German rule things *had* got better. Similar treatment, this agency suggests, might have been given to technological progress ('for instance, the whole European Community would be getting to the moon by now, rather than the Americans'), or to the absence of strikes which, though allowed in theory, would in practice have become infrequent, if not unknown, and to the absence of party political strife now there was a dictator to take clear decisions.

An underlying theme of the whole of such a campaign would be that the British and the Germans were not so very different and, in the agency's view, this might effectively be put across by a commercial about an Englishwoman who had married a German. Worked out in detail, this would show a blonde, glamorous housewife of about twenty-eight, who might in appearance be either English or German, wandering round a typical 'dream home' tidying up after her man had left for work, engaging in such reassuringly homely tasks as carrying his egg cup and coffee cup to the sink, and clearing up the mess which her typical family, of three appealing small children, had left all around. The German himself would never appear, though at one point his wife would pick up a photograph of him —showing a pleasant, kindly-looking, reliable type of face, distinguished

[1] The television audience became larger than the radio audience soon after the coronation in 1953, though it was not until 1958 that the number of television licences surpassed the number of radio-only licences.

only by its German cap from that of a million Englishmen. Over this charming, familiar scene with which vast numbers of women could identify, would be heard the voice of this model housewife and mother:

I married a German boy. It was terrible at first. No one would speak to me. I lost all my friends. I didn't care. It was worth it. *He* was worth it.

And then, of course, people started to forget a bit. So gradually we made new friends. Kurt gets on well with all of them. Like they do with him.

(*She picks up the portrait and looks at it.*)

I suppose it's because basically he's no different from any Englishman.

(*She looks round at the untidy litter left by the absent Kurt.*)

Not really.

This message might then have been underlined by a male English voice repeating the theme of the whole campaign, 'New people for a new Europe'.

In normal times the British people might have felt able to resist such appeals but life during an Occupation would have been far from normal, as several of those who experienced life under German rule in Jersey would certainly agree. 'There's a sort of general numbness that comes over one', one man remembers. 'You can't think, you can't feel, you don't know what's happening. You can't plan for tomorrow. You're frightened to talk to anybody and there's this sort of clamp down on top of you that makes you dry up.' 'You developed a fatalistic approach to life', another resident found. 'If you went, you went. It was Kismet, there wasn't much you could do about it. You were quite resigned to the fact either that you were going to stop here, be deported, or shot.' 'I should say the worst aspect of the whole thing was the unknown,' agrees a local businessman. 'You get a knock, you open the door and somebody would say "Come" and you went and that was that.' Anyone having to live in such an atmosphere, not for five years, but ten, fifteen or twenty, might well being to feel the attractions of the German offer of stability and security even if he did not succumb to them.

Unless the British Isles had had an exceptionally lenient Occupation, like Denmark, most of those organisations which strengthen a man's own opinions, or enable him to voice them effectively, would, of course, have disappeared. The political parties would have been dissolved or powerless, the trade unions allowed to exist merely on sufferance so long as they did not thwart the Germans' wishes. Social gatherings would not have been banned—amateur theatricals and private entertainments round the family piano flourished in the Channel Islands, though one either had to get home before curfew or stay the night—but once 'politics', as the Germans understood them, intruded, even the most harmless-sounding chess club or play-reading group would have been in trouble. Undoubtedly, as in other occupied countries, there would have been pressure from their friends on those who wanted to challenge the Germans, urging them not to do so for fear of endangering the progress back towards normality already achieved. The argument not to 'rock the boat' is a powerful one, especially when the waters ahead seem increasingly smooth and the surrounding sea is full of sharks.

One activity which would certainly have been permitted was church-going, though no foolhardy vicar who used his pulpit to denounce the Nazi Party or the Occupation authorities would have lasted very long. Provided, however, that he confined himself to conducting services and counselling Christian acceptance of the inscrutable dispensations of the Almighty he would have been allowed to retain his living. Hitler despised Christianity, whose coming he described as 'the heaviest blow that ever struck humanity', and his only recorded religious observance was on the evening that the French armistice was signed when, apparently without irony, Field-Marshal Keitel 'addressed a few words to the Führer as our victorious lawlord', and the company joined in singing 'Now thank we all our God'. Nazism preached, of course, the very reverse of the Christian doctrines, which were frequent subjects for scorn when Hitler had his sycophantic audience gathered round him at the dinner table. 'Christianity,' he told them one day in October 1941, 'is a rebellion against natural law. . . . Taken to its logical extreme, Christianity would mean the systematic cultivation of the human failure.' 'What nonsense it is,' he said on another occasion, 'to aspire to a heaven to which, according to the Church's own teaching, only those have entry who have made a complete failure of life on earth.'

True to his principles, Hitler had refused, back in 1933 when the Nazis came to power, to attend the usual religious service to mark the assembly of the Reichstag, and clergy were not accepted as party members. But he rejected atheism, which he described as 'a return to the state of the animal', arguing that 'an educated man retains the sense of the mysteries of nature and bows before the unknowable'. His solution was 'to let Christianity die a natural death. . . . Religion will have to make more and more concessions. Gradually the myths crumble'—though Hitler proposed to help them do so by making recruitment to the Church's ministry more difficult. 'In the long run,' he considered, 'National Socialism and religion will no longer be able to exist together. . . . It's impossible to escape the problem of God. When I have the time, I'll work out the formula to be used on great occasions. We must have something perfect both in thought and form.'

Hitler never did get round to inventing his new religion, but he did try out his economic ideas with a fair degree of success. The essence of the New European Order, or the Greater German Economic Sphere as the Germans called it, was that it was based on a united Europe, built round what was now the major Continental power. Germany had developed, she could claim with justice, a new system of production which had raised her from the poverty of 1933 to unheard-of prosperity, and she argued that, given the chance, it could do the same for those countries fortunate enough to enjoy German rule. The important person in the new system was the worker—the Nazi Party had begun as the German Workers' Party—not the financier, and it offered him real freedom, the freedom of security and employment, in contrast to what German radio described as 'the abstract and dying idea of English freedom'. Capitalist laissez-faire, said the Germans, was clearly finished and the basis of the economic relationship between countries was trade in goods, not paper transactions based on their possession of gold. Under Germany, claimed Goebbels's propagandists, Europe could enjoy what she had not enjoyed in the past, unbroken peace, a steady advance towards affluence and even a cultural renaissance. Both economically and politically the New Europe would be strong enough to deal on equal terms with the United States, and the Monroe Doctrine, that European states had no concern with the American continent, could now be practised in reverse, with 'Europe for the Europeans'.

Great Britain had no place in this tidy scheme, except as an uninvited guest. She had always tried, the newly conquered nations were told, to divide Europe, while Germany's interests, like theirs, lay in her being united. England was 'decadent', and had no real interest in Europe, which could very well get on without her, her interests lying in her empire overseas. Whether a place would have been found for Britain in the New Europe if she had been successfully occupied is not clear. A senior wartime official of the German Ministry of Economic Affairs, which drew up and operated this scheme, confirmed in 1972 that no plans to absorb her permanently into the new economic community, as distinct, of course, from the immediate removal of the booty mentioned in an earlier chapter, had been drawn up. This expert believes that Britain had 'too big a population, too big an industry' to have been 'dominated the same way as the European countries' and that she might, therefore, have been allowed to go on trading with the Commonwealth countries, obtaining her raw materials from them and selling them her exports, though whether the Commonwealth would have been willing to continue to send goods into a German-occupied British Isles seems highly doubtful.

It seems more likely, however, that Britain's economic future would have lain with the other German satellites in Europe, and, in strictly economic terms, it might not have been too grim a future. This official, concerned with drawing up the economic blueprint for the New Europe, believes 'we could have done without the United States', though there would have been 'certain bottlenecks in minerals, metals . . . seeds [and] oils of different kinds', as well as 'in textiles, because there wasn't much cotton or wool in the whole of Europe'. But he also considers that, given time, all these could have been overcome, 'through new raw materials like plastics or in building up a big industry of producing synthetic fibres'. Natural rubber, he thinks, might have been bought from Indonesia, to supplement the Germans' own expanding production of artificial rubber, and 'certain types of metals that were very scarce', and oil and minerals could have been found in 'Arab and African countries'.

Nor, this man believes, would imposing central control from Berlin on the allocation of raw materials and the type of output on which each factory was to concentrate have created any insoluble problems, for in imposing this policy between 1940 and 1945 there were no 'difficulties to amount to anything with industrialists and none with the workers at all'. The former welcomed a guaranteed supply of raw materials and an assured market while what the latter 'wanted was work and earnings and food'. There were, he admits, 'irritating and disagreeable' strikes in Holland, encouraged, he believes, by the Dutch government in exile, but they rarely lasted long because the strikers 'didn't get any pay and they had no food cards'. In France, where 'there was a real government and we could talk over problems as they arose', cooperation was complete, though 'in Belgium it was not quite so easy because the government was out of the country and there was not very much cooperation from the civil servants', although the King was still there. The Ministry of Economic Affairs in Berlin, however, suffered no real anxieties—as the production figures for German industry confirm, for they went on rising throughout the war, despite allied bombing. 'The necessities and resources of the whole of Europe', this economist found, 'had a tendency to balance each other.' Had the New European Order lasted, 'there would have been enough agricultural production and there would have been enough industrial capacity and there wouldn't be too many conflicts of interest'. As for the factory-owners and managers and workmen on whom the whole edifice rested, some of them 'worried a lot' about the fact that they were working for the Third Reich, 'but they couldn't help it. There was no other way out.'

A good deal of other evidence bears out these conclusions, including that from a German industrialist who was then working in the same ministry in charge of the allocation of steel, and was sent to Italy to try and develop additional sources of supply of various special types of the metal. Although this was 1943, and the Italian government was suing for peace, the German experts he later despatched there 'found very good cooperation. We had no sabotage, we had good friends who, after the war all agreed that we helped them a lot in those troublesome days'—indeed the postwar Italian steel industry owes much to the Germans' wartime efforts. The Germans achieved what they wanted here by setting up a special company to organise the supply of raw materials and to give firm orders for the finished product, and though the Germans who arrived to 'advise' the Italian factory managers and industrialists encountered 'a certain resentment in the beginning', before long the Italians 'found out that we had come to help them in using their full capacity by supplying the necessary raw materials', and became 'very cooperative'.

This is not hard to believe, for German industrialists too, for similar reasons, had very early on come to terms with Hitler, but more opposition might have been expected from the Italian labour force, who later acquired a reputation for left-wing militancy. But the Germans did not encounter it. 'I don't think I ever ran into a problem with a trade union', says this official. 'Strike in those days was not a term you thought of. I mean, what would they strike for? They got paid according to their wage agreements, we didn't care whether their wages were increased, that was none of our business. . . . The main thing for working people in general is stability. Whoever gives it to them I don't think they care so much.' But he admits that the Germans enjoyed two advantages: they could offer a man the security of a well-paid job at a time of uncertainty, and, since they were already working for the Germans, the men in the steel works were exempt from the danger of being sent to work in Germany.

The Italians were, until 1943, at least allies of the Germans, but experience in other countries seems to have been little different. What happened in Denmark, where there was an active resistance movement and most of the population never mentally accepted German occupation, while fitting neatly into the place in the New European Order for which they had been cast, is even more revealing, for the Danes in their general approach to life have often claimed some affinity with the British. The basic fact here, as in every occupied country, was that whatever one's patriotic sentiments one had to eat, and this meant finding employment, which meant in turn being able to sell the country's products. The Danish government adjusted itself with remarkable facility to the new situation. Before the Occupation more than half the country's exports went to England and only one fifth to Germany, but within a few months, instead of the shiploads of Danish butter and bacon crossing the North Sea, trainload after trainload was pouring into Germany to feed both the civil population and the Wehrmacht, while the Army of occupation also filled its needs of food through local purchase. Eventually, and up to the very end of the war, Denmark was supplying ten per cent of all Germany's needs in butter, meat and sugar and nearly twenty per cent of its salt-water fish, leading to a saying among the Germans that occupying Denmark was as good as having an extra ration card. One of the leading Germans involved in the occupation of Denmark believes that 'basically the farmers were glad', since they now received far better terms from the Germans than they had done from the British. 'Production increased, income increased and the farmers got out of debt', claims this official. 'Naturally they . . . liked that; they were the ones who were reconciled the quickest' to the Occupation. Whether they were so pleased at the end of the war when they found the Germans had run up a debt of 7000 million Kroner (about £350 million) through the Clearing Account handled by the National Bank seems more doubtful.

Denmark was, of course, a small country with no hope of liberating itself, but its reactions show clearly the pressures to which a beaten people were subjected, as this German, who was in charge of propaganda and press matters in the newly conquered country, discovered:

I remember on 15 June 1940 there was a great party given by the Danish Publishers Association. The guest of honour was the Danish Minister of State and I was the German guest of honour, the only German present. I was sitting next to the Minister and he was asking me what was the latest news I had. I replied, 'Well, minister, I can tell you that Paris has fallen.' Then he said, 'Well, thank heavens, things will be finished soon.' At that time the Danes believed that England would give in, i.e., would make peace with Germany and then the whole episode would be over and done with. It was under this impression that the Danes issued a declaration in July:
'The great German victories, which have caused astonishment and admiration all over the world, have brought about a new era in Europe, which will result in a new order in a political and economic sense, under the leadership of Germany.'
And this declaration was not just handed over to the German government by the Danish ambassador in Berlin, no the second highest man in the Danish Foreign Ministry . . . went to Berlin and accompanied the ambassador to the German Secretary of State.

A similar spirit was reflected in another conversation the same German had with another member of the Danish government, whom he asked, ' "Minister, really and truly you would not want the Germans to win victory?" He replied, "Oh yes, but only a small victory", which meant that Denmark wanted to go on [benefiting from] the rivalry and competition between England and Germany, because by this she would gain most. And he told me further, "You see, there is the heroism of the lion, which you, as the great German nation have, and then there is the heroism of the hare, who has to know when to flatten his ears in danger; and we are a small nation, and for us the heroism of the hare is appropriate." ' So enthusiastically did the Danes carry out this policy that there were even, later in the war, discussions of a possible currency and customs union between the two countries, though they came to nothing, as 'in the meantime . . . England had not given up, and eventually it was said, "Well, it is probably better if we decide after the war." '[1]

[1] In fairness to the Danish minister concerned, it should be pointed out that these accounts of the conversation come solely from the German side, but certainly views of this kind were then commonly held in Denmark, and the Danish government statement was indeed issued on 8 July in even more effusive terms than quoted here.

Chapter 20:
The end of the nightmare

We begin to think that we shall end our days in bondage.

Entry in the diary of a Guernsey farmer, July 1943

The cooperation (to use no harsher word) of so many in the occupied countries with the Germans does not, of course, mean that it would have happened in the British Isles, for it seems inconceivable that the British people would have accepted the philosophy of the hare (if not of the rabbit) practised by the Danes. But however bitter the aftermath of a successful invasion, sooner or later some form of civil government would have had to be set up in the conquered British Isles, and some method of working with the Germans would have had to be evolved, however reluctantly and however much those old enough to remember a time when there were no Germans in the streets longed for liberation.

But would liberation ever have come? The oppressed people of the British Isles, and the British government in exile in Canada or the Bahamas, would naturally have looked to the Commonwealth, but its resources were scattered about the globe and would have been totally inadequate for the unprecedented operation of landing a million or more men on a hostile coastline from the other side of the Atlantic. As the British Army had learned in France, air-cover was now vital to successful operations on land, but the fighter aircraft of the time had a range of no more than ninety miles, and this was also as far as most landing-craft could travel under their own power. Neither the men, nor the shipping, nor the aircraft for such a venture existed in 1940, nor would they have been available for several years to come. Nor was the United States in 1940 yet powerful enough to have come to a defeated Britain's rescue, even if it had not been unthinkable—as Americans of that period from both parties now readily admit—that she would ever have made the attempt. If the American people were not prepared to become involved in a European war to help the British while they were still fighting, they would, the authorities are unanimous, not have dreamed of doing so when their would-be ally was already occupied and intervention could only be an empty, but costly, gesture.

So obvious did it seem to the British people in 1940 that Hitler had to be stopped, that the strength of non-interventionist sentiment in the

United States was never appreciated. The distinguished American historian, Arthur Schlesinger, an interventionist himself, looking back in 1972, believes that 'President Roosevelt and his administration would have wished very strongly to do everything possible to assist the British resistance and would have continued regarding the government in Ottawa [assuming it had gone to Canada] rather than any Vichy-type government in London as the British government. . . . On the other hand, there would have been very bitter opposition to this view. Isolationism was very strong in the United States. The "America First" Committee and those who supported that view would have felt, first, that it was essential to come to an accommodation with Hitler and to accept this conquest of England . . . and second that we should abandon any interest in the rest of the world outside . . . the Western hemisphere, and try to make ourselves as strong as possible there. The power of isolationism', Professor Schlesinger recalls, was such 'that in the 1940 [election] campaign Roosevelt himself had to make concessions to it by promising that American boys would not be sent abroad to fight in foreign wars. . . . It would have become much stronger had Britain fallen. The bitterest debate I recall in my own lifetime in the United States . . . was the debate between the Isolationists and the Interventionists in 1940/41.'

To many Americans in those years, when inter-continental missiles had not been invented and no military or civil aircraft regularly flew across the Atlantic, those 3000 miles of ocean seemed very wide indeed. Many people, Professor Schlesinger recalls, 'felt that Europe was very, very far away. . . . Others felt it would be possible to do business with Hitler; in no case did they feel that the conquest of Europe by Hitler represented so deadly a threat to the national safety as to make it worthwhile for Americans to get involved in the war against him.' And there was, too, a great sense of disillusion in the United States at the results of American intervention in the first world war: 'We'd entered the First World War to make the world safe for democracy' and what had followed had in fact been 'the rise of Fascism and the rise of Communism. . . . And the people who supported England did so not only because they had a sense of solidarity of political views but more fundamentally because they felt that the conquest of Europe would be a threat to the United States. Thomas Jefferson said, more than a century before all this, that the United States could not afford to have all the forces of Europe wielded by a single hand and it was this . . . belief that that force would move out into the Atlantic, into Latin America, and menace the United States . . . more than the desire to rescue democratic principles which led Roosevelt and his administration to believe that our interests were involved in stopping Hitler.'

Britain's best ally in securing American aid had been Hitler himself, for he had blatantly violated his own professed policy of 'America for the Americans'. President Roosevelt, explains Professor Schlesinger, 'knew that the Nazis had been for some years systematically penetrating Latin America, using the German colonies in Latin America as their bases for Nazi propaganda; preparing radio networks and airlines and so on; that in 1939 they'd been quite active in Mexico, and he was under no illusions about the fact that Nazi victory was really creating a serious threat to America'. But there were many who preferred not to recognise the disagreeable truth in front of their eyes: the sizeable colony of Americans of German descent, and businessmen 'who had cartel or other arrangements with German firms', and who 'thought Hitler was someone they could do business with, that he would discipline the workers and extirpate the communists and the like'. Ironically, too, as well as the 'reactionary right', the far left, then far more powerful in the United States than it later became, was opposed to intervention. Its members' opposition to Hitler, like that of British Communists, only began when he attacked Russia in 1941. Finally Winston Churchill himself, although personally admired by many Americans, was violently distrusted by others, who saw him 'as the embodiment of British imperialism. . . . There was great feeling at that time that America must not go to war to save the British Empire.'

Had Britain fallen in October 1940 such views would have been widely heard during the campaign which led up to the presidential election of the following month. The Republicans in fact chose, to challenge Roosevelt, Wendell Wilkie, an admirer of Britain whose views on foreign policy were not so far removed from his opponent's. In a different situation, however, they might later have opted for a thorough-going isolationist—at least one had been a strong contender for the nomination— who 'might well have taken a position that we should not alarm Hitler by continuing relations with the British exiled government and that it was to our best interests to accept the finality of the Nazi conquest, stop all aid to British resistance, and make the best terms we could'.

This somewhat pessimistic, though no doubt realistic, view of the prospects for an occupied Britain, is borne out by a then Congressman who was, and indeed still is, an unashamed non-interventionist, Hamilton Fish. The term 'isolationist', he insists, is 'a misnomer. An isolationist is a person who doesn't want diplomatic relations or trade relations or goodwill. . . . There was no such person in America', only 'honest to God American citizens who believed in peace and who did not want to become involved in European or foreign wars unless attacked'. This group, of which Congressman Fish was a leading spokesman, was not, he points out, a small untypical minority. 'They represented all ranks and files, Democrats, Republicans, rich and poor of every denomination.' The impression of pro-British sentiment visiting Englishmen gained from their contacts in New York and in the newspaper, radio and film worlds was misleading. 'In New York there were a lot of very rich people . . . who'd intermarried with England or France and had business relations with them. Many of them were pro-war,' points out Mr Fish, while other Americans stress that both the city of New York and the communications media contained a high proportion of people of Jewish origin, who were far more anti-Nazi than most of those around them. A truer reflection of the nation's attitude was, he believes, given by a Gallup Poll which in the spring of 1940 showed 93% of the population opposed to America's entry into the war, a figure which 'the Roosevelt propaganda machine' never, until America was actually attacked, managed to bring down below 85%. Ex-Congressman Fish still regards America's involvement in the war as unfortunate. 'If England had fallen', he considers, 'Hitler would have turned all his armaments against Russia and probably would have defeated Russia and crushed communism and . . . it would have been the greatest thing that could have happened', freeing the world both from the postwar threat from Russia and the immediate danger from Germany, for 'Hitler would have had a lifetime's work putting it in order'. To British ears such a conclusion comes as a surprise, but it is true, as has been mentioned, that Hitler's real interest lay in colony-making to the East.

Hitler eventually solved Roosevelt's problem of persuading a reluctant nation to fight by declaring war on the United States in December 1941, at the same time as Japan attacked America's base at Pearl Harbour. The United States, having begun to mobilise its full power, then decided to crush Hitler first, but, even with British help, it still took three and a half years. If Britain had in 1941 already been out of the war, it seems probable that Hitler would not have intervened—and even had he done so America's first aim would clearly have been to win the war in the Pacific. Eventually, such was his ambition and the basic conflict between Nazi tyranny and American democracy, the two great powers must surely have come in conflict, but even then Britain might have had a long, long wait before her turn came to be rescued. One American general, concerned with strategic planning in 1940 and reappraising in 1972 the military problem involved, concluded that the task of reconquering the British Isles would have been so fraught with difficulty that almost any military authority would have advised against it. A base near at hand would, he believes, have been essential, and North Africa—which was in fact successfully

invaded by a powerful force sailing direct from the United States in 1942
—would have been the obvious choice, but mounting from there a major
expedition to southern England, beyond the range of friendly fighters and
with shipping having to pass through the narrow and vulnerable defile of
the Straits of Gibraltar, would have been an appallingly hazardous
undertaking.

But lurking in the background, unknown to everyone except a tiny
handful of those close to the seat of power, was the 'Manhattan Project',
the codename for the manufacture of the atomic bomb, which reached its
triumphant conclusion in August 1945. If British scientists, with their
precious knowledge, had arrived at Los Alamos in 1940, as they did a
little later, and Hitler's researchers, as happened in reality, had failed to
search out the secret of making an effective bomb, this vital weapon might
first have been used against Berlin instead of Hiroshima. How long it
would have taken to manufacture sufficient bombs to force Germany to
surrender is a matter of guesswork, but in the bomb seems to have lain
Britain's best—if not only—hope of rescue.

And, as the liberating Canadians, Australians and Americans stormed
or stumbled ashore, what sort of a Britain would they have found?
Whether it was poor or prosperous, strife-torn or peaceful, would have
depended on the resistance Hitler's plans had encountered and the extent
to which, with Russia in their grasp, the Germans had lost interest and
relaxed their rule in the other conquered territories. But that the liberated
islands would still have been British in spirit as well as in name seems
certain. During five years, when it must often have seemed that they had
been forgotten and that the war would last for ever, the loyalty of the
people of the Channel Islands to their own race and their own country,
their pride in its past and their faith in its future, had never wavered. On
the mainland, too, it would surely have survived, to quote Churchill's
phrase, 'if necessary for years, if necessary alone'. Let the final word be
with Hitler, half-grudgingly, half-admiringly uttered in February 1942,
eighteen months after the invasion and victory that never were: 'The last
thing these Englishmen know is how to practise fair play. They're very
bad at accepting their defeats.'

A note on sources

*The place of publication of books is London, unless otherwise stated. Most of
the documents, including* Directive No 16, *on the invasion plans, and* Orders
concerning Organisation and Function of Military Government in
England *were collected by the BBC for use in the television programme of the
same name. The other principal source is the transcripts of interviews recorded
by the BBC for the same purpose, though not all these were finally broadcast,
and in other cases I have quoted more of the text than could be included in the
programme.*

On the general history of the period, and at numerous points throughout
the book, I referred to Alan Bullock, *Hitler, A Study in Tyranny* (revised
edition, Pelican Books, 1962) and Winston Churchill, *The Second World
War* (Cassell, 6 volumes, 1948–54). For Hitler's opinions throughout I
consulted *Hitler's Table Talk* (edited by Hugh Trevor-Roper, Weiden-
feld and Nicolson, 1953). For Chapters 1 and 2 I consulted, on the
Germans' military plans, Ronald Wheatley, *Operation Sea Lion* (Oxford
University Press, 1958), and on the British defence plans, Basil Collier,
The Defence of the United Kingdom (Her Majesty's Stationery Office,
1957). On numerous aspects of the preparations on both sides, in these
chapters and in Chapter 3, I used Peter Fleming, *Invasion 1940* (Rupert
Hart-Davis, 1957) and my debt to this excellent book will be apparent to
all who have read it. Fleming is the source of most of the information
about German 'black' radio, but I also used Ernst Kris and Hans Spier,
German Radio Propaganda (OUP, 1944), which provided most of the
quotations from German bulletins. The firsthand accounts of caring for
the soldiers from Dunkirk, the French refugees at Weymouth, the treatment of the Italians in Londonderry, the Scotsman who wanted a machine-
gun and Mrs R, who was concerned about the washing-up, came from
private information supplied to me by contributors to my book, *How We
Lived Then, A History of Everyday Life during the Second World War*
(Hutchinson, 1971). This was also my main source, along with material
collected for it of which full details can be found in the exhaustive biblio-
graphy to *How We Lived Then*, for background information on wartime
shortages, etc. Only in a very few cases, however, mainly relating to the
Channel Islands, have I used in the present book material that has already
appeared there. The account of building an anti-aircraft obstacle was by
Hector McQuarrie, *Front to Back* (Cape, 1941, to whom I am indebted

for permission to quote from it), and the LDV recruit who described his first route march was F. Howard Lancum, *Press Officer, Please!* (Crosby, Lockwood and Co, 1946). The policeman who said 'This may happen to us' is mentioned by F. Tennyson Jesse and H. M. Harwood, *London Front* (Constable 1940). On the early days of the Home Guard I used previously collected private information and Charles Graves, *The Home Guard of Britain* (Hutchinson, no date, but in fact 1943), which is confusing and inadequate but indispensable. The publications on irregular warfare mentioned are John Brophy, *Home Guard Handbook* (Hodder and Stoughton, 1940), which mentions swearing at dive-bombers, John Langdon-Davies, *Parachutes over Britain* (Pilot Press, 1940), which deplores the lack of obvious sites for barricades in British villages, and Tom Wintringham, *New Ways of War* (Penguin Special, 1940), which recommends consulting boy-scouts. The information on arming the police is contained in extracts from the Cabinet minutes, recently available under the 'thirty-year rule' and collected for the television programme, and the accounts of the ways in which the police planned to control refugees are from interviews filmed for it.

In Chapter 4 the minister quoted is Hugh Dalton, *The Fateful Years* (Frederick Muller, 1957) and other information comes from the Cabinet papers mentioned above. The account of American and Canadian reactions to Britain's possible defeat can be found in C. P. Stacey, *Arms, Men and Governments: The War Policies of Canada 1939–45* (Department of National Defence, Ottawa, 1970). The account of the shipment of the gold reserves is based partly on Peter Fleming, partly on the narrative prepared for the programme and partly on an interview recorded for it. The details of the Battle of Britain, and of the weather during subsequent weeks, are taken from Derek Wood and Derek Dempster, *The Narrow Margin* (Arrow Books, revised edition, 1969). The description of the despatch of the codeword 'Cromwell', and the first-hand accounts of those involved, are taken from material I collected for my BBC radio programme, *The Night the Germans Didn't Come*, broadcast on Radio 4 on 7 September 1971. This was supplemented by information in Peter Fleming and in David Lampe, *The Last Ditch* (Cassell, 1968), the source of the incident at Lincoln. Chapters 5 to 7 are based on the military sources already mentioned and on the narrative of imaginary events referred to in the Foreword, though I obtained some information about the government's underground headquarters from James Leasor, *War at the Top* (Michael Joseph, 1959).

In Chapter 8 and subsequent chapters I made extensive use of *German Occupied Great Britain: Ordinances of the Military Authorities* (first printed in Leipzig, 1941, reissued in England by Scutt-Dand, Foord of Lancing, Sussex, on an unspecified date, probably 1967), and of the military government *Orders* mentioned earlier. On Sir Oswald Mosley my sources were his over-long but revealing autobiography, *My Life* (Nelson, 1968), supplemented by an interview he recorded for the programme. Mr Coldwell's opinions were also specially recorded and other information about the Canadian attitude came from C. P. Stacey, previously cited. The so-called 'White List' was one of the documents collected for the television production, while the suggestion about Sir Samuel Hoare occurs in David Dilks (editor), *The Diaries of Sir Alexander Cadogan 1938–1945* (Cassell, 1971). The *Proclamation to the People of England* was one of the documents supplied to me by the BBC, as was most of the material used in Chapter 9, though the biography of Dr Six is based on David Lampe. The informants still living in Liverpool were interviewed by the BBC. Chapter 10, apart from some material, including the cartoon about nuns, in Peter Fleming, is also based on programme material. Chapter 12 is based largely on the *Ordinances* and on source-material assembled by the BBC. Most of the material on the Channel Islands was collected in interviews for television, or supplied to me privately for *How We Lived Then*, but I also constantly consulted Alan and Mary Wood, *Islands in Danger* (Evans Brothers, 1955), the source of the 'Mrs Churchill' story; on Guernsey, Frank Falla (frequently identified in my text as 'a Guernsey journalist'), *The Silent War* (Frewin, 1967); and, on Jersey, L. P. Sinel, *The German Occupation of Jersey* (*Evening Post*, Jersey, revised edition, 1946). The sources for Chapters 13–15 are similar. Conditions at Biberach, in Chapter 14, were described for television, and the quotation which ends the same chapter occurs in Alan and Mary Wood. On Chapter 16 I used, beside the BBC interviews, David Lampe's book, and I interviewed by telephone, and corresponded with, the under-cover agent in Sheerness. I also acknowledge with thanks the assistance given me by Mr Richard Body, a former member of an Auxiliary Unit. The Channel Islands material, including the hostage sent to jail, the man reprimanded for being uncooperative, the cheeky girl in Boots, and the colonel who spat at Hitler, was recorded for the BBC. The same source, and documents collected by the BBC, was used for Chapter 17. Chapter 18 is based on all the Channel Islands sources, published and unpublished, previously mentioned, and the account of the last few months of the Occupation owes much to Alan and Mary Wood. The interview with Albert Speer which opens Chapter 19 was recorded by the BBC, which also provided details about the 'Newhaven experiment' and the way in which a contemporary advertising agency would 'sell' Nazism to the public.

I also referred to *Hitler's Table Talk*, while Hitler's singing of 'Now thank we all our God' is described by an eye-witness, Field-Marshal Wilhelm Keitel, in his *Memoirs* (William Kimber, 1965). The economists and industrialists quoted were interviewed by the BBC, as were the Americans referred to in Chapter 20. Hitler's tribute to the British which ends the book can be found on page 307 of his *Table-Talk*.

David Littlejohn, *The Patriotic Traitors, A History of Collaboration in German Occupied Europe 1940/45* (Heinemann, 1972) was published while I was writing the present book, though I did not read it until the manuscript was complete. Although Mr Littlejohn's book omits the Channel Islands, and does not speculate as to what might have happened in Britain, I saw no reason, after reading it, to alter any of the conclusions given in this book.

Index

Compiled by F. D. Buck

Academic Assistance Council, 141
Admiralty, German, 66
Aham, Lt.-Col. S. S. G., 140
airborne landings, 19
aircraft, British:
  Airship R100, 97
  Blenheim, 30, 65, 97
  Defiant, 65, 97
  Fairey Battle, 97, 98
  Gloster Gladiator, 97
  Hampden, 70, 97
  Harvard, 97
  Hurricane, 64, 65
  Spitfire, 64, 65
  Swordfish, 98
  Tiger Moth, 97, 99
  Wellington, 30, 70, 97
  Whitley, 70, 98
aircraft, German:
  Dornier, 53
  Heinkel, 29, 53
  Junkers, 29, 53, 65
  Messerschmitt, 53, 64, 65, 97, 99
  Stuka (i.e. Junkers 87), 53, 64
Air Force, British (*see* RAF)
Air Force, German (*see* Luftwaffe)
Air Staff, German, 19
Air Transport Auxiliary, 97
Alderney, 20
Aldershot barracks, 95
All-Ireland Council, 50
'America First' Committee, 259
American aid, 260
American Forces Network, 153
Ancient Order of Foresters, 198
Ancient Order of Rechabites, 198
Anderson, Sir John, 143
Anglo-Spanish Society, 145
anti-German conspiracies, rooting
  out, 138
anti-Jewish edicts, 199
anti-semitism, 200, 201, 225

Armistice, French, 19
Army, British:
  Auxiliary Territorial Service, 210
  Auxiliary Units, 100, 109, 207,
    208, 209, 210, 211, 212
  Catering Corps, 95
  Devon Regiment, 73
  GHQ Home Forces, 70
  Royal Irish Fusiliers, 178
  Royal Signals, 213
  Somerset Light Infantry, 73
  1st Armoured Division, 90, 91
  7th Corps, 91
  7th Division, 72
  7th Parachute Division, 71, 72
  9th Army, 68
  12th Corps, 207
  12th Training Battalion, 95
  16th Army, 68
  17th Infantry Division, 72
  35th Division, 72
  (*see also* Home Guard *and* LDV)
Army, Canadian: 1st Division, 90
Army, German:
  Army Group A, 64, 68, 71, 73,
    79, 93, 99, 122, 123, 207
  Army Group B, 64, 99, 122, 123
  'Das Vaterland' Division, 81
  General Staff, 18
  High Command (OKH), 16
  Waffen SS, 81
  1st Mountain Division, 78
  4th Panzer Division, 104
  6th Division, 73, 74
  7th Army, 90
  7th Panzer Division, 93, 94, 96
  7th Parachute Division, 76, 104
  8th Division, 27, 74
  8th Motorised Division, 93
  8th Panzer Division, 96, 104
  9th Army, 73, 75, 79, 122
  10th Panzer Division, 93, 96

Army, German—*cont.*
  16th Army, 73, 122
  16th Division, 72
  17th Division, 76
  24th Division, 73
  26th Division, 73
  28th Division, 74
  34th Infantry Division, 81
  38th Corps, 26
Army, New Zealand:
  28th Maori Battalion, 76
ARP (Air Raid precautions), 43
Ashford, 68, 79
Ashmolean Museum, 136, 138
Associated Press, 146
Athenaeum Club, 142
atomic bomb, 262
atrocity, 89
Australia, 51

Baden-Powell, Lord, 198
Bahamas, 258
BBC, 13, 103, 152, 153, 154, 155
  Forces Programme 71
  German-controlled, 153
  programmes, 156
Belgium, 16, 18, 19
  co-operation, and, 254
  defeat of, 36
Belsen, 199, 206
Berlin, 254
  air raid on, 64
  atomic bomb, and, 262
Best, Dr, 246
Bexhill, 28, 73
bicycles, 234
  tyres, 234
Biggin Hill, 53
Birmingham, 104, 246
  Gestapo offices in, 128
  Information Bureau, 144
Blackburn, 104
black market, 231–42
  offences, 149
'Black Monday', 66
'black radio', 227
Board of Trade, 218, 245
Bock, General Fedor von, 122
Bohle, Ernst, 118

books, black list of, 160
Boulogne, 68
Boy Scouts, 43, 198
Brauchitsch, General Walther von,
  18, 23, 24, 28, 64, 99, 103, 110,
  116, 120, 122, 165
  invasion plans, and, 61
Bridlington, 17
Brighton, 23, 24, 66, 68, 73, 75
Brighton Bay, 22
Bristol, 105, 246
  BBC, and, 152
  Gestapo office in, 128
  University, 144
Britain, Battle of, 53–5
  opening shots of, 53
British Expeditionary Force 18, 23,
  34, 115
British Government in exile 258, 259
British Museum, 136, 137, 224
British Union of Fascists, 111, 112
broadcasting, 152–6
Brooke General Sir Alan, 59–60,
  61, 73, 79, 91, 95, 100, 104, 107
Brooks's Club, 142
brothels, 164
Brüning, Heinrich, 139
Büchsenchütz, Dr, 132
Buckingham Palace, 31, 32, 107, 118,
  178
  German occupation of, 110
Bund Deutscher Mädchen, 32
Busch, General, 72, 99, 122

Cadogan, Sir Alexander, 117, 139
Calais, 68
Camber, 72
Cambridge, 18, 19
  Archaeological Museum, 138
  occupation of University, 143
Canada, 52, 100, 114
Canterbury, 68, 79
Canvey Island, 213
Cardington, 97
'caretaker' government, 117
Carlton Club, 142, 143
Central Committee of National
  Patriotic Associations, 141
Central News, 146

Chamberlain, Neville, 112, 118, 138, 140, 142, 247
  appeasement policies, 139
Channel Islands, 147, 159, 168, 173, 247
  broadcasting, and, 154
  brothels, and, 165
  church, the, and, 172
  denouncement, 219
  deportation, and, 189–95
  Freemasons, and, 197
  German behaviour, 246
  German misbehaviour, 174
  Gestapo, and, 196–7
  home entertainment, 251
  journalists in gaol, 148
  loot, 176
  'milking' cars, 176
  non co-operation, 221
  occupation of, 11 *et seq.*
  occupation policy, 182, 183, 184
  rationing, 237, 238, 239
  sabotage and spying, 166
  tobacco starvation, 236
  transport, and, 176, 177
Chatham, 92, 213
Chartwell, 100
Cherbourg, 23, 67
Chesil Beach, 23
Chief Supply Officer, 182
Childers, Erskine, 11, 60
Chilterns, Battle of, 99, 103
Christian Peace Movement, 37
Churchill, Winston, 12, 20, 31, 34, 38, 46, 51, 60, 66, 98, 100, 102, 107, 114, 142, 144, 152, 196, 208, 247
  American distrust of, 260
  broadcast, 89, 90
  death of, 108
  German capital ships, and, 66
  invasion, and, 61
  invasion fear, 59
  request for destroyers, 50
  speeches, 218
cinema, 157–9
  no smoking in, 159
Citrine, Sir Walter, 151
Civil Service, 235

Cleary, Sir Joseph, 133
clothing shortage, 235
coal, 248
  supplies, 187
codes, 215
Cohan, R. A. Z., 140
Coldwell, M. I., 114
collaboration, 223–30
colleges, occupation of, 143
Collier, Basil, 11
colonies, German, 15
Committee for Jewish Refugee Children, 202
Commonwealth, the, 155
communications, 214–16
Communism, 259
  British, 260
Communists, 131, 212
  German, 221
Conservative Club, 142
Cooper, Duff, 142
Coutanche, Lord, 167, 191, 199, 216, 217, 233
Coventry, 104
Criminal Police, 124
Cripps, Sir Stafford, 151
'Cromwell', 55, 68
curfew, 157, 251
Czechoslovakia, 15

Dachau, 199
Daily Express, 143
Danish Publishers Association, 256
Darlington, 104
Daventry, 103
D Day, 218, 221
Deal, 66, 68
Defence Economic Commands, 179, 180
Defence Economic Staff for England, 123, 179
defences, 48, 56–8
  S.E. England, 39–47
Denmark, 19, 22, 66, 114, 223, 246, 247, 251, 256
  air attacks from, 53
  Jews, 200, 204
  resistance movement, 255

Department of Information
    Intelligence Bureau, 138
deportation, 186–95, 212
Derby, 104, 180
Derby, Earl of, 142
Directive for Military Government,
    165, 186, 208
    No. 16, 22
    No. 17, 21
Ditchling Beacon, 75
Dollis Hill, 105, 106
Dover, 29, 36, 61, 65, 66, 70, 72,
    78, 79, 93
    Straits of, 20, 24
Dowding, Air Chief Marshal Hugh,
    65
Drage, Sir Benjamin, 202
drive to the north, the, 104
Droitwich, 103
Dunkirk, 23, 38, 60, 68, 95, 207, 213
    British evacuation of, 19
    progress since, 57
Dutch government in exile, 254
Dymchurch, 72

Eagle Day, 53
East Anglia, 18, 29, 60
    proposed landings in, 21
East Hoathly, 91
Economic Defence Staff, 182
Economic Officers, 180
Eden, Anthony, 40, 142
Edinburgh, 100, 101, 104
    Gestapo office in, 128
Edward VIII, 115
Eichmann, Adolf, 248
Eindhoven, resistance workers, 154
Eire, 49, 50
electricity supplies, 187
Emergency Association of German
    Scientists Overseas, 141
Enemy Information Department, 126
England, great air offensive against,
    21
*England, Preparation for the Invasion
    of*, 20
Etchingham, 68, 79, 91, 95
Eton, occupation of school, 143
European Anti-Jewish Congress, 127

Evaluation Commando, 142
Evening Post (Jersey), 148
Evening Press (Guernsey), 149

Farnborough, 53
Fascist League, 225
Feder, Prof. Gottfried, 28
fifth columnists, 49
Fish, Hamilton, 260, 261
Fishery Rights, 162
'Flame Fougasses', 58
Fleming, Peter, 207, 211
Folkestone, 22, 28, 65, 68, 69, 72, 77,
    78
Fontainebleau, 61
food, acute shortage of, 240–2
footwear, 235
Foreign Office, the, 142
Forester, C. S., 11
France, 16, 18, 19, 27, 39, 53, 60, 258
    co-operation, and, 253
    defeat of, 36
    loot from, 126
    unoccupied zone of, 190
Freedom Radio, 153
Freemasons, 131, 132, 167
    Gestapo Commando Group and,
        197–8
    suppression of, 197
Freud, Prof. Sigmund, 225
Friends of the Basque Children
    Society, 140
Fritzsche, Hans, 31
fuel oils, 234

gas-chamber, 186, 249
gasoline, 234
gas supplies, 187
General Staff, German, 19
General Strike, 201
George VI, 32, 52, 101, 102, 110,
    112, 115, 172
    in Canada, 113, 114
    leaves for Canada, 102
Gestapo, 128, 132, 138, 139, 141,
    142, 143, 145, 151, 163, 164
    'Black List', 196, 198
    blueprints for occupation, 121
    Channel Islands, and, 196–7

Commandos, 143, 176, 196, 202
intelligence, 131
local branches, 224
Section III, 197
swoops, 144
Gibraltar, 22, 155
Straits of, 262
Gillard, Frank, 152, 153, 154
Girl Guides, 198
Glasgow, 38, 101, 104
Gestapo office in, 128
Gloucester, 105
Goebbels, Dr Paul Josef, 30, 42, 43,
249, 253
on British food stocks, 183
gold reserves, 53
Goring, 99
Göring, Reich Marshal Hermann, 16,
32, 64, 65, 82, 98, 125, 126
Gosport, 68
governments-in-exile:
flee to Canada, 100
Gravesend, 68
Great Britain:
German plans for, 186
Greater German Economic Sphere,
253
Guernsey, 36, 147, 154, 155
books and, 160
collaborators, 224
deportation, and, 189, 191–5
food shortage, and, 184
food stocks, 183
friendly societies, 198
Jews, 199
non co-operation, 221
occupation, 233
rationing, 237, 238, 239
sabotage, 216
transport, and, 177, 178
water shortage, 233
Guernsey Star, 148, 149, 234

Halder, Col.-Gen. Franz, 24, 110
Halifax, Lord, 142, 143, 196
Handley, Tommy, 85
Harrow, occupation of school, 143
Harwich, 17, 70
Hastings, 29, 73, 79

Haushofer, Prof. Karl, 132
Hawkinge, 53, 76
Heathfield, 86, 90, 91
Henderson, Sir Nevile, 139
Henley, 96
Herschel, Sir William, 136
Hess, Rudolf, 244
Hetherington, Prof., 130
High Command of the Armed
Forces (OKW), 16, 17, 20
High Wycombe, 105
Himmler, Heinrich, 81, 82, 125
Hiroshima, 262
History of the Second World War, 11
Hitler, Adolf, 15, 16, 20, 21, 22, 24,
25, 31, 37, 41, 44, 49, 80, 106,
112, 113, 117, 118, 123, 125, 127,
153, 158, 161, 201
American aid, and, 260
atomic bomb, and, 262
Battle of Britain, and, 55
Brüning, and, 139
Channel Islands obsession, 191, 216
Christianity, and, 252
conquest of Europe, 259
declares war on USA, 261
hatred of Freemasonry, 197
industrialists, and, 255
international conspiracy belief, 198
invasion, and, 21, 64
murder of Röhm, 248
Nelson's Column, and, 135
new palace, 243–4
new religion, and, 253
Russian campaign, and, 261
Second Front, and, 154
slav races, and, 246
speeches, 245
strategist, 20
Hitler Youth, 29, 32
Hoare-Laval Pact, 117
Hoare, Sir Samuel, 117, 118, 142
Hohl, Sonder-Führer, 161
Holland, 16, 18, 19, 27, 53, 60, 114
defeat of, 36
Jews, 200, 204
looting from, 126
Royal Family, 100
strikes in, 254

Hollesley Bay, 18
Holyrood House 178
Home Guard, 12, 36, 40, 41, 42, 43,
    46, 55, 56, 57, 58, 68, 80, 82, 83,
    84, 85, 86, 95, 100, 106, 208,
    212, 213, 214, 215
Horam, 82, 86, 91
Hore-Belisha, Leslie, 202
hostages, 220
Hull, Cordell, 115
Humber, mouth of, 66
Hythe, 71, 72, 76, 78

If Hitler Had Invaded England, 11
If the Invader Comes, 44
Intelligence, German, 29, 72
internment policy, 186
invasion of Britain, 66–75
    break-out, the, 76
    preparation, 27
    stop-line, 59
    warning, 56
Inverness, 104
Ireland, 22
Ironside, General William, 55, 59,
    60
Isle of Wight, 21, 23
Ismay, General 'Pug', 49
Italians, 255
ITMA, 85, 156
Ivychurch, 72

Jakobovitz, Dr, 204
Japan, 261
Jefferson, Thomas, 259
Jehovah's Witnesses, 167
'Jerrybags', 188, 223
Jersey, 147, 148, 155, 167, 168, 173
    alcohol, and, 174
    bicycles, and, 176
    black market, 231
    brothels, and, 165
    curfew, 157
    deportation, and, 191–5
    foodstocks, 183
    friendly societies, 198
    home-grown tobacco, 236
    hostages, and, 220
    income tax, 184

Jews, 199
    'milking' cars, and, 176
    occupation, 233
    prisons, 169
    rationing, 237, 238, 239
    sabotage, 216
    suppression of Freemasonry, 197
    transport, and, 177, 178
Jersey Evening Post, 234
Jeschonnek, General, 23
Jewish organisations, 140
Jews, 131, 167, 198, 206, 212, 246
    Freemasonry, and, 197
    protest against persecution, 140
    refugees, 196
Joad, Prof. C. E. M., 196
Jodl, General Alfred, 16, 21, 22
Joyce, William, 38

Kailan Mining Association, 202
Keitel, Field-Marshal Wilhelm, 16,
    21, 24, 25, 43
Kennedy, Joseph, 50, 51
Kiel Canal, 17
King, Mackenzie, 50, 113, 114, 115

Last Appeal to Reason, A, 15–16
Laval, 117
Layton, Sir Walter, 140
LDV (Local Defence Volunteers),
    31, 36, 40, 41, 46, 95, 213
Le Havre, 24, 68
Leeds, 18, 104
Leeper, Sir Reginald, 138
Lewes, 75, 90, 91
Lidell, Alvar, 37
Link, The, 112
Linz, 243
Littlestone, 72
Littlington, 74
Livermore, Harry, 134
Liverpool, 104
    German community in, 131
    Gestapo office in, 128
    Security Service Provincial HQ,
        129
Liverpool International Society,
    132

Lloyd George, David, 113, 196
Local Defence Volunteers (*see* LDV)
London, 60, 76
  capture of, 18, 105–8
  clubs, seizure of, 142–3
  communications, 18
  cut off from north, 100
  German advance round, 104
  invasion stop-line, 59
  princesses departure from, 52
  refugees, and, 35
  University, 144
Londonderry, 35
long-term political aim, 144
loot from Continent, 126
loot, potential, 176
looting, national museums, 136–8
Lord Haw Haw, 38
Los Alamos, 262
Lowestoft, 18
Luftwaffe, 21, 53, 66, 82, 91, 93, 98
  High Command, 16, 18, 19
  invasion, and, 64
Lullington, 74
Luxembourg, 162
Lydd, 72
Lyme Bay, 23, 24, 67, 70
Lympne, 53, 69, 71

Macclesfield, 180
Macpherson, Sandy, 71
Maginot Line, 59, 64, 80
Maidenhead, 99, 108
Maidstone, 92
  invasion stop-line, 59
Malta, 155
Manchester, 104
  Gestapo office in, 128
'Manhattan Project', 262
Mannheim, 180
Manstein, General Fritz von, 26
Manston, 53
Maquis, 204
Maresfield, 90
Margate, 39, 79
Marquis, Sir Frederick, 140
Marshall, W. H., 176, 218
Melchett, Lord, 202

Memorial Crypt of the Field-
  Marshals, 244
Meuse, the, 64
Michael, Dr, 139
MI5, 111
*Military-Geographical Data about
  England*, 29
*Military Government in England:
  orders concerning*, 110
  Commander-in-Chief's *Directive*,
    179
Ministry of Economic Affairs,
  German, 253, 254
Ministry of Food, 86
Ministry of Information, 144
  closure of, 146
Molotov cocktail, 58, 80, 90
Monroe Doctrine, 253
Montreal, 52
Morrison, Herbert, 46, 49
Mosley, Sir Oswald, 111, 112, 116,
  118, 131, 201, 224, 225
Muller, Max, 136
Münchener Neueste Nachrichter, 139
Munich, 243
Munro, H. H., 11
Mussolini, Benito, 112, 117, 153

National Gallery, 136, 137
National Joint Committee for Spanish
  Relict, 140
National Registration Card, 169
Navy, British, 20
  Birmingham, HMS, 66
  Furious, HMS, 67, 102
  Home Fleet, 18
  Hood, HMS, 66, 91
  Manchester, HMS, 66
  Naiad, HMS, 67
  Nelson, HMS, 91
  Newcastle, HMS, 70
  Revenge, HMS, 52
  Rodney, HMS, 66, 91
Navy, German, 18
  E Boats, 66
  Graf Spee, 18
  High Command (OKM), 16
  Hipper, 67

Navy, German—*cont.*
  Scheer, 67
  Staff Operations Division, 16, 18,
    19
  (*see also* U Boats)
Nazi Party, 252, 253
Nazis, 30, 55, 157, 161, 225, 247
Nazi shrines, 243
Nelson's Column, 243
  planned removal of, 135, 136
Newcastle, 104
New European Order, 253, 254
Newfoundland, 50
Newhaven, 27, 48, 66, 78, 91
'Newhaven experiment', the, 249
New Romney, 72
News Chronicle, 146
Nicolson, Sir Harold, 139
North Africa, 261
Northampton, 104
North Sea, 21
  German bases on, 17
'North-West' study, 18, 19
Northwood, 105
Norway, 19, 49, 66, 111, 114
  Royal Family, 100
no surrender pledge, 100
Nottingham, 104
Nuremberg, 243

occupation:
  Announcements, 170
  cultural-political sector, 146
  Orders, 178, 179, 181
  Ordinances, 121, 162, 163, 165,
    168, 169, 174, 176, 177, 178
occupied countries, role of, 246
offensive to the south, the, 104–5
OKH (*see* Army, German, High
  Command)
OKM (*see* Navy, German, High
  Command)
OKW (*see* High Command of the
  Armed Forces)
'Operation Yellow', 16
'Opponents of Germany', 140
Ostend, 60
Ottawa, 113
'Overseas Office', 225

Oxford, 104
  occupation of university, 143

Pangbourne, 94
Panzers, 72
  Mark III, 29
  Mark IV, 29
Paris, German victory parade 29
Pas de Calais, air attacks from, 53
Peacehaven, 75
Pearl Harbour, 261
PEN Club, 143
Perth, 104
Petersfield, 92, 93
petrol, 234
Petroleum War Dept., 58
Pevensey, 73
Phipps, Sir Eric, 138
Plymouth, 105
Poland, 15
  decision to attack, 16
  Jews, 200
Polegate, 84, 91
population, effect on, 186
Portland, 20, 91
Portsmouth, 24, 92, 93
power, source of, 188–9
Press Agencies, closure of, 146
*Proclamation to the People of
  England* 120
Pulitzer Prize, 89
Punch, 37, 149

Quisling, Major Vidkun, 111

Radio confiscation, 219
Raeder, Admiral Erich, 16, 24, 27,
  64, 67
RAF, 17, 21, 57, 64, 79, 93, 96, 97
  Bomber Command, 70, 105
  Coastal Command, 105
  control of skies, 61
  Fighter Command, 64, 65, 105
  ground crew, 95
  invasion and, 64
  last stand, 98, 99
  11 Group, 64, 65
  12 Group, 65
Ramsay, Captain, 225

Ramsgate, 21
rationing, 233, 235, 236, 237, 238, 239
Reading, 71
Reform Club, 143, 196
refugees, 35, 196
  anti-Nazi, 196
Reich Central Security Office (RSHA), 123, 124, 127
Reichstag, 243, 252
Reith, Sir John, 155
resistance movement, 255
Reuter, 146
Ribbentrop, Joachim von, 116, 139
Riddle of the Sands, The, 11, 60
Ringmer, 74
roadblocks, 39
Röhm, Ernst, 248
Rommel, Major-Gen. Erwin, 94, 96
Roosevelt, President Franklin D., 12, 50, 51, 114, 115, 144, 259, 260, 261
Rotary International, 198
Rottingdean, 68, 75
Royal Antidiluvian Order of Buffaloes, 198
Royal Asiatic Society, 145
Royal Canadian Navy, 102
Royal Institution of International Affairs, 140
Royal Military Canal, 72, 76
RSHA (see Reich Central Security Office)
Runciman, Lord, 143
Rundstedt, Field-Marshal Karl von, 64, 71, 73, 79, 91, 93, 99, 103, 104, 105, 108, 122
Rye, 72, 78

sabotage 166
'saboteur's handbook', 209
St Leonards-on-Sea, 68, 79, 91
Salisbury Plain, 29
Salmon, Isidor, 142
Salvation Army, The, 140, 198
Samuel, Sir Herbert, 202
Schlesinger, Prof. Arthur, 259, 260
Schniewind, Admiral, 24
School of Oriental Studies, 145

SD (see Security Service of the Nazi Party)
S Day, 25, 58, 65, 93
Seaford, 66, 74
Sea Lion, Operation, 20, 22, 23, 24, 25, 31, 65, 92, 93, 104, 121, 122, 125, 127
Search Commissions, 118
Search Group, 142
'Secret Field Police', 123
Secret Service, British, 198
Secret State Police, 124
Security Service of the Nazi Party (SD), 124, 125, 136, 137, 141, 142, 152, 196, 197, 198, 225
  Department III, 135, 136
Sevenoaks, 92
Sheerness, 70, 212
Sheffield, 104
Sheppey, Isle of, 214, 216
Shoreham, 66
Siegfried Line 28
'Silent Column', 38
Singapore, 51
Six, Dr Franz, 125, 126
  appointed Chief of Security Police, 125, 126
  head of RSHA Sect VI, 127
slave-labour threat, 189–90
Slav races, 245
soap, 233, 234
Socialists, German, 221
Sociètè des Amis de L'Espagne, 145
Society Asiatique, 145
Society of Friends, 140
Solent, 68
South Africa, 31
Southend, 213
Spanish Civil War, 42, 131, 217
Spears, Brig.-Gen. E. L., 140
Special Search List, 196, 224
Speer, Albert, 243, 244, 245
Spengler, Dr, 132
Spring Offensive, the, 18
spying, 166
SS, 81, 82, 89, 90
  regalia, 249
  troops, 143
Stanmore, 64, 105

States, the, 168
Static Flame Traps, 58
steel, 246
Stirling, 104
Stock Exchange, the, 139
Stockton-on-Tees, 57
Stoke Abbott, 56
Strang, William (Sir), 144
Strauss, General, 73, 122
Streatley, 94, 96
strikes, 254
Stroud, 105
suspect organisations, 196
Swanage, 102
Swindon, 209

Tangmere 92
Tenterden, 68
terror attacks, 106
theatre 160
Thyrolf, Rudolf, 129, 131, 132
Times, The, 78, 146, 202
tobacco, 235
    rationing, 236
    substitute, 236
trade unions, 186
Trafalgar, Battle of, 135
Trondheim, 67
Truro, 105
Tunbridge Wells, 93

U Boats, 66
    offensive, 22
    operations, 24
    schnorkel, and, 28
Uckfield, 68, 79, 84, 90, 91, 95
Ukraine, 246
United Dominions Trust Ltd, 140

United Kingdom, Invasion of, 22
United States, 50, 115, 253, 258, 259
    Canada, and, 113
    enters the war, 261
    non-intervention sentiment, 258
    self-defence, 51
universities, occupation of, 143

Valera, Eamon de, 49, 50
Vansittart, Sir Robert (Lord), 138,
    139
Versailles, Treaty of, 113
Versailles 'Diktat', 226
vice-squads, 165

War Office, German, 179, 182
war shortage, 233
Warlimont, Major-General, 21
West Indies, 50
West Malling airfield, 92
Weymouth, 34, 70
When William Came, 11, 50
'White List', 224, 225, 228
Wilkie, Wendell, 260
Wilmington, 74
Winchelsea, 72
    beach, 73
Winchester, 111
Windsor, 94, 96
Windsor, Duke of, 115
Winter Hill, 84–90
Woodland Folk, the, 198
Woolton, Lord (see Marquis, Sir
    Frederick)
'Wormwood', 214

'Yank-bashers', 188
York, 100, 101